Overcoming a los‗ ‗ ‗

Katrina Jeffery was born in Brisbane, Australia in 1962. She spent her high school years in Sydney and returned to Brisbane in 1981. In 1984 she moved to the far north coast of NSW. Feeling at home for the first time in her life she stayed.

The first edition of this book was published 18 months after the loss of her husband Chris, to motor neurone disease (also known as ALS or Lou Gehrig's disease).

Front cover

The front cover background is the photograph I took as the sun rose on the first day of my life without Chris.

The cornflower is the universal flower for motor neurone disease.

The butterflies are a symbol of metamorphosis – the changing of life through death. These butterflies are a part of the memorial candleholder Chris gave on his last Christmas with us. The flame shining through the butterflies symbolises the love we shared.

For information on caring for someone with MND/ALS, visit
www.alsgardens.net.au

ISBN: 978-0-9944649-0-3

This work is a personal memoir. All details described in this book are from the memory of the author only.

I have written about my feelings concerning my experiences and memories of an incredibly stressful time in my life. I have been faithful to my memories, but acknowledge that others may remember things differently.

All poetry written by Katrina Jeffery

KATRINA JEFFERY

~

Overcoming a loss
by 1000 deaths

~

ACKNOWLEDGEMENTS

This book would never have been possible without the love, support and expertise of many people.

Pamela Learned was a constant source of inspiration for me while Chris was ill. We formed a beautiful friendship through an online support network for carers. This gentle-spirited lady cared for her own husband who displayed the same incredible grace of spirit through his own horror. Their ability to face the monster together with love continues to inspire me daily.

Pamela gave her time generously to assist me in placing this book on indiegogo to fund its publishing.

Marny Bonner and I have walked many paths of love and pain together over the years. She inspired me constantly to go for my dreams regardless of the hurdles in my path. Her enthusiasm when I announced my book and idea of crowd funding gave me the guts to make my dream a reality. Marny then gave her time generously to the indiegogo campaign relentlessly editing and helping with the design.

Kerry Davies of Kerry Davies Publishing Services turned my rambling memories into a book. Handing a deeply personal story like this over to a stranger was incredibly daunting. She massaged the text with care and respect for the true story it contained.

Ree Maloney from Cherry Jam Web and Graphic Design came forward during the campaign on indiegogo and generously donated her services to produce the book cover. She took my ideas and created a cover that captures my story.

Through the indiegogo campaign I was overwhelmed by the support I received from around the world to get this book from my head to publication. Without a shadow of doubt, this would never have been possible without every one of you.

"I met Katrina when she, like me, was in the thick of caregiving for a husband with ALS/MND. With declines came numerous injuries to his body and her heart.

MND takes mobility and breathing from someone faster than any human can adapt to. As Katrina poured her heart out, it was hard for anyone in our care group to tell if her husband was suffering from dementia or just being willful and mean! With love's care and time's wisdom, she's told an uplifting and helpful story for carers and family members who need help—now!"

Pamela Learned, Philadelphia, Pennsylvania, USA
Caregiver of husband with MND 2009-2015

"Katrina was such a wonderful support and a life line as a fellow caregiver. Both of our partners had MND with frontotemporal degeneration, which is a rare, but not uncommon condition, but one which people are rarely prepared for as the professionals say MND does not affect the thinking brain. Katrina has wonderful experience to share with readers which will bring many as much peace of mind and sanity as her help during the journey with MND/FTD did for me."

Shawn Bracebridge, Albany, NY, USA.
Cared for Chipp one year.

For all those who care

~

until there is a cure.

Preface

No one should have to go through their life with this disease affecting them, and yet every single day people are doing their best to live with it all over the world.

We all cope with disaster in our lives differently, and we are all at different places in our own self-development at any single point. I have often reflected on how I would have coped if all that had happened five, ten or twenty years earlier, as I know where my own self-development was at then. I would have had far fewer resources inside myself twenty years earlier, that is for sure, and I still didn't have as many as I would have liked when my time to go through this did come.

Every person who came into contact with Chris has had their life and soul touched by him in some way. No matter how any of us battled to cope with what unfolded for him, we have all grown personally through the time of his illness and since he left us, as we struggle to grieve and move forward again.

I am sure that every person in this world feels that if they were given their time again they would do better, more or differently. Each situation we face in life is an opportunity to grow as a person, and increase our ability for love and compassion.

CONTENTS

Any one story
is but a weaving
of the threads
of many stories
too numerous to separate

Why do we feel alone?
we forget
that we are part
of many other stories too

1.   Before we start

What is it like to find out that the love of your life has a degenerative, terminal illness that has no cure?

There are so many emotions and reactions, and most people may imagine that they would feel a certain thing in particular or a range of things. But what does it really feel like to sit in an office and have those words pronounced?

Perhaps the most famous description went viral, raising so much money and awareness: 'It's like having a bucket of ice water tipped over your head.' That was a great catchline and the challenges were awesome, as they took on a life of their own. It's a gross understatement nonetheless.

It's funny how many words we say during our lives, and how much we think we mean them, and in many ways of course we do mean them.

Words like: 'You never know what is around the next corner, so you must live every day to its fullest,' or 'The day we are born we begin to die, so live every day like it is your last.'

But do we really live that? If we are honest we have to say, 'No, I waste a lot of my time and expect that tomorrow is another day like this one.' I know that I have wasted a lot of my life, even though I have always been very active, busy and involved. I still feel time slipping past like an oiled rope, and have to remind myself constantly that life is an amazing gift. I have to remember that it is not endless, and it should never be wasted.

How many times do we feel little aches, pains or oddities about our bodies as we age, and either ignore them or think something terrible is happening to us, only to forget about them later?

I could tell you of a range of pains I've had for years, and of all kinds of things another might race to a doctor about. I've been fortunate in that I've rarely been sick. I've had little to do with seeing doctors for myself, and I tend to avoid doing so if at all possible. I rarely get a cold, let alone the flu. Chris was the same; he had been ridiculously healthy all his life.

I was vaguely aware that there was a disease called motor neurone disease, or MND. If you had asked me what it was, I would have said that I think it affects your legs, and maybe your arms, it would put you in a wheelchair, and it is a degenerative disease. I had never known anyone with the disease, and I wasn't aware of knowing anyone who had any family members or friends with the disease. It was something vague that was out there, and it was nothing to do with me, so I didn't even know I was ignorant. I certainly had no appreciation for what it means to have a degenerative disease.

It's odd how much we don't know that we don't know, and don't feel we need to know. You may have come into contact with this disease, and are just realising that you don't know anything about it at all. If you ask Dr Google, you will quickly become frightened out of your wits – I know I was the first time I started researching what was going to happen. I make no attempt anywhere in this book to downplay the hideousness of this disease, it is the worst thing I can ever imagine. I still find myself in some shock at what happened every single day, and find it hard to believe that it did happen. And yet I discovered that hundreds of thousands of people are living with and dying from it all the time.

There is a group of diseases that attack the motor neurones in the body and are collectively known in Australia and some other countries as motor neurone disease (MND). In the United States it is known as amyotrophic lateral sclerosis (ALS) or Lou Gehrig's disease. There are some differences in how the disease works on any one person's body. Each individual experiences a different range of effects from the disease, order of progression through parts of the body and speed of the progression. If you were to put a group of a dozen affected people together in a room you would be amazed at the vast range of differences you would find in that room, while also noticing sets of similarities.

This can make the diagnosis difficult, and as there is no definitive test for the disease, say a blood test that picks up a specific organism in your system. The path to the diagnosis you never want to receive can be arduous and frustrating - and frightening. There is a test called the EMG that is used as an important diagnostic tool, but it isn't always simple to get to the point of having this test. Doctors have to eliminate other diseases that could cause your particular symptoms, and then watch the progression. Finally getting the diagnosis, oddly enough, can almost be a relieving end to the first part of the journey. I say almost because, once you do have that diagnosis, you have to face the fact that there is no cure.

This is my true story about the personal effects of this disease on real people, living real lives, with real families. Anyone who has been through a terminal illness with someone they love will find they can resonate with so much of what they read here.

Too often when terminal disease strikes, the medical profession forgets that these are people with incredibly deep feelings, hopes and aspirations. Their lives are shattered, changed forever, and they struggle with so much more than the medical calamity that has struck. Health professionals mostly do care about this, but they are often unable, for so many reasons, to address this with you. In Australia we are incredibly fortunate that our health system and the MND Association of Australia do provide us with many health and support services, for both the physical and personal aspects of the disease. I am in the debt of many wonderful professionals whose services were provided to us free of charge.

There are other people who can give valuable support, and peer support can be one of the most powerful. The internet has provided an incredible avenue for this support, giving people a way to communicate despite distance or physical limitations. The power of peer support cannot be overemphasised and I was fortunate to have this support through online groups.

I have written my story in the hope it will help people who are struggling to cope, whether they are the primary carer of a loved one, or another family member or friend. The internal struggles are different and deeply personal for each person, but we share many commonalities.

Having a loved one struck by MND is like having them suddenly seized, ripped out of your arms, and put into a glass cylinder. You get strapped into a chair with your head pinned and your eyes propped open. Your loved one is also strapped to a chair. You realise that there is water dripping into the cylinder, and with horror you have no choice but to watch as the cylinder fills to the top.

As a child I played
and in playing I dreamed
and in dreaming I created

And as my creations
took on a life of their own
in turn, they
created the person I became

That must be the reason
I find so much pleasure
in the creativity of playing

2. Where we came from

All through childhood I dreamed of living on a 'farm'. Now don't laugh, but by this I meant what was shown on *Play School*. My earliest memory of life is waiting for them to look through the windows thinking 'show me the farm, show me the farm'. To me, a farm was a bit of land with just a few of each animal – two cows (the milker and her calf), a horse maybe with a foal, two or three sheep, ducks, dogs, cats and a dozen chickens. You would stroll around this lovely little barnyard-type area and throw a bit of feed to them all and give them a cuddle.

As I grew, my love for animals only increased, especially as the most we got in that area was a budgie, a few mice, a few guinea pigs and, finally, a kitten. I dreamed of a life with animals and became interested in working with them. When I would pine for a dog of my own or chickens or something, my father would say, in what seemed to be a sincere voice, 'When we get our farm you can have that.' It took me until I was nearly finished school to realise he never had any intention of buying anything remotely like a farm.

At fifteen I finished my school certificate and went to study and work as a veterinary nurse. I was in my element and working with animals in a humane fashion made perfect sense. I loved working with the animals. I loved learning about how a body works and was particularly interested in surgery.

When I was seventeen I changed to study nursing. One of the places I trained at was a nursing home. It was huge and they took in patients that most nursing homes would not take. I was deeply affected by the inhumane way many were treated, institutionalised for long periods with chronic illness. Many patients lived there for more than twenty years.

I also did part of my training in the palliative section (although this term wasn't in use yet), and noticed the amazing attitude of many terminal cancer patients in the end stages. I was struck by their acceptance of what was imminent, the peace so many had reached, and the acceptance of staff and family when each passed.

I felt a small fear growing in the back of my mind of ever becoming so disabled that I would need to be cared for in a medical facility, and developed my own very clear set of boundaries on what I would consider quality of life. I couldn't help but compare how we had cared for animals in my first line of work.

I did eventually get my 'farm'. It wasn't quite like *Play School*, and yet it was just a small hobby farm. It was idyllic, and I felt that I was living my dream. I had a small herd of dairy goats, and I supplied raw milk to several outlets around the area. I did the whole process myself –fed and milked the goats, and bottled, labelled and delivered the milk to the shops. I had farm cats that kept the rats, mice and snakes away from the house and feed, and I had chickens to provide eggs. I also fell in love with the dog breed that seemed made for me, the maremma sheepdog, and these dogs guarded my goats from wild dog attacks brilliantly.

So there was my little farm, a few more of each animal than my *Play School* dream farm, but I did feel at peace with the world as I tended my animals. I have four wonderful children and raising them on this little farm felt to my soul like the kind of childhood I had dreamed of for myself.

With my background, I solved most birthing emergencies, and was often called out to other goat farms to help. I could sew up injuries, provide basic nursing care and get help fast when it was beyond me.

As a farmer I gently held any seriously ill or injured animal and agreed with tough decisions. I would be sad, but never consider they should suffer.

I saw palliative care as being similar. It was all about acceptance, comfort and dignity. I knew that if I were to suffer any terrible accident or illness I would rather be nursed in a palliative way than have the medical profession force 'life'.

I could never have guessed that some of these things that shaped me in my early years would be called upon the way they were in this story.

I had been married for twenty-seven years in a very tempestuous relationship, and we split up numerous times, one or the other breaking free, but always we were drawn back together.

I finally emerged, divorced by my ex-husband, angry, bitter and cynical about love. To most people I emerged rather well and was innovative, fun, hard working and moving on brilliantly.

Farming on a small scale is no way to create true income, and as my children grew I studied computer programming and worked in the IT field and teaching adults. As situations changed with my marriage ending, I moved from my little farm into town, just for five years, with the intention of going back to the land. Circumstances, however, dictated unforeseen changes that saw the sale of that first piece of land but I vowed that I would own a small acreage again.

I spent some years on my own, healing and getting to know myself as an adult without a partner or young dependent children. I even came to like myself. The process was slow and happened on many levels. I didn't want to go through any of the 'bad' stuff again, any of the pain again, and felt that the cost of a relationship was too high to pay.

I had a great circle of friends and began a lovely social life going to live music and doing fun things either with other single girlfriends or with groups of friends. In many ways I was the happiest I had been for much of my life, and in many ways I felt satisfied. But I did feel it was a shame that I didn't have someone to share that with. I have always found it strange that we can live in paradox and accept it.

As a single person I felt so free and in control. There was no one to disapprove or want something different and lots of great things happening in my life. And yet – the paradox – I also wanted a true partner. I did not confuse that with just wanting someone, anyone. Maybe it wasn't such a paradox in truth. Maybe it was that I was happier being single than I had ever been when going through the many ups and downs of the marriage. I was not prepared to 'settle' for anything. If I was going to have the ultimate – a true partner – then great, but I felt that he had better find me, because I wasn't up to the task of whisking through all the chaff. I didn't want to just have boyfriends and try to make something work. I wanted it all, or I was happy on my own, thanks for asking.

I had tried meeting men a few times but found it took a great deal of energy. I felt that I would probably live alone and enjoy the peace and safety of not daring to try again. I felt I was graciously bowing out of the dating arena, without having participated much.

I still find it incredibly ironic that the only reason I agreed to meet Chris for that first coffee was because he was a widower. My reasoning was thus: here is a man who 'did' until death do us part, not someone who just walked away when things got tough. I wondered what he might be like, and then wondered, what would he think of me? Divorce is a very different way of ending a marriage – in fact, the two ends to a marriage cannot be more opposite!

The first time I met him, he talked nearly non-stop for a good two hours and finally drew breath to ask if I wanted another coffee. I almost never drink two cups of coffee in one afternoon, but I said yes! I had heard few people that could have out-talked him, and yet I admit he had me hanging on every word.

A couple of weeks later, he told me that I was the first woman he had met for a coffee since his wife passed who had looked into his eyes, rather than just looked 'him' over. The thing that bowled me over was that he had seen 'kindness' in my eyes. To this day, that very statement still sums up for me the kind of man he was – a man who looked inside for real beauty and understood it.

Over the next four months I came to know the man that was my soulmate. I didn't really believe in that concept for myself, personally. Oh, I knew that amazing people seemed to meet amazing people and that they had something wonderful. I knew that there are older people who have been married for fifty or sixty years who still gaze at each other with love and say they are best friends. But to me it was like hearing a fairytale, not the cold hard reality of my life.

I was stunned to find how fascinating I found this man, and even more stunned to discover we were truly becoming friends. In fact, often I felt more like I was having perpetual sleepovers with school girlfriends. We would giggle and laugh and be silly and talk deeply well into the wee hours of the morning. We would be so tired, laying there talking and giggling, that one or both of us would start dribbling onto the pillow and yet we would still have more to talk and giggle over.

I loved his attitude to life – live it all now, you don't know what is around the next corner. It became infectious, and I was caught up in this whirlwind that took us on a journey where we felt we just held our arms out and rolled along with it. We felt that all our lives we had only waited for this moment to arrive. And here it was. We felt we were living a fairytale, and we lived it in every fibre of our being.

My youngest son was the first to meet Chris as he was still living with me at the time. He was very open to me having a relationship and warmed to Chris quickly. Later, when he gave his speech at our wedding, the things he said about Chris's obvious effect on me told me that he had been taking notice and approving more than I realised at the time.

My youngest daughter turned up hours early for a visit one day and caught us in bed. There she was, banging on the front door, and there we were, with all this rustling and exclamation until I got to the door to let her in. As she hugged me, she ran her hands down my back and suddenly exclaimed, 'You aren't wearing any underwear!' Poor Chris then sheepishly emerged from my bedroom to meet her. We laughed about that many times later and she told the story in full detail at our wedding, much to everyone's delight.

We went to Canberra to meet my eldest son and have some time away together. I never realised until his speech at our wedding that his first impression was – who is this long-haired lout with my mother? Very quickly however, he found that Chris was a wonderfully deep and loving man he grew to respect and love.

I was probably most nervous about him meeting my eldest daughter because she does not tend to warm to new people quickly. I was amazed to see that on the first day they ended up alone and deep in easy conversation together for hours.

It was another confirmation for me of how right this man and this relationship was. All of my children took to him as though he were family from the very beginning.

It wasn't quite as easy when I met his children, as I was so nervous. I kept wondering if I would come across as some idiot. Once I had been there for a little while it got easier – and harder at the same time. It seemed to me that they were all as nervous about meeting me. I wondered what it must be like for them to meet me, given they had lost their mother, and I didn't have experience of something like that to really be able to relate to. But they were gracious and I left feeling that we had all been able to get things off to a fairly good start. Each time I saw them after that certainly became easier and I felt that they were truly accepting me, and genuinely happy to see their father moving forward with someone with whom he was happy.

At the time he was working as a short-order cook six days a week in the restaurant of a pub. He worked split shifts, so was very tied down to his job. Early in our first conversations he mentioned that he had run a café with his wife, whom he had loved, but he had sold it when she was diagnosed with cancer in order to look after her.

One day he was walking down the arcade where his old café was and found a sign on the front saying it was up for lease. He began talking wistfully about how wonderful it would be to have his old café back, and within a week he began enquiries with his bank and the owner about the price. When the bank said they would back the venture he began to talk with great enthusiasm and animation about what it would mean to him to go back there. He felt it was like coming around some kind of full circle. He had been through the illness and death of his wife, had spent several years mourning her and caring for their children, and now had met a woman he felt was his soulmate – and suddenly there was the café opportunity becoming a reality.

I fully supported him and we talked for hours on end about business, and the way he felt when cooking homemade food for a person with a smile and listening to their woes. He radiated this beautiful depth of soul in his need to make an impression on individual people and provide a service he could be proud of.

As a business owner for many years myself, it was such a joy to watch him sort out and organise all the necessities, negotiate and secure the lease on his old café. I listened to him dream of what he would do and how he would run it, seeing joy on his face as he felt his life opening up again. It was a balm to my own soul.

We had both lived on acreage in the past, but now were both living in houses in a small rural city. As we got to know each other and talked about life and visions of futures, our discussions turned to the love of living on a small acreage. I was excited when he spoke of his love of a piece of land, making gardens, the privacy and all the things I missed and loved about small properties. My ex-husband had really never liked living on our farm. He liked living out of town, but he took no enjoyment in doing all the tasks. This man, though, would be hard to hold back from the tasks this life would entail.

Before I knew it we were opening up the real estate guide on Saturday mornings and messing around looking at what was on offer, talking about our dream property. It was a pleasant way to spend a morning together. However, when we spoke seriously about how much we would like to live on small acreage again, we were aware that his eldest daughter was in her last year of school and felt it would be best not to disrupt her by moving house. We mused that maybe the following year we would sell our houses and buy a property.

One Saturday morning a lovely property was advertised in the paper. The agent was holding an open house. On a whim, we decided to go out for a sniff around the place, just for some fun. We had a great time walking around, discovering that we disliked all the same negative features and that we loved all the same positive ones. It felt like having a conversation with myself in many ways, total agreement without having to explain why. There were quite a lot of negative features for us in this place and we came home and rolled about laughing at the way the agent had presumed we were married and how much fun we'd had.

A few weeks later as we continued our Saturday morning study of the real estate we found another likely-looking property having an open house. We quickly agreed that we could enjoy another trip out to agree on all the negative points and eagerly headed out.

We parked outside the front gate and as we walked in we both looked at the set of cattleyards and said at the same time that they would buy a nice spa! We laughed, but as we walked down the driveway we both became a little quiet. We met the agent and she was keen to show us through the house, but we were more interested in the actual land. Still, not wanting to appear rude, we followed her in and walked dutifully through the house. Neither of us was particularly impressed as we both love older houses and this was a newer kit home. The rooms were very small and the house was boxy, but we agreed that the kitchen bench space was impressive and the fully screened back verandah was a bonus. We then begged to have a walk outside on our own. I don't think the agent was into walking the hills, and was ready to pack up, so she readily left us to explore our own way.

We almost didn't speak at all, we just walked, and I felt like I was holding my breath. The property itself was beautiful and it gave the distinct impression of a place that had been much loved. We headed to the top of the hill.

It is so clearly etched in my mind, standing up there, looking out over the countryside, looking down on the house, the breeze and the sun on our faces. Quietly I finally whispered, 'I *really* like this place.' Just as quietly he simply replied yes.

We wandered down to the front paddock and looped back to the house. We found the back verandah unlocked and sat on the three-seater swing inside. We talked quietly, enjoying the beautiful view, and suddenly realised we had been there for an hour. It was just starting to lightly rain. We jumped up, realising we had better leave. We would have looked very strange if the owners had turned up home so long after the open house had finished to find us swinging away there. We giggled like schoolkids as we scurried down the driveway back to the car.

We kept coming back to talking about how much we liked this property over the next few days. We agreed that this property was what we had both always dreamed of owning one day. We also knew that we were in a new relationship, he was just getting his café up and running and his daughter finishing school. We had lots of rationalisations as to why we would not be doing anything about it. But, hey, we could enjoy dreaming that this was the kind of place we just may be able to buy the following year.

Two weeks later we encountered the agent in the street and she asked us what we had thought of the property, pulling us into a conversation. It was hard to explain that we loved it but weren't in a position to purchase. I think she saw that we could be worked on.

We started receiving phone calls telling us more about the property and that it was coming up for auction and that the owners would really prefer to sell it before then. Each time we spoke with her we couldn't quite mask how much we were interested in it, even as we said we weren't truly ready to buy yet.

Finally she phoned and asked us if we would come out one evening with her and meet the owners. They were willing to offer us a six-month contract, as they were planning to build their next house but could wait there that long if they knew they had the sale. They were aware that we needed to sell both our houses and so they were also willing to offer us the long contract with only a $5000 deposit, something like ten times less than it would normally be. I still laugh to think that we really both wanted that place somewhere inside, because we found ourselves agreeing to meet them. Now it is not common for an agent to get the buyer and seller together. The role of the agent is normally to be the person in between.

So we went out and met the loveliest couple, about ten years older than us, who had an aura that made us feel at home. We went for a ride in his four-wheel-drive ute, and found it even more stunning, with a rainforest pocket at the base of the property.

Once back at the house we had tea and pretty cakes, and then the two men walked off for about an hour, talking non-stop all the stuff men talk about concerning tractors, water and fences.

We women sat on the verandah and literally talked about life, the universe and everything. It was past dark when the men stopped wandering about and we all sat down to the business side. We knew our budget and ended up making our highest offer. It was obvious that it was far below what they had expected and so we left with them thinking about it.

We laughed all the way to my house, feeling a bit relieved that we hadn't found ourselves buying our dream property, and disappointed at the same time.

It was a fifteen-minute drive home, and as I put the key in the front door the agent phoned.

It took five more phone calls back and forward, and in between we were frantically saying, 'Should we, shouldn't we? Would we, wouldn't we?'

On the last call we agreed to a price and the ball was rolling. Truly, it seemed like one of those 'too good to be true' offers. We had six months to sell at least one house and, even if all went flat, we had only lost $5000. It seemed like it was still a bit distant – it was going to take six months after all.

The next week I put my house on the market, expecting to settle in for the ride, as the real estate market was pretty slow in general. Chris held off putting his house on the market because his son immediately said he would be very interested in trying to buy it. We didn't see that as a problem because we weren't expecting anything to happen too quickly, so told him to find out what his bank would need him to do. It would be his first house, so getting that first home loan approved would be a bit of a process.

Two weeks later my house sold. It was such an easy process and so fast that it was a bit of a shock. It suddenly meant that we were going to have to get ourselves up and moved into that amazing property in only four weeks. This made the owners very happy as they could get on with their new plans too.

The thing about packing up is that you never feel like everything is going to be ready and then suddenly the removalist walks in to begin loading the truck. Somehow I got my house cleaned out and culled in time and the van picked up items from Chris's house and what was left at mine. On 7 May 2010 we moved to our dream property and into our less than dream home, but it all seemed dream enough for us.

We held a fabulous house-warming party, complete with a live band and nearly all our family around us celebrating. Chris's two daughters moved in with us. The eldest completed her final year of school with success and moved out of the area for university.

I had never had a partner living with me who was simply my best friend. He was as keen to take on some big project for a new garden as I was. In fact, he would end up expanding on everything we started because he would get so excited. We worked outside, filthy and exhausted, and then climbed into the spa and felt like we were on top of the world. We had been correct, the cattleyards sold for nearly the exact cost of the spa.

One of the things I loved most was the laughter. And he could talk for hours and never run out of something to say. I could simply sit and soak up his conversation, which could leap topics, from serious to belly-hurting silly, from one second to the next.

He was off to his café early every morning and I was in my home office, working for my clients and taking my breaks, walking around all the gardens we were creating. If I went into town I held every meeting I could at the café, and loved all the happy people there eating his food, laughing with him and watching their regard for him. He constantly inspired me to want to be the very best person I could be.

His talk turned towards marriage and he was slowly softening me. I had come out of divorce so hard and cynical, and now I was slowly melting down to a human being again. My first reaction to the mention of marriage was, 'I don't "do" wife!' But as the months passed I wasn't really objecting any longer when the subject came up. I found myself thinking about what it would mean to be his wife, both to me and to him. I kept thinking about 'until death do us part' and how I respected him because he had done that. From the start, the family was able to bring their mother into a conversation as a natural thing and I enjoyed hearing their stories. This doesn't often happen after divorce, and I found myself affected by the way they were honest about her, not putting her on some pedestal. Over the months I was coming to feel almost like I had known her, through their memories of her.

As I got to know this man even better by living with him and watching the kind of man he was, I began to realise that I had truly found someone incredibly special.

When he raised the subject of marriage again one night I realised I didn't have any objections left. I think he sensed that as he took the conversation along and the last of my walls crumbled.

This man who could talk about anything and be so silly, yet showed such depth of understanding.

This man who frolicked in gardens of flowers and could describe the subtle colour differences of every one of them and tell you its full name and how to propagate it.

This man who loved driving the tractor as much as I loved the ride-on mower, so we covered all the property waving as we came near each other.

This man who delighted in baking fruit-and-nut breads and making every kind of jam, pickle, chutney or relish you could think of.

This man who carved 'love hearts', as he called them, into every bit of concrete we poured, with our initials inside.

This man who would pause a movie to point out a vase of roses in the background.

This man who just wanted to lay back and hold me in his arms for hours at a time.

This man truly and deeply wanted me to be his wife, and he had an excellent track record.

He told me seriously that he was going to formally propose to me but that he had to get a few things organised. After more than a week I admit I was starting to wonder what was going on. I had made it clear that I did not want a ring. I am not a big jewellery person, and it seemed a waste of good money to me, so it's not like he was doing something sneaky with a jeweller.

When nearly another full week passed I began to wonder if I were mad as he was still behaving the same, but there had not been a further word said about a proposal. I thought that it would sound decidedly odd if I were to ask him when he planned to do this, so I kept it to myself and wondered instead.

On 10 October 2010 (10-10-10) he had everything in place, although he wasn't able to control the weather and it poured rain all day. I hadn't even considered that he was waiting for this date but it turned out that he felt it was a 'lucky' date. He had planned far more than I had imagined, and the torrential rain was wreaking havoc on his plans as they hinged around us being out in the gazebo. As the day moved along there was no sign of the weather changing. I was unaware of his rising unease at being thwarted in how to carry off his plan. I felt we were both getting a bit of cabin fever so decided I would have a nice hot shower, wash my hair and scrub the shower out.

Unbeknown to me, he decided to devise and execute Plan B and scurried about while I was in the shower, preparing everything in the dining room. I took my time and finally wandered back down the hallway, stunned to find the table set out beautifully with fruit, nuts, chocolates and champagne glasses. Beside the table was a pot containing a tree. He sat me down and in the most romantic way asked me formally if I would agree to become his wife.

I solemnly told him that nothing would make me happier than to accept.

He broke open the champagne and we raised a toast and he began to totally blow my mind. He knew I did not want a ring, and he also knew that the Moreton Bay fig is my favourite tree in the world. He picked up the pot and told me that this was my 'engagement ring' and that we were going to have to go out in the rain and plant it that very afternoon. I laughed and agreed we could handle the weather for such a planting. Then he opened a cupboard and brought out a wrapped gift. I was surprised, as it seemed to me that he had already put together the most romantic proposal. I opened the package to discover a heart-shaped plaque to go under the tree. It announced that on 10-10-10 this tree had been planted on the day of our engagement to marry, may it flourish, as we will for the rest of our lives. I cried as I read the plaque, in the way beauty and happiness can bring tears. I was amazed that for the past two weeks I had wondered why he was dragging things out, and now saw that he had been working with great care for detail.

So we ate a little, and drank a little, and I was feeling like a princess when he returned to the cupboard and brought out yet another wrapped gift and a card. Now I was starting to feel a little overwhelmed as he handed these to me with a smile of sheer delight. I opened the card to find that it was not a bought card, but one he had actually designed himself and had printed professionally. He had written out his feelings towards us becoming man and wife. I felt shaky as I turned to open the second gift. It was beginning to feel like some kind of dream that I was going to awaken from. No one goes to this much effort to propose, surely!

The second gift was a silver heart-shaped jewellery box, with overlapping hearts on the top. I was a bit taken aback for a moment, as there was to be no jewellery, but as I looked at what a lovely item it was he said gently, 'I wanted you to have something that would sit in plain view, so that every day you can look at it and remember this moment. It doesn't matter if it is empty; it is for you to enjoy the memory.' Well, I was crying again, unable to believe that anyone would go to this kind of effort for me. It seemed like something you would see in a movie.

We did indeed head out into the rain and it was something we laughed about so many times afterwards. Gumboots, rain and mud followed the beautiful setting of the proposal and gifts, as we chose where to plant 'our tree' and battled through the task.

We later found a beautiful sandstone rock with a flat side and mounted the plaque, and we would often walk to the tree as it grew, indeed thrived. On some nights the moon shone on the plaque and from the back verandah it looked like a star under the tree.

As we mused over choosing dates, tossing ideas back and forth, we realised that 7 May 2011 would be a Saturday, and would be exactly one year since we had moved onto our property. It was obviously the perfect choice. We would have seven months to prepare and it was likely to be good weather, not hot but not yet cold. And May is usually a fairly dry month.

My man began to blossom, like a flower that had been hidden, as we planned our wedding. He was involved in every single detail. In fact, he had more creative ideas than I had, and dragged me around craft shops, excitedly explaining his latest ideas to me.

He insisted that we would make the invitations ourselves and somehow had a pretty good idea of how to go about that. We must have spent hundreds of hours laughing as we devised invitations, details of how the ceremony would proceed and making all kinds of things we needed. We wrote the entire ceremony ourselves and emailed it to the celebrant. It must have been the easiest money she had made, as usually the celebrant has to help the couple out a fair bit to get everything in order. It was an important aspect of the wedding for us to do it ourselves in our own way. And yet Chris insisted that I would have to leave the property the day before the wedding as he intended to do all the decorating of the gazebo and reception area. I was not to see any of this in advance – it would be a surprise for me.

I decided to organise where we would stay on our wedding night as a surprise for him and to design my own traditional white wedding dress. He decided that he would therefore not allow me to know anything of his suit. Even though we would not know exactly how we were each dressing, we knew already that we would complement each other regardless.

We had been given a discount on a wonderful unit down at the beach as a wedding present from a friend, where we would spend the next week for our honeymoon.

All of our children and closest friends took part in some way so that it was a ceremony created completely by us, but carried off by all that were dearest to us, working with us.

Of course there were a few hitches along the way, a few mild panics, but I guess a wedding wouldn't be complete without some dramas. The person making my dress decided to move states halfway through and posted me a dress that was nothing like a finished product, or truly matching my specifications. I was able in the last few weeks to have it corrected and completed by a very talented local lady. The band that was going to play for both the ceremony and the reception pulled out at the last minute, but we were able to find the most delightful guitarist and singer, who made the wedding music even more than I could have hoped for.

The day before the wedding, I dutifully packed a bag after breakfast and a very nervous man kissed me tenderly goodbye and said he would see me 'at the altar'.

I slept fitfully and finally rose quietly just before dawn, made a cup of tea and went out on the back verandah and watched the sun rise to a perfectly clear sky that quickly became a vivid blue, without a breath of wind. It was the most perfect weather we could have hoped for and I felt alternating calm and nerves.

The wedding was perfect; every single thing happened on time and in sequence. To say the decorations were stunning would be an understatement. The inventive way he had attached cascades of living flowers everywhere, with mixes of white and purple lengths of material making graceful scallops over every doorway and around the gazebo, glittering hanging hearts and heart confetti strewn around gave a magical wonderland effect.

After the perfect ceremony we climbed onto the tractor in our gorgeous wedding clothes and went down to our rainforest pocket with our photographer. We had a small reception and all left by 6 pm so that we could actually relax and enjoy our wedding night. We went to our private cottage with our dinner and champagne all ready for us, and reflected on what a perfect day we had created and what an amazing life we had already lived in only sixteen months. We were in total awe that so much love and happiness had been given to us. What a team we were.

We spent the next ten months poring through the 2000 photos that had been collectively taken of the wedding day, and the video footage, and put together a DVD of our life leading up to and including the wedding day. It was a huge task, but we worked on it three to five nights every week and it never felt like a chore. We were constantly talking about our day, remembering details and finding photos that gave a laugh or another memory of the day. We reflected on our awe at finding each other at this point in our lives. We were immensely proud of the DVD once it was complete and had the cover and jewel-case jacket professionally printed. We even had personal postage stamps made from a wedding photo and sent the packages out to everyone dear to us.

One of our favourite sayings was, 'It just doesn't get any better than this, except that it just keeps getting better!'

It was almost a letdown to finish the project as we had enjoyed the focus on our perfect wedding day, but a relief as well because we wanted to share it. We decided to take a little break and then begin working on a wedding photo album that we would create online and have professionally printed.

We never did complete or print that album. The loss of an amazing future was soon to unravel the simple joy of things in our short past.

3. A monster creeping up on its prey

In retrospect, I had noticed some of the earliest signs of the disease. But I had no idea that what I thought of as little oddities that we all have would turn out to be the early onset of such an insidious disease.

They were things we laughed about. My hips ache if I sit about for too long, but Chris would get burning pains if he had to walk far, particularly up any incline. He would mumble that he never used to be that way, and I would laugh, as actually I'm not so good going down inclines. Walking around our property, he strode confidently downhill while I lagged behind, then I would pass him easily going up the other side. We thought these were just irrelevant details of life.

I always noticed that his hips looked 'thin' but couldn't really put my finger on what it was about them, just that they seemed awfully 'bony'. He never carried any real fat, but it was just how I knew him from the age of fifty-one and I didn't give it much thought.

A few months after we moved onto our property Chris took on a huge vegetable garden project. We had a lot of rock on the property and he spent many hours digging this garden out by hand. While he worked he was happy and didn't seem to find the work too hard or tiring, at the end of the day feeling that wonderful tiredness that only a good workout can give. But at night he began to wake with burning sensations in his hands that would disappear within minutes of getting up. They were disturbing his sleep and I suggested he see a physiotherapist.

The physio checked him over and told him that he had muscle wastage in the back of his shoulders. Chris didn't mention it to me and didn't really take much notice of what the physio had said. The physio worked on him, gave him exercises and after a few sessions the hand burning at night stopped and never returned.

This symptom was nothing to do with MND; it was the mention of muscle wastage that far back that was important, although it couldn't have registered as such at the time.

When I massaged his shoulders I noticed he felt strange between the shoulder blades – it was like long cords rather than normal muscle but, again, I hadn't known his shoulders before this time. He would comment that he never used to feel like that and we would laugh about old age creeping up, not giving it much further thought.

We just lived our fairytale. He felt strong working outside, and we took on any project on the property, making new gardens, laying down paths or whatever. We loved working outside together, and creating beauty.

We still laughed a lot, and he still talked constantly. We still stayed up too late at night, talking and laughing as though we hadn't seen each other in weeks. He would amaze me with the way he seemed able to work out how nearly anything worked and fix it with some bit of something he had in the shed.

In October 2011 Chris had a nasty dose of influenza, something very unusual for either of us. He was sick for two weeks and over the next few weeks I noticed that he would often give a funny little throat cough. It wasn't related to eating, drinking, talking, exerting himself or anything that I noticed, he would suddenly give a funny little cough. I had been with him long enough to know that he had never done that before. It ever so slowly increased. It was not a true cough; it was more like a sudden little throat spasm.

He also had exaggerated reflexes in his feet. I didn't think of his reaction as a reflex in a neurological sense. All I knew was that if I was giving him a leg massage I could not easily take hold of either of his feet. If I did his toes would pull up sharply towards the ankle and his foot would jerk out of my hand. I had to work my way carefully to his feet and gently but firmly take hold of them, holding against the reflex, and be still for a few moments. Even then there could be a milder version of the reflex at any time during the foot massage.

Now who would go to a doctor and say, 'Doc my hips ache when I walk uphill and my wife thinks they are bony, my shoulders are odd, my feet are jumpy and I give a funny cough now and then?' Who would even connect any of these things? At the time they were hardly noticeable; it is hindsight that has burnt the significance of them into my mind so that I can connect them now.

He began to seem mildly depressed. The café was not making the kind of money he had hoped, and I put it down to this. If I asked him if he felt at all depressed he would say definitely not. I still felt, as months passed, that he either was depressed or his personality was changing from a very happy, silly, energetic, hopeful man to a sometimes annoyed, slightly lethargic man. At the time I was not alarmed, but it was in the back of my mind. He started coming home from the café earlier. He had always told me all the funniest stories of what had happened in his day, and café owners seem to have quite a lot of funny things happen. But as each month went along he began to talk about the annoying things in his day more than the funny ones.

Internally I felt a little annoyed at this myself. More often he was arriving home before I had finished my work for the day. Even though I was engrossed in the task at hand, if I had another hour or more of work left I would stop and have a cup of tea with Chris so that I got to have a little break with him. In the earlier days he would then go off to do something around the property and I would finish work. As he seemed to turn more often to what had annoyed him or been difficult in his day, I began to feel I was not taking a break and that he was putting negative energy around me, when I still needed to be focused on my work, finding solutions to problems.

He began to become annoyed at me as the months went on, because he felt that I wanted him to always be jolly and happy instead of being able to tell me all sides of things. I felt that when things don't go so great at work, the best thing is to leave them behind, at work, rather than bringing them into your personal life. I wasn't expecting him to be always jolly and happy, but I didn't want him perpetuating the negative stuff. Instead of doing things around the property after that cup of tea, he began to sit on the verandah doing nothing. He would say he was just so tired after being on his feet all day and mark off all the things he had to do in a day.

I was the opposite, as so much of my work revolved around being fairly physically inactive, but being very mentally active. For me to have a break and listen to the negative of another's day was draining, particularly when I was going to go back to work straight after.

I didn't feel this was a big issue. For all I knew he could have turned around after a couple of months and become his happy, positive self again, back doing things outside, whistling a tune and telling me stories that would have me laughing for hours. If this had happened, I would probably have forgotten that there had been a few months when he wasn't as positive as usual. With the benefit of hindsight, however, I see that a slow but definite change was happening, and it never got better as we slid down that MND hill.

He decided that he would not continue the café lease when it expired in a year's time, at the end of February 2013. The economic climate was poor, people were tightening their budgets and the price of so many ingredients was rising. Once he came to this decision, he became even more critical of every negative detail of his day. He closed the café two hours earlier than he had in the first year. So he was coming home earlier, in a complaining mood, and I was feeling more pressure to work harder.

He noticed one day that he could not whistle. It began to really disturb him, but he did not tell me for some months. At first he was just puzzled, because he used to whistle quite a lot and was far better at carrying a tune than I am.

He began grinding his teeth in his sleep, in increasing frequency. It's a most unnerving noise, especially in the middle of the night when everything else is so quiet. In the mornings he would wake and find either he had bitten the inside of his cheeks or that his jaw was tense from the grinding. The bite areas would ulcerate, and he began to bite his mouth or tongue more frequently as he ate. These little symptoms creep up on you and, by the time you notice them, you realise they have been happening for months.

Around the same time he found that any breeze, even a warm breeze on a hot day, would set his teeth to chattering uncontrollably. Again he did not tell me this for months, and the first time I saw it happen I was quite stunned that it was so severe.

By June 2012 Chris found at times that taking a drink of cold water would cause his palate would drop down, closing his throat off, when it hit the back of his throat and the water would come spraying back out. Next sip of water, no problem. This happened maybe once a week. His workmates were starting to laugh at him, and he laughed along. Around this time, he got it in his head that he was going to give up caffeine and cigarettes, all at the same time. I'm sure that he suspected something was wrong and wanted to get a bit healthier. It was a disaster with the cigarettes, but he did keep his caffeine consumption lower for good after this.

He started to find that, without warning, he would begin to laugh hysterically at something in the shop, and couldn't stop himself and would have to walk out the back alone to control it. The first time the uncontrollable laughing hit him was when he failed to swallow a large mouthful of water and apparently covered a large area of floor with the force of it leaving his mouth. Everyone put it down to him being a little crazy as he tried to stop smoking. After some weeks of this behaviour increasing in severity and frequency, his staff began to mention it to me. Oh it was said with a laugh, but also with that hooded look of worry in the eyes that people use when they aren't sure if they should even tell you, or if you will believe them.

In July he began to notice that at times during the day he would seem to be slurring, maybe lasting for an hour or a little longer. At night, within the first few sips of a beer he would feel himself starting to slur. By August people at the café could hear the slurring but it would come and go, often not too bad during the morning but becoming noticeable as the day wore on. It was only a light slurring, but it concerned him, although I didn't think it sounded too bad. By September he was slurring nearly all the time, worse at different times of the day, and it was not going away. I remember a girlfriend phoned me one late afternoon and Chris said a few things in the background. She said in surprise, 'Is he drunk?' That was the first time it hit me that his speech really was slurred, as I think I had become accustomed to it. I explained to her that he was having something very strange happening with his speech and we didn't know why.

Finally, by October 2012, I could no longer deny that there was something medical going on. I knew he was concerned and that his odd symptoms were slightly but persistently getting worse. On top of the speech and water-swallowing issues, I had now noticed that a couple of muscles in his upper arms would often twitch. And I mean they could twitch for hours. I didn't see how any of these things were connected. I certainly made no connection between these symptoms and the slow changes in his attitude and behaviour that I had noticed. My birthday was coming up and we were having a party, so I decided to wait until after this to talk to him about it all and suggest we seek medical advice.

When I discussed my concern, he began to tell me a few of the details that he hadn't mentioned earlier. I suggested it was time to see a doctor, and he reluctantly agreed. I thought it would just be a trip to the doctor, maybe a test or something, so we could sort this out and get back to our fairytale. I made an appointment and together we went to see our GP.

By now he was reporting that his nose felt dry and blocked and would not clear properly by blowing it. After a physical examination, the doctor announced sinusitis and prescribed Amoxicillin, garlic and horseradish, and gave us a referral for a CT scan of the sinuses if it didn't improve after a week.

She felt the problem was a post-nasal drip, probably a mild sinus infection, and that it explained what she described as 'hyper-nasal' speech and the throat issues.

To be honest, one of my first thoughts was that she had probably hit the nail on the head. I felt it could also explain the teeth grinding and the strange little throat things that had been going on for a year now. I figured that he had probably had some low-level something left over from that flu, and it had been slowly building a chronic reaction. Garlic and horseradish would help loosen up and clear the sinuses and antibiotics would clean out any infection. I came home feeling quite positive about the direction she was taking and the treatment ordered.

We sat and talked that evening and he confessed that he had been convinced he had a brain tumour. I was stunned to think that he could be carrying a worry on that kind of level, and that I hadn't known. His first wife had died of cancer only seven years previously, and it had moved to her brain in the last stages, so he knew first hand where that kind of diagnosis could take him. I kept thinking how awful it was that this had been on his mind, and he had worried about it alone. It reminded me how much we really do experience our lives inside our own heads and hearts. He stated he felt that maybe it would turn out to be something simple after all, but he didn't look completely convinced.

I had an uneasy feeling, however, that something had been bothering him for at least a year, causing personality changes. Yet, whenever I had approached him he had said all was fine. It felt like my ship of courage had sprung a slow leak.

After a few days on the antibiotics, he realised that a back molar had been feeling aggravated for some months and now felt a little better. It was strange as it was like he hadn't consciously realised that this tooth was unhappy, until suddenly it started to feel better, but the difference was now obvious. So he saw a dentist who X-rayed his teeth and did a thorough examination. He noted a bad gum infection, where an old filling had fallen out, and filled the tooth. He said the previous filling had been leaking for a long time and was likely the cause of general aggravation. It explained a low-grade infection in the sinus region.

The tooth felt great, but he continued to worsen, so we booked in for the CT scan of his sinuses. The results showed mild sinusitis and the doctor prescribed a new antibiotic, advised him to keep up the garlic and horseradish, and wrote an ENT referral, saying we should go to him if it did not clear within two weeks. Still his speech and swallowing slowly but definitely worsened, so we made the ENT appointment for December 2012.

This time, within a few days of starting the new antibiotic, the molar that had started feeling good last time began to ache fiercely. We made an urgent dentist appointment and he ordered the dentist to pull the tooth out.

The ENT examined him, checked the CT results and announced that he could completely fix this. He explained why we needed a different antibiotic for this type of infection and that we needed to move up to Bisolvon to help his body clear the extra fluids out. He made an appointment for us to return in January to review, but assured us that this was easily solved and he would be cured by then. So now he was on the third lot of antibiotics within two months, but we had been assured that this was the cure.

Two weeks after the first tooth was removed, the molar directly underneath began to inflame and cause a lot of pain. Another trip to the dentist and more X-rays showed that there was a huge hole over the nerve of the tooth and he ordered the dentist to remove this tooth also. Looking back, I think he was fearful and hoped that ripping a few teeth out would magically sort everything. I admit I was also feeling that maybe the issue was more dental in origin and had been causing all his problems, even after the assurance of the ENT.

One day early in the New Year a regular customer came into the café and, hearing him speak, told him that some years back a friend had experienced similar speech problems and it had turned out to be MND. So Chris went straight to Dr Google and researched. He messaged me and told me what had been said, so of course I immediately looked it up too.

This is where denial is such a powerful thing. It became quickly obvious that MND is a fatal disease with no cure, so my mind was jumping up and down telling me there was no way it could be anything like this. Yes, he was certainly having trouble speaking, but no one in their right mind would believe this meant he was going to die. As I looked at the information on the screen I could see that bulbar-onset MND starts with the tongue failing, and this is the cause of the speech and swallowing issues.

Denial jumped up in satisfaction saying, there you are, it can't be this because he is not having problems with his tongue at all; he is having problems with his nose, sinuses and jaw. That is not the same thing at all; it is impossible. I became quite angry that someone would just say this in the café, pronouncing such a hideous illness. I let him know that it did not seem like what he was experiencing. He went along with me, but I could tell that he now had this lodging itself in his mind as another terrible cause of what could be happening to him.

There was no improvement, of course, so he started syringing tea-tree oil into his nose and found that it did give some relief. However, his speech was still declining and anyone hearing him talk could notice it at any time of day. The dentist suggested that he should be referred to see a facio-maxillary surgeon to have the issues resolved once and for all.

In January we went to the surgeon, who took everything very seriously, saying that he would get to the bottom of it. He ordered a series of tests. He also made a point of saying that his clinic liked solving a real challenge and they would not rest until they had the answer.

The tests included 3D imaging of the brain and neck, which showed all to be completely normal. An MRI came back completely clear. An ultrasound of carotid arteries showed no obstructions and blood tests showed all within normal range. In short, he was given a totally clean bill of health and the surgeon did not want to know anything more about us. So much for his insistence at the first meeting that they were going to stick to this until it was solved. He walked us out of his office and as he put my husband's file on the desk he looked at the receptionist and said clearly, 'No further appointments.' We walked out wondering what we were going to do next, as he had been prodded and poked by four different people now, and had pretty much every type of image taken of the insides of him, and everyone said he was perfectly healthy and normal.

Due to some local floods, we were unable to keep the ENT appointment in January 2013. Chris decided he didn't want to book another appointment as it wasn't worth pursuing – he did not believe the ENT specialist was going to solve anything either. In early February a part of his mouth became increasingly painful and he returned to the dentist, who found that a bony growth that had been there for years had begun to ulcerate. We were referred back to the facio-maxillary surgeon, who removed the section of bone.

As his mouth healed from the surgery, he continued to experience worsening speech and the sensation that his palate was not opening or closing properly when drinking liquids. When the sutures were removed and we discussed the continuing symptoms with the surgeon, he referred us back to the ENT, saying clearly that he could do nothing more for us. He suggested Chris was just stressed and needed to take some time off and we should go for a nice holiday.

I don't know how I held my tongue when he said that, as it seemed to be such a disparaging remark. Once I got over my anger at this later, I did begin to wonder if Chris was depressed, causing a physical reaction. So many people think that psychosomatic illnesses are 'not real'. However, I knew that symptoms caused by stress are just as real as those caused by some organic issue. If you have a severe headache because of stress, rather than because you have a neck injury, you have pain just the same. The treatment will be different but the pain is just as real.

I tried to talk with Chris at home about whether or not he felt depressed or if the stress of the café situation was getting to him at all. He probably felt angry at me, like I had at the surgeon earlier, and said that of course he was stressed. He had planned to leave the café in only another month or two and find a job, and now he couldn't even apply for a job when he sounded drunk. He was beginning to worry that he would never be able to apply for a job at all. It was getting hard to turn up at the café and work with people who kept asking him what was wrong with his voice. His feelings in those situations were valid, but it was starting to feel rather like the chicken and egg debate.

The lease ended, and he secured a buyer for the business at a greatly reduced price from what he had paid.

Now, not only did I have a husband who was having a very hard time working out some health issues, but I had him at home all the time as well, and more debt from the low-priced café sale. Because I do much of my work from home, it was like having to bring my sick husband to work with me each day. He saw no prospect of looking for work until this was resolved. He also became convinced that there was something serious going on, fearing they had missed finding a brain tumour or some other very serious issue.

One day as we talked about all that was happening to him, he confessed again that he truly felt he either had a brain tumour or a neurological condition such as MND. Without thinking much about it I asked him to stick his tongue out. I felt sick to the pit of my stomach. He stuck out his tongue and it looked like a little sock filled with a hundred live worms. I had never seen anything like this tongue that was constantly wriggling and rippling. I told him it looked strange but I tried not to let on my fear. In my heart, I knew at this point that we were looking at something insidious and the ship of courage was now sinking.

I suggested we get a neurologist referral and he said he would go back to see the ENT specialist.

We returned to the ENT and he examined his throat again to find that one side of the palate was not functioning correctly. He organised an endoscopic examination. I asked him to look at my husband's tongue. The ENT did not seem to think that what he saw was anything of any real note and dismissed it. I felt that my fears over his tongue must have been unfounded and so we agreed to the procedure, the date set for late April.

We always seemed to be waiting another couple of weeks or a month to get to someone new, or go back to someone again, or have some new test or other, and yet he was steadily worsening. His speech was now noticeably impaired and he had to be careful swallowing anything. By the time he would have the endoscopy, we would have been seeing doctors for six months and he would have been having symptoms that had concerned him for nearly a year. We thought at this point that living in limbo was the worst thing we could imagine.

A friend recommended a doctor specialising in alternative medicine to us. Chris had heard amazing reports about him, so I made an appointment. I was given the name of specialists further out of our area and made appointments with another ENT and a neurologist a couple of hours' drive away. We were starting to feel desperate – when was someone going to understand what was going on and give us a clear diagnosis so we could start getting him better again?

We went to the alternative doctor who took his history, gave him an examination and said that he worked on the basis of what caused disease to take hold of a body. He explained that an injury sustained by walking through a plate glass door some fifteen years earlier was the cause of all his problems now, as the vulnar bone in the roof of his mouth was not functioning correctly and that he could fix this. He also said Chris was suffering depression. He did a 'treatment' that can only be described as like a 'laying on of hands'. He had Chris lying on a table for a good hour, and came in at intervals to do the laying of hands.

He refused to charge us any money for the treatment and said he wanted to see him again in six weeks' time. He gave no indication as to what would happen, how he would improve or how fast it would happen, but seemed confident in his diagnosis and treatment.

To be honest, that evening was the best in many months. Chris felt light in spirit, like a weight had lifted, and we talked and laughed and loved. He still felt very good the following day, but over the next few days it slowly wore off, as there was no difference at all in his speech.

He began to experience weakness in his left hand, particularly between the thumb and index finger, causing him to have problems holding a fork or anything small, not being able to keep it steady. His left arm was beginning to look markedly thinner than the right, and he was a left-handed person.

The twitching that had started in a couple of muscles was spreading down his arms.

In early April, I had a client working here who had worked with children with multiple issues in schools. She had not been here for a couple of months and, after hearing Chris speak, later turned to me and said, 'If that was one of my children, I would get them to a speech pathologist. I think you should try this.'

At first he resisted the idea as he was being shipped around from doctor to dentist to doctor, but after a few days he saw there could be some value in it. We decided that we had been to so many places and had so many things done and tested it would be worthwhile to write down a history of all that had been going on. With Chris's speech continuing to deteriorate, it was difficult for him to tell the story, and it was getting hard to remember everything in order and not end up leaving parts out and having to backtrack to fill them in again.

It was getting hard to work up any hope about seeing anyone new, as we had hoped so many times over the past six months. It felt like this would probably be just another waste of time, but we were too desperate to not try.

On arrival we handed her the written history, and Chris said hello, but not much more. She asked if she could start by reading what we had written. I was thrilled that, after all the time and effort it had taken to write this, someone was actually going to read it. I had been a little fearful that health professionals might pay very little attention to the detail we had written out.

She read carefully the first half page, then started to scan read. She looked directly in his eyes and said: 'I'm not a doctor so I cannot diagnose you. In what I've heard in your voice so far, and what I'm reading here, I believe this is MND. I want to get you straight in to the specialist MND clinic in Brisbane so that you can have the experts give you a true diagnosis.'

That day, having a speech pathologist so quickly speak the words that changed our lives, remains a blur except for the time sitting there with her. I will never forget how calm she was when she looked us in the eyes and simply said, 'I believe this is MND.' I felt myself start screaming in the back of my brain somewhere with the first overtures of panic. Yet somehow I sat there pretty calmly. I was trying to keep my breathing slow and controlled, and my hands were carefully clasped in my lap. I was thinking of the need to keep them held together in case they went flying off, but not to hold them too tightly either, so that I would look calm. I felt that if I moved I may well fall completely apart, but somehow, sitting very still, I felt like I had some kind of control, and that this would become normal any minute and she would realise she was wrong.

She asked if she could examine him a little more thoroughly and proceeded to have him poke out his tongue, and did some speaking and swallowing tests with him. I remained silent and 'calm', but it was like sitting in the middle of a whirlpool.

If I stayed very still then I would not be caught by the whirlpool and flung into a downward spiral and smashed to pieces. Just sit still, think about breathing slowly and evenly, be very calm, it's going to be alright in a moment, you'll see, just stay still no matter what.

I must have kept on saying inane things like this to myself the rest of the time we were in her office. She phoned the clinic while we sat there with her to make the appointment. She was unable to get through and left a message, assuring us she would follow this up and phone us the moment she had an appointment.

She recommended that there was absolutely no point in going through with the endoscopic procedure or seeing another ENT, and that the neurologist we had made an appointment with was also not worth pursuing as we needed one who specialised in MND. Most neurologists do not.

We were silent walking to the car. We got in and I drew a deep breath and we looked at each other. I was in full-blown shock, but Chris simply and quietly said, 'You know, I feel relieved. I knew it was this, and the waiting and wondering while no one could diagnose me has been worse than knowing it is something even this bad'. I did cry then, not the blubbering, screaming and wailing that was happening inside me but a quiet little cry, then another deep breath and I drove us home.

'Us' would never be the same again, nothing would.

This was still not even an official diagnosis, just a provisional one given by a health professional, but not by a doctor, certainly not a neurologist. Hope that it could still be wrong tried to clamour through to my consciousness, but somehow the long winding path we had been treading seemed to have reached the final fork and there was no mistaking or hiding from it.

The innocence of childhood
oh how sweet the games
a hand over the ear or the eyes
and all manner of monsters
are forever banished
If I can't see you
then neither can you see me!

~

If life is an ocean
and I am but a drop
If I drown
will I become more
or less
or will I simply 'become'?

4.   What you never want to hear

Is there a right way to react to a diagnosis such as MND?

All I can say is that my experience was nothing like in the movies. I'm no hero; I don't have some magic way of knowing how to do everything right in the worst of situations. The shock produces so many effects on you that you are not in full control of yourself. I often had the eerie feeling of watching myself going through it all from a slight distance, as though it was happening to someone else or I was watching it as a movie or as though I had ceased to exist and was just a shadow in a world that no longer made sense. I knew it was really happening to me, but it is an overwhelming situation. So many emotions all clamour for first place in line, including that demon denial that still wanted to convince me that it would all go away if I refused to accept it.

There was no way to accurately measure time. There was the time we had not been here, there was the time when we would be somewhere else, and there was this time in between. The wait in this time seemed interminable. Time took on a whole new meaning within MND space.

Bulbar symptoms are just so rottenly obvious. My wonderful man who could talk under water with a mouthful of rocks was barely able to get out any word with more than two syllables. He was becoming withdrawn because talking was so hard and he was so self-conscious of how he sounded. Now added to this was the certainty of a diagnosis, not just terminal, but also a progressively degenerative illness with no cure.

A huge aspect of the disease is the progressive degeneration. Terminal is one thing, but you could live for a reasonable period of time. Some people live up to twenty years with invasive ventilation, some live five years or more, declining slowly. It is the way this disease takes your loved one away a little bit at a time, each bit seeming like its own little death.

This was definitely the hardest part for me. In my working life I solve problems. I excel at taking a problem, pulling it to pieces and formulating a solution, making life easy and workable for my clients.

I have always believed that if there is a problem, there is a solution. If there is no solution, then you don't have a problem, you have a fact. I desperately wanted Chris's health issue to be a problem! But what I had to face was that his disease was a fact. The only problems we would be able to find solutions to concerned how to live each day to the fullest, make the most of whatever we had every day, and try to keep him as comfortable as possible as it progressed.

How quickly days slip by if we don't take notice and cherish them and use every hour in them wisely. Even faced with a diagnosis such as this, I know I wasted time in the early months because I was in shock and I was grieving both the immediate loss and the losses that were to come.

We were both overwhelmed with emotions and reactions, and the mixture of numbness and panic caused a lot of inefficiency and so days and weeks were slipping by as fast as ever.

Chris did not want to tell anyone about this provisional diagnosis. This is a common difference between the person afflicted with MND and their partner. For all my denial, I wanted to be able to tell close family, and indeed they had been worried for months, and receive a bit of support and feel less isolated. For him, even though he had been expecting it to be very serious, and said he was relieved to know what it was, he wasn't ready to deal with the reactions of others, and maybe felt it would make it all too real.

We spent hours talking over the next day or two and suddenly he said that he wanted to go and visit his sister. This surprised me as they had not been close and rarely spoke. I believe now that it was a need to put things into order that he had left tangled up for many years. I immediately told him that he should do what he felt was right and got out my diary.

We were seeing the neurologist in only a few weeks, and our second wedding anniversary was coming up in between, the choices were to go straight away, wait until after our anniversary or wait until after the clinic appointment. I told him that he should just up and go right away. We had no idea what was going to happen now in the way of timeframes, but we did know that he was only going to become worse. Going now gave him the option of seeing her again; if the disease did not progress rapidly, maybe even several times. I did not want him never getting there and regretting it.

In a flurry we had him organised to go and he was adamant that he would drive, even though it is a sixteen-hour drive without taking breaks into consideration. He would stay in a motel overnight and take two days to drive each way. This was really quite amazing given he had been finding it difficult to go into town on his own to run errands because his speech was so hard to understand. Suddenly he was taking off on an adventure.

In fact, the trip did him a lot of good in many ways. The long drive gave him some time to process what was happening, with the freedom of not doing so in front of me. He organised himself with a pocket notebook to carry with him and wrote several pages of items he would commonly ask for – what coffee he liked and so on. I was impressed, as he had resisted using any kind of communication aids. I think it is harder to walk into shops in your own town, run by people you know, and either not be understood or have to write down what you need. Suddenly he was stopping at places he had never been before and would probably never come back to again, with strangers serving him. It seemed that this allowed him to feel freer to practise communicating with pen and paper.

Suddenly, only nine days after this provisional diagnosis was given, I was alone. It all happened so fast I hardly had time to realise that I was going to be alone for nine whole days before he was actually gone. I worked the morning he left and had a lovely afternoon off, made a nice dinner and had a couple of drinks. Then I sat down at my computer and for the first time started to truly research, going to an online forum for people with MND and carers of those people. I sat in horrified fascination, reading through information posted by people and watching YouTube videos, and scared myself totally out of my wits. How the hell was I ever going to be able to do this? How can anyone bear what was going to happen to them? How could I possibly watch this happen to my own husband? I felt sick, my heart was racing, and yet I couldn't tear myself away from it all and I kept on scaring myself. I spent hours in this torture, telling myself I was researching to become educated.

The next day I gave myself a stern talking to and promised myself I would not repeat that exercise. Of course there is the old question – if no one hears a promise being made did it really happen? I didn't ever quite scare myself to that same point again, I learned to limit my reading on the forum to the types of topics I felt more able to deal with and stayed away from topics about dealing with the later stages of progression.

When Chris came home from this visit, he was in better spirits in some ways, but we were both still very much in shock. Our second wedding anniversary was nothing like I could have ever imagined it would be. We went out to dinner and, while the restaurant was lovely and the food was nice, it was a sombre evening. With his speech problems, sitting in a noisy restaurant meant there was little conversation.

It was the first time it really started to hit home to me – we couldn't plan any future together any more. We could plan to do something in the coming week, but we couldn't take on any big projects again, we couldn't plan any kind of activity for the long term. Being our anniversary, I would have expected us to tell the stories of our magical wedding day again, talk about how wonderful our second year together had been and how much better the next year coming up would be. We didn't talk about any of those things. In fact, I don't remember what we did talk about. I know that we talked very little.

Only two weeks now to wait until the MND clinic. I worked long hard hours and we tried to believe we could keep living life as normally as possible. We had another appointment with the speech pathologist and Chris had a lot of questions for her about the disease and the diagnostic process. He made it very clear that he would not be satisfied unless a neurologist could completely rule out anything else this could be, and prove to him that he had this. I was surprised by what he said here. Two weeks earlier he had been saying that he knew this was what he had and that he was relieved to finally be told. Now he had all these rules on what was required to convince him. Denial is a powerful thing and it can always lead to surprising tactics.

We were led to believe that we would be at the clinic for at least a couple of hours and would have many more tests done and would probably then have to go back another day for the diagnosis. We updated our written history and wrote a list of questions so that we wouldn't forget anything, as we were nervous and scared.

The neurologist was a kind man who gave us his full attention and a suitably concerned smile. He went over the reports from all the previous tests and the referring letters from both our GP and speech pathologist. He asked to examine Chris and proceeded to check his reflexes and examine the muscle atrophy. Every time he tapped his jaw with the reflex hammer it would do the chattering motion that Chris had noticed as one of the early symptoms. The neurologist asked permission to bring in some others. Five other doctors came in and most of them had a go with the hammer themselves.

Apparently this clear reaction isn't common, though they never really told us why they all wanted to see and try it for themselves. It felt demeaning to be treated this way. This was the life-changing diagnosis we were here to pursue, we were highly stressed and scared, and yet my husband was just this interesting set of symptoms for others to observe. We had been asked if we minded, and we didn't, but we could have been included and had it explained to us. I learned what it was they were observing and what it meant months later with my own research.

Afterwards we sat down with the neurologist, who looked us in the eye and said that he had no hesitation in telling us that it was MND. In the United States, it is pretty much unheard of to diagnose this without a test called an EMG as the final diagnostic tool. The test involves placing needles into muscles and running electrical signals through them in order to detect electrical currents being transmitted and record their speed and strength. We had expected he would whip this machine out and do the test, but he hadn't even mentioned it. It was eerily similar to our first appointment with the speech pathologist – read the history, take a bit of a look and a listen, and it was obvious. What stunned me most was that Chris accepted the diagnosis without question. The neurologist filled out Centrelink forms for the disability pension, stating this as the diagnosis, and not a question of 'Are you sure?' was raised.

I found out some time later that the EMG is not performed by simply whipping out some machine in an office and doing a simple test, but at this point we were so ignorant about everything I didn't know what to expect in a 'diagnostic appointment'.

We were told there was no cure, to come back every three months, have some breathing tests done and an EMG would be organised in a few months' time. We were given a couple of prescriptions and we could decide if he wanted to fill them and try the medications. He couldn't predict how long Chris would live or how quickly he would lose the function of any particular parts of his body. We were given some information sheets to take home, and an 'I'm so sorry'. What eye-watering words these were.

Next thing we were walking out of the clinic again and once again it was surreal. That's how someone totally turns your life upside down and inside out. It only took a little more than half an hour and we were on our own, feeling like the world had gone a funny kind of washed-out black and white, and the air had turned to water. We were staying the night at my daughter's house in Brisbane, and we returned in a haze.

We all tried to have a nice evening together, but the atmosphere was strained after this news and Chris got on the phone and told one of his daughters, leaving us to all sit and stare at each other in shock and try to talk enough so we would not be listening in on his phone call.

It's hard to explain how many times I simply felt like I was in shock, from the very early times of realising that we were facing something serious, to the very end of his life. I guess it's partly because we have coping mechanisms, and they are a bit different for each individual. I tried to focus on certain things I felt I could cope with. I tried to take it all a little bit at a time so that I didn't become completely overwhelmed, finding that a good coping strategy. I just couldn't quite put my finger on what was going on, because my finger was way too scared.

The reality of the situation, what was really happening in front of my eyes, to my own husband, would kind of hide behind me and jump out and slap me in the face over and over when I was least expecting it. It would hit me hard every time, and no amount of repeating that slap would make it seem less shocking. It was like finding myself suddenly clinging to the side of a wall, and there is no way to bluff a wall.

Amidst the struggles of life
be still oh my soul
listen to the silence
bathe in the pools of quiet
surrender to the peace

Remember the path to stillness
where the meaning of beauty
the nature of being
has taught me to know and accept
It is what it is

5. Finding life after diagnosis

How do you stay strong? Ah, the eternal question. If only I had a dollar for every time I was asked that.

In the first month after receiving the diagnosis this question kept coming back to me and was a common discussion with my online peer-support crew. I was discovering that there were oh so many ways of still finding yourself to be alive, even as you felt yourself being poured out like liquid onto the floor.

I really don't know or remember ever feeling very strong at all, but somehow I managed to seem that way much of the time. I sat and cried with Chris in the early months, and that was good for both of us. I found that, despite how I felt about appearing weak, it was best not to be afraid to show Chris that I was devastated, let him comfort me as I cried, then pick myself up and march along with him again.

In those last weeks leading up to diagnosis, we talked a lot, very gently, to each other and cried our fears and held each other. We seemed to be drawing closer together as we prepared to face our worst fears. We talked about concepts like 'living with a disease' rather than 'dying from a disease'. Chris seemed to have a deep philosophical grasp of the whole situation, far more so than I had. He would talk about what it was like dealing with the terminal illness of his first wife, and how she withdrew from him emotionally when he needed them to be close. He insisted that we were going to get through this together, and how hard he knew my role, as his carer, would be.

He was philosophical about accepting the diagnosis and living all we could while we could, while knowing it was going to take him out. Having already faced the decline and death of his first wife may have given him an extra depth of strength. The more he talked of his past experience, the more I was in awe of how deeply he could grasp both sides of the situation. I was determined to give him all I could for what time we had left.

I couldn't imagine how I would feel if it was happening to me. I did not feel strong at all and his apparent strength did not last long either.

I battled every day, but Chris soon began to have bad days when he became morbid and that was hard as I tried to stay as positive as I could. I decided to take up the attitude of 'fake it til you make it'. If I could fake that I was strong enough to do this with him, then maybe one day I would find it had become truth indeed. I admit as I look back that I became excellent at faking it, but I didn't really become strong at all.

People use many ways to draw strength and each of those is valid for that person. A special thing about online peer support is that each person can give you ideas of how they draw strength. Getting to know these people, their perspectives, so honestly shared, helped me find the way through, bit by bit, to ways that worked for me. There are no true right or wrong ways but, as individuals, we needed to work out what would give us the best chance of making the most of what we had left. Just being able to talk honestly and be understood was one way of garnering the strength to go on each day. A lovely attitude fostered in the online communities centred on the concept of 'lean hard, lean often'.

I could get up on any given morning feeling like I was ready for another day, ready to love and support and make the best of the day. As the snowball of consciousness began to roll, however, by the first cup of tea I could be a sobbing mess, or exhausted, wondering how I would even get through the next hour, let alone the entire day. The range of feelings that threatened to swamp and drown me were valid in the light of what we were facing. At the time, all I knew was that I was in the midst of this maelstrom and I just wanted to go back to sleep and hide in some dream, because the light of day seemed to be the nightmare.

Chris began to experience times of high frustration and fear and his anger would overflow and result in some very hurtful statements such as:

'You will just find me dead on the floor one day because I've choked.'

'You will be relieved to see the back of me when I die.'

'I can't stand to look at myself, hear myself talk or feel myself.'

'I grow more revolting every single day.'

'Oh you are such a martyr aren't you – you don't even know what it means to feel vulnerable!'

I wondered how much of this he meant. To a degree, he probably meant every one of those statements, and each one showed a high level of fear. In the early days after diagnosis when we talked about the disease, I think he was trying to fake it, show me bravado. He would say that he did not really fear what was coming. Did holding that fear back only make it come out in sneaky outburst ways he didn't mean? It's like putting the fears into a pressure cooker and hoping that if he held the lid hard they would never escape. Instead, when they escaped the pressure they had built up caused them to rush out in a burning, scalding steam that moved faster than a streaker through a convent, and left a trail of destruction in its path. Sometimes I would back out of the room, relieved simply to get away.

As his wife, I had a hard time coping with these outbursts. They were very hurtful statements, and I had to learn to take a deep breath, take a step back and try to imagine what he was really feeling. I believe he did not really think about how it felt to me to hear these things. He had some very dark fears and was trying desperately to cope with them, and the pressure could only build for so long before it had to be released. Sure he wasn't getting them out in a healthy way – he was lashing out spitefully at me – but are these kinds of statement really a way of screaming for help?

I believe they were, and telling myself this helped me immensely not to just feel hurt and retract into myself or lash back out in response. Sure, I felt like responding in kind sometimes but I determined that my role as his wife was to love him through better or worse. Well here we were, at worse. So how do you love someone who is hurting, scared, in many kinds of pain and not able to fully explain or even acknowledge all those feelings? If only I had known how to respond or what to do to give him the help he really needed, but I was as lost and scared as he was. I felt there had to be some key to opening a safe door to let him release his fears to me, without just spewing them out in a hurtful way. I began to feel totally inadequate to the task ahead of me in helping him deal with the emotional side of what was happening. I knew that when the time in his progression came that he would need personal and even nursing care I would learn to do these tasks easily. All my past experience as a mother and nurse and in animal husbandry gave me confidence in how I would fulfil that role. But where would I find the resources and reserves to help him with his mental health when I felt so desperate myself?

I would try to gently ask him more questions to help him explain what he was really feeling. Try to direct the questions so he could talk about himself, rather than lashing out at me.

Now, I'll be honest, it didn't always work. Some of these talks ended with more lashing out and a lot of anger directed towards me. But I would try to then go back over the conversations in my mind later, and see where things went awry and try to find some clues as to how I could help him better.

I had to accept that my role with him had completely changed. This is critical, no matter how strong your relationship is. Changes are going to happen. When your partner is facing a terminal illness, and you are not, the illness affects you both, and you both go through it, but the difference is that you are going to be alive when this ends and your partner is not. I would constantly remind myself to keep this clearly in mind, as this was a key to the turmoil he was in – facing his death as the end for him, but the beginning of something new for me.

I didn't want to face something new; I wanted what I had back. But of course I couldn't have it back, so it's true, I was going to 'survive' and he wasn't. The turmoil was possibly heightened for Chris because he had lost his first wife, and had been the one who survived. Possibly it played on his mind that not only did he survive but had ended up meeting me, and this amazing relationship, romance and marriage had blossomed. I couldn't even begin to imagine what surviving after he was gone was going to be like. I couldn't even imagine what the next day dealing with this disease was going to be like, let alone look beyond that.

He would tell me that, if it were reversed and I was the one who was dying, then when I was gone he would want to meet someone new as soon as he could. This stunned me and I know it came back to haunt me many times over the months after he died, as I tried to understand his attitude towards me. I've read in books about relationships that people accuse the other person of things that they would do or think themselves. If one person thinks or believes along a certain line then they will use this as a basis for fearing that their partner is actually acting on that same belief. If I tried to tell him that meeting someone else was the absolute last thing on my mind, and at this point I couldn't even imagine that I may even want to meet someone else at all, he would sneer at me and tell me I was lying.

Why wouldn't my damned magic wand work? All I wanted was the man I had married, that romantic man who had treated me like a princess and given me a relationship based on friendship. If I couldn't have him any more then I didn't want someone else. I could agree that I had no idea if one day down the line I might meet someone with whom I could form a relationship, but that is a very different thing to saying I would be actively looking for someone as soon as he was dead.

To my way of thinking, that was the same as saying that I already saw him as dead and was just doing what I had to until it was over and I was set free from the duty.

I would sit alone at night and my head would reel trying to make sense of things he said along these lines, particularly because he had said that this is what he would have been doing if the situation had been reversed. Did he really mean that after all the things we had done together in the past few years, the way he had proposed to me, the way we had planned and executed that amazing perfect wedding, all these things had just been because I happened to be here, but if I was not he would just pick up with someone else? Did it mean that had he met someone else instead of me he would have done and said all the things that I had cherished as being his feelings only for me? I had to force myself, after some particularly bad days, to put these thoughts aside as I knew that they were only more torture and I could not answer these questions.

These hurtful statements, I concluded, had to be the result of his overwhelming fears as he battled to accept the diagnosis and find his place in what was to come. I determined to fortify myself and refuse to let these things take me down. I knew that this was 'worse' and I was going to love him just as I had when it was 'better'. It sounds so much easier a task when I write this down two years later, but at the time of this heart-wrenching turmoil, I would have to battle it again afresh each time it rose to swamp me beneath the dark waves of despair.

It was so isolating. I have an amazing circle of friends, but part of me never wanted to betray him by talking about these dark things, and part of me was ashamed of the darkness. I wanted desperately to make everything right. No matter how desperately I wanted this, I just couldn't find the way to what would be right. I couldn't fix the situation because he was going to die and there was no treatment or cure. I wanted to make this journey we were forced into one that is shown in beautiful, sad movies. You know, ones where the terminally ill person totally accepts the illness and their fate with grace, and everyone involved just glows with love and making everything wonderful through to the end. The wife is this amazing, positive, energy-filled goddess who manages everything brilliantly. Through all the pain and suffering, the husband looks at her adoringly every time she walks in the room and never makes a complaint.

You know what I found? That's just a lovely movie and people flock to see these movies because they all crave something that is rarely the reality of life.

Instead, this disease robbed us both of everything. I have met many people afflicted with this disease since my husband's diagnosis. I know I have spoken at length with them, and so many were amazing, strong, courageous people. I also know that in the privacy of the home, alone with your partner, there is despair, anger, sadness and hopelessness. I know the hour-by-hour struggle when your body is failing you, and you are left helpless and full of fear. I have talked to many couples that can attest that they deepened and strengthened their love for each other through facing the illness together. As I went down this path with Chris I often questioned whether the fault was mine, preventing us from growing closer.

Almost worse was that in the months attempting to obtain a diagnosis and in the first month or so after diagnosis, I did feel that we were growing very close as we talked about what the disease is and our devastation at the prospect of the progression. We both shared our devastation at the loss of our perfect fairytale. I know the turmoil I was in; I can only try to imagine the turmoil he was in. I found it hard to see how we lost the growing closer and headed to the situation that was developing, where he seemed to be angry towards me, even though I was sure he was truly angry towards the disease.

He would never have wished the illness on me, but that didn't stop the fact that, in trying to come to terms with his own situation, only he was going to die at the end of it. I knew that I was also going to die one day. In fact, I often said to him that we didn't know what was ahead and I could still die before him. We both knew that there was a much higher chance that he would die before me, and that was what was on his mind.

I know from my experience with Chris, and from talking to other people in that first month, that for anyone in the early months there is a huge fear of 'how' they will die. The fear of choking and dying in terror is probably the highest on their list. It can happen, I've personally known carers who lost their partners this way, and it is a horror beyond imagining, but it is rare. It is more common for a choking incident to result in aspirating something into the lungs, bringing on pneumonia. This does not give anyone much comfort at all; pneumonia is also a cruel way to die.

The process of dying was, to me, even bigger than the end result. I don't mean the end stage but, with a degenerative illness, being in the process of dying, bit by bit, day by day for months or years. It's like a teaspoon of you is taken away every day, every teaspoon lost another little death – loss by a thousand deaths. Sure we all begin to die the day we are born, but I'm talking about obvious degenerative processes that you can track and that you grieve as a long continuous process.

Losing the ability to speak, swallow, use your arms and hands, your legs and feet, and to breathe, this is what is to be looked forward to in some order or other. Each person progresses differently and you don't really know what order these losses will happen in, and you don't know how fast any loss will happen. It is the loss of the ability to breathe that is the final loss and for some this comes before the loss of arms or legs. With the advance of science there are ways to prolong life with feeding tubes and breathing assistance, but in this early stage we couldn't contemplate serious discussion on these things as it still seemed too incomprehensible.

Just sit back for a few minutes and try, honestly, to imagine a life where every single day you find something a bit harder, things a bit heavier, people understanding you less, so many simple tasks requiring more effort. And to top this all off, you will never get any better – today is the best you will ever be; you will only get worse.

I will never forget the day Chris said to me, 'The biggest thing to get my head around is that every time I find I can't do something any more, I know I will never be able to do that again, ever.' That statement seared through to the core of my being with the full force of its injustice. Again it isn't so much about death, but about losing your body, losing your independence, losing your dignity, losing yourself. I felt the weight of the truth of this against the fact that he could possibly live for years. If you find one day that you simply cannot pick up a knife and butter a piece of bread, for however long you continue to live, you will never do that simple task again.

Chris ran cafés for many years and he found many inventive ways to use equipment to assist him in the kitchen in the early months. But he went from someone who could cook ten meals at once and hold three different conversations while doing so to not being able to even butter a piece of bread, not even being able to lift a spoon to his mouth, and not able to speak, in only a matter of months. These losses are the core of the horror of the disease, more so than the eventual death.

My initial reaction to the diagnosis first was plain anger, shock and disbelief, even though the effects the disease had been having on him had been in my face for nine months.

The first month after diagnosis is definitely the hardest emotionally, facing that there is no hope of cure or even effective treatment. I can't say it gets easier but there is something about that first month and dealing with the raw emotions hitting you. During this turmoil you have to tell family and friends, so you are reliving that shock and anger each time, and trying to deal with their reactions.

That is one of the harder bits – not so much telling, but dealing with their reactions, their raw emotions. It's amazing how huge the range of variation is. Some people start to say things that seem totally ludicrous, particularly if they have no knowledge of the disease. By the time Chris was diagnosed and we were ready to tell people, we had crammed a lot of information about the disease into ourselves, and had formed barriers around ourselves that we needed in order to cope. It was exhausting to constantly have to compose myself to give the news to the next person, and discover where in the spectrum their reaction would lie, remaining composed to answer questions and explain that there is no hope he will ever get better and what it means that he will only continue to become worse.

Some people simply broke down crying uncontrollably, and I found myself trying to comfort them. That's a surreal feeling as I didn't feel up to the task at all, but probably the 'mother' inside me would kick in at that point. It was like trying to survive on my wits against the most powerful of enemies. The people were not the enemy; the ignorance of a hideous disease and their desire to hide in denial were the enemies.

Some people would become angry or start to go on about how unfair it all is. That's valid too, but I found it difficult to get into a big anger fest. Anger is a valid early reaction, but it sucks your energy faster than a dry sponge in a bog. I knew from the start that I could not give way to anger and allow it to start ruling me or I would be sucked dry and never be able to look after my husband. I learned to allow myself to express anger at carefully controlled times and only ever against the disease. It became paramount to clearly separate Chris from the disease, and allow myself to be angry at the disease, but never towards him. After all, he never chose this; it stole our choice away and was taking him against both our wills.

Some people, particularly family, did take it personally and start to become very upset about how this was going to affect their own lives. That was always the hardest one for me to cope with. I knew that he was going to die from this, and that down the track this meant I was going to be a widow and alone, but I never brought that to the front of the situation as it was then. I was primarily concerned about what this disease was going to do to Chris, and how he could be helped, loved and supported during the time he had left with us. It was difficult for me to offer comfort to someone complaining about how awful the loss of him would be for them. This loss was valid but, to my mind, the time for this kind of grief was after he was gone.

While he was still here with us, I felt that his needs were of prime importance, not others. Even for myself, I was more concerned about what this disease was going to be like for him to experience than how it was going to be for me as a carer.

Then there were all the questions we had thrown at us. They wanted answers, understandably, and we had spent months researching, talking to others online and learning. We were still trying to come to terms with 'no cure', 'no treatment' and 'terminal'. Usually at the time of telling people they would be too shocked to ask too many questions on the spot. But, over the next few months, people would maybe talk to others, or look things up online themselves, or just think about it. Then the questions would start, often with these people looking for some hope that I could not hand to them.

Worse, for me, was that Chris had taken the stand that 'he was fighting this'. He would say, 'I'm not dying of MND, I'm living with it.' He would tell me what I was allowed to tell people who asked after him, and what I was allowed to tell them even of my own thoughts on it all. I believe it was a part of his denial – if it was all talked about in a certain way, then that would make it so. I can admit now that I only partly carried out his wishes. Sure, to people we did not know well, or who were just asking after him briefly, I would say what he wanted. But to be honest I believe I had the right to express my own views and feelings, and to give honest updates on his situation to people close to me. I had the right to receive support from people I needed it from, in the way I needed it and when I needed it.

The worst was when people would come up with things that we could do to give some hope. They meant well and I appreciated that they meant well, but they were simply plain wrong. So we were told of diets, exercise regimes and natural remedies and supplements, and I felt cruel to say bluntly that some of these would actually harm his situation and others would simply be a waste of our precious time left together, and of our money.

One of the important things requiring attention immediately was the legal stuff. So we dragged ourselves to our solicitor and ensured our wills were in order, drew up enduring power of attorney and guardianship, then saw our GP and drew up an advanced healthcare directive. This was a difficult thing to do as it was being done in light of possibly needing to be executed far sooner than later. These documents take on a very different meaning when you know you are facing a progressive disease. When you decide under what circumstances you would agree to medical intervention and when you would not, you know that these events could actually happen very soon. I've always had strong views on what I would or would not want to happen medically in certain situations. Chris seemed to find some questions were quite difficult to answer. I had to work hard to ensure that I helped him understand the questions well, but not lay any of my own opinions on what his decisions should be.

For someone like me, always focused on solutions, that first month was a constant mission to find out everything I could about this disease. I joined online groups, researched, coordinated and attended appointments with many health and service-providing professionals. I knew that I was being overloaded with information, and some of it was scaring the pants right off me. I often found doing online research resulted in scaring myself silly and I would sit and cry, wondering how it was humanly possible to bear this burden, either for Chris or for myself. Even though I had done this that first night Chris went away to see his sister, I could not afford to stop researching and talking to others online, no matter how much it scared me.

Chris was also spending a lot of time researching, and had more time for this. He constantly bombarded me with complex information on supposed treatments, trials and differences between progressions in the different onset types. Never did we read anything anywhere that gave any kind of comfort or hope. There were some obvious predators out there offering things too good to be true for huge amounts of money.

He quickly developed an understanding of many medical terms concerning the disease, and he seemed to be gaining a grasp on what progression meant and what kinds of equipment and therapies could give relief of secondary effects. I marvelled at the depth of the information he was absorbing in those early months. I was reading online whenever I could, but he seemed to be absorbing so much more and retaining it. For me it was some kind of complicated bendy education thing, but for Chris it was just a learning curve.

What I found next was that, even though we had been watching his speech and swallowing decline for nine months, its intensity had seemed to level out after the first six months. It wasn't getting better, but it wasn't getting worse at the same rate. The twitching in his arms was still slowly spreading, but it was 'only' twitching. I hadn't really connected yet what the twitching meant in terms of what was happening to the nerves.

Within a month of the diagnosis, we started to see rapid decline in his hands and arms. His hands and arms began to waste, more so in the left. I wasn't really prepared for this change. His arms would tire quickly and he developed problems with fine motor skills. Opening lids became difficult, opening cardboard packaging even more so. Other things also quickly became difficult, and could just happen overnight – using a spoon to get sugar out of a jar, turning a screwdriver, moving a toothbrush around his mouth, turning a door handle, writing or getting a key into a lock.

It is strange how I processed information compared with the reality in front of me. No matter how much information we were taking in, despite seeing fasciculations in his arms and hands for months, I was not prepared to see them worsen so suddenly. He had been showing signs of wastage for many months, but had remained strong. Nothing had prepared me to watch him begin to lose these fine motor skills. This man could do anything, fix anything, and would take over and do a great job of anything he tried.

For most people, if they saw him once every week or two, they could agree his talking was difficult, but they thought he seemed pretty great otherwise. This is how insidious this monster really is. The losses, taken one at a time, are tiny and it's only when you are living with the person that you see the importance of these tiny losses. If people didn't see him for a couple of months they were shocked to see the decline. When you consider he was gone eleven months after diagnosis, it was even more shocking.

We couldn't explain it easily to other people. I sometimes wondered if they were stupid, or was it just a hard concept to grasp if you were not living it daily. Of course people were not stupid, it's just that our entire world became focused on what was going on right in front of us. Other people had all this other complex life stuff happening, and I think denial is a factor yet again. It's not the same for other people to be told that he has a degenerative, terminal illness. They clucked their tongues and said that it was oh so tragic, then went back out into the world and somehow thought that he had years, he would be good for ages yet, or he would even get better. Hey, they may even find a cure any day.

Already we knew that, even if a cure were found, the nerve damage he had already would not repair, and every day that went by, and every loss each day brought, meant that even if a cure were found, it wouldn't be a cure for us. It is hard to accept there is no cure, without just throwing the towel in and giving up.

We had a mouthguard custom made to try to stop the teeth grinding and biting of the inside of his mouth. It was a bright green colour and, as we were getting ready for bed that night, he began to play silly games with it and we rolled about laughing. Suddenly his laughter became strange, and he was breathing oddly and then he couldn't breathe and was making awful noises attempting to draw breath. It was incredibly frightening. I didn't know what to do and he pushed me away from him. It must have taken him five to ten minutes to fully recover, but it seemed like hours and I had found my phone and was about to dial emergency when he began to breathe on his own again.

He had aspirated some saliva laughing. It was the first truly sobering moment since diagnosis for both of us. It hit me for six as the reality of what this disease meant for us both sank home. From that day, we never, ever, relaxed and laughed together again. Oh yes, at times we had a laugh at something. But never again could we just let go and laugh in a deep and true way, as always there was the fear of what a simple laugh could do. Dealing with aspiration became another part of our lives with MND.

He could climb onto a tractor and hold the steering wheel, driving it around easily. But he couldn't pick up a pillow, as all the muscles between thumb and forefinger were gone. Once he had his hands on the steering wheel, he didn't need the fine motor muscles, and the four-wheel-drive tractor could be put in low gear to move along steadily at a slow pace. It was similar with holding a brush cutter or pushing a wheelbarrow. He may have trouble getting his hands positioned on them, but once that was done and he had a grip he was fine. Doing up a button on his shirt, well forget it or use a button-helping implement. Not much later, forget that too and simply accept that your wife has to do buttons. He kept a fork on the windowsill in the toilet to pull up the zip on his fly, then he had to get me to do it for him, then he had to wear elastic-waisted pants with no fly, but soon he couldn't pull his pants up himself.

To someone watching occasionally from outside, he still didn't seem too bad, but they didn't see him being dressed or trying to do anything that required fine motor skills. He quickly learned to just sit with people if they did come and not attempt to do things in front of them so that they would not realise. But to watch this incredible man fumbling with such simple tasks, and yet being able to perform some far more complex-seeming tasks was a paradox that was always hard for the brain to reconcile. I know that it did his head in, as well as mine. He would say that when he got on that tractor and rode off into the property he felt like there was nothing wrong with him at all.

He wanted to live life in as normal a way as possible. I tried to support him in doing this. But I think that this was another form of denial taking hold. Every day, as the weeks and months moved along, it took increasing time and effort to complete the simplest of tasks. The more effort these tasks took (get up, dress, eat, brush teeth), the less energy and enthusiasm there was for what the day could hold. As the muscles wasted, every task took more effort. More effort required more energy. More energy burnt more calories to perform the simplest tasks so he needed to eat more calories.

The act of eating became so difficult for him in two ways. First his poor swallowing ability meant that he had to eat slowly and carefully, with no distractions at all in order to avoid choking. The painful result, and a source of deep sorrow for me, was that meals became a silent time. No longer were meals a time to discuss the day, laugh about things and plan future things, let alone enjoy the meal together. We had to eat in silence so that he could concentrate. Even if I attempted to speak to him, it would be distracting and therefore dangerous. Every day, each meal he ate increased the danger that he could choke and aspirate, and succumb to pneumonia. The fact that he had to eat so slowly and carefully meant that he used more energy to eat.

Second, as his hands wasted he had difficulty in holding a knife, fork or spoon. We used adaptive cutlery for a while and this did help. It was not just holding the cutlery but the coordination of getting a fork or spoon successfully to the mouth that became so difficult. This made the need to concentrate even more important, as he had to get that food into his mouth very carefully to ensure that he didn't choke by it going in a bit sideways or rushed. Because his lips and tongue would not work properly, and he could not seal his mouth shut properly, getting a spoonful in with hands that were failing was a mammoth effort. Before long it could him take half an hour to eat a meal, then forty-five minutes or longer. His food would be cold, and by the end he was exhausted. I'm sure that he didn't receive as many calories in the meal as he had used to eat it. He really needed a second meal just to get enough calories to have energy for anything else. He would deny that it tired him to eat this way or that there was any problem with taking so long to eat a meal.

It could be compared to a wolf having to hunt for an hour to find a herd, then chase down a deer and kill it, then drag a large, heavy carcass back to a den a kilometre away so that the cubs could be fed. The cubs would wake hungry and keen to eat this wonderful fresh meal, but the wolf would have used so much energy it would need to be a large deer indeed for her to get enough calories from it after her litter of cubs had taken their share. The disease was like the cubs that were going to steal most of the calories the meal provided.

So much of his life had revolved around the preparation and sharing of food. So much of our life had revolved around talking and laughing together, particularly over meals. First he needed help to prepare a meal, then the need to eat in silence, with my eyes averted and yet my ears fully trained on him, fearful that on any mouthful there would be a choking episode. I found it heartbreaking to eat with him. Every single meal I could not help but wonder if he would have a choking episode that would result in pneumonia and his death. I would feel guilty even as I wondered, would this meal be the one that would tip us over the edge of the cliff towards death?

It is so embarrassing for an adult who has always been so capable and independent to watch their body failing. They don't feel weak or incapable; their body simply won't do what their brain tells it to. This is distressing for both the person and the people who love them and are watching. I remember how I used to love sitting at a table in his café, enjoying a coffee and cake he had baked that morning, and watch him bustle about cooking and talking to people. He was always able to give everyone a smile, listen to anything they wanted to talk about, feed them well and leave them feeling good. Suddenly he began to feel that everything that made him a person of value was being taken from him.

As his arms became weaker, the ability to raise them became difficult. He would say that hanging out the washing was good exercise to keep his arms working. All too soon he could not lift them high enough to reach the line. One day I found him standing on a milk crate and my heart leapt to my mouth.

'I'm fine' became his standard response to everything.

6.   Visits and crashes

I was working in my office only a couple of weeks later, and had an ear tuned on that washing line. I heard the unmistakable sound of him aspirating. As I raced through my office door I could see him teetering on the milk crate and barely caught him in time to steady and hold him until he could breathe again. As my senses returned from whatever corner they had fled to, I was relieved to realise he was agreeing that he would hand all washing duties over to me. He was able to tell me later that as he had reached up to the line, he had just slightly tipped his head back, and saliva that had built up in his mouth had shot down the back of his throat.

I began to see twitching in the muscles between his ribs, not long before he was sent for respiratory tests. These tests showed that his lung function was 90 per cent but the functionality of the muscles around his ribs and his diaphragm was only at 30 per cent capacity.

This began to cause another change in my emotional state as I began to face the reality of the terminal nature of this disease. I was beginning to learn how MND affects the muscles of the body and it was becoming rapidly real to me that this was not just a situation of Chris losing his speech, but it was going to completely incapacitate him. But how could it be that so quickly his strong, young body was being attacked so relentlessly? I'd always known there were such things as avalanches, but had never expected that first stone of slurred speech to have this kind of result.

I was only fifty, Chris only fifty-four, and our life had been turned totally upside down and he truly was going to die from this. But I still had the idea in my head that somehow he had a few years ahead of him and we would both adapt and get used to all this and make many more wonderful memories. I talked to many different people online – I was coming to know and love so many as friends – who were in their second and third year of the disease. Some of them could not walk but otherwise were doing far better with their independence than

Chris, only months in. Some of these people were taking holidays and doing bucket-list things together, making the most of what they had left. It seemed that we were being propelled along a path at a frightening speed and I could not predict anything about how he would be the next day, let alone the next week. So how could I plan anything we could do even in a very short time?

At first I put my energy into finding health professional supports and services and advice as possible, to make his journey as comfortable as possible and keep him as well as possible. I had this idea that if I could do this well, we would in fact have at least a couple of years to enjoy together with excellent care and advice. He resisted this. Often when health professionals gave him advice he would nod and accept, yet when we returned home he would be angry and say he wouldn't do these things.

I was deeply concerned and disturbed by his paradoxical attitudes, and for a while there I pushed a bit, and he resisted. He didn't want to spend what was left of his life in doctors' surgeries and hospitals. I began to accept what he was saying and understand this view. They can't cure him, and we should be living what we have. Why should we spend too much of the time we could have together in waiting rooms, being prodded and poked and examined, when they really couldn't do anything except explain scientifically what we were experiencing and already knew was happening? He felt that we should use the medical profession for what was needed, but that we were not going to be drawn into a lot of long medical battles.

A significant change happened about two months after diagnosis. I purchased an iPad for him with an app on it that allows you to type what you want to say and the app will speak for you. These are called 'text to speech' apps. He agreed it made sense to get this early, while he still had some speaking ability, get used to using it, and then have it mastered when it would be needed. You can save all kinds of text and phrases in the app to use again for things you commonly say and put them into categories, and it offers you words as soon as you start typing, so it allows you to put sentences together quite quickly.

But he put a Facebook app onto the iPad and began to make contact with other people afflicted with MND or ALS around the world. He spent large portions of his day sitting and using Facebook, and hardly touched the speech app. If I asked him how he was going with mastering the app he would say that it was okay and that he must spend more time using it.

One day he told me that he had been talking to people in the United States who had been living with the disease for twenty years. These people were completely paralysed, except for their eyes, and on invasive ventilation. This is a tracheotomy with a ventilation machine breathing for you. He talked about how it would be better than being dead and he intended to be the longest living person with MND in the world.

I was shattered, but I never told him this. How do you look your husband in the face and say, under no circumstances can I imagine that you want to commit me to a twenty-year sentence of looking after you in such a high-care situation. But it felt like a jail sentence to care around the clock for a totally bedridden quadriplegic person for such a period of time. One who would suffer pain, bedsores and who knows what. I was fully aware that a person on a ventilator could never be left alone, so it is twenty-four-hour care.

I know that I started to feel the beginnings of true panic at this point. Inside I was screaming while outside I was asking polite questions and pretty much just letting him talk. I felt like my sanity was sprouting wings and flying off, and that, if it succeeded in getting out of the door, it may never return to me. On top of this I felt a strangling guilt rising that I could be so heartless as to consider even thinking that I would not want to give Chris every chance at a long life despite it being in a high-care situation with this horror disease. But the internal screaming was winning; linked as it was to the old fears I had carried since nursing people in high care who lived many years in institutions. I knew the reality of what a person could suffer.

He began to talk aggressively of 'fighting this disease', of how this disease 'did not have him' and of how long he could live.

I am being totally honest here, and I am talking about my own internal reactions. I would never tell anyone else where quality of life begins or ends for them, or what any other person should or should not do. This is about my reaction to facing what this would do to our lives.

It was at this time that I began to have trouble coping on my own. The next morning I emailed our MND NSW adviser and asked about the option of invasive ventilation. She quickly replied that this is not offered in Australia. Even this news was not enough to calm my internal distress at the change in Chris. I just could not join in with him and it was deeply troubling me. I knew that he was not going to live a long life, and it upset me that he was going into a new form of denial.

I saw it as denial, because it simply was not an option for him. I had no idea how to open a conversation and dash his hopes. I didn't even want to calculate the enormous cost of providing twenty-four-hour care financially. I could not see that anyone could expect our free health system could provide this to a person, and would not expect it to. We obviously did not have the money it would require even for a single year, let alone decades. But the financial cost was not my real concern. What I could never get my head around was the impact of being trapped in a body with only your eyes working would have on a person. It was my personal worst nightmare.

I went to a homeopath I respected and was prescribed a remedy to help me cope emotionally. Many carers take antidepressants to help cope, and I wanted to see if I could avoid this path with homeopathics first. After a long consultation I started on a remedy and I could feel the effect very quickly. I still felt all the same emotions, but they were not as overwhelming now.

A remedy was also prescribed for Chris. It is designed for terminally ill patients who are experiencing a high fear of death, to help calm them. I admit, I did not fully describe to him what the remedy was exactly for, but I gave him a basic indication and he agreed to take the remedy. You take three doses – night, morning and night – and then stop.

The day after completing the remedy Chris suddenly decided that he needed to see his sister again, and this time his mother as well. I booked him plane flights and before I knew it he was going away for two whole weeks. I couldn't believe it – two weeks respite, all to myself, to recover, to get myself together and be ready for whatever was coming. I also knew it was strange as he had kept so little contact with them for so long, except seeing his sister just after his diagnosis. That previous time he had ensured his mother didn't know anything about the visit so that he would not have to see her at all.

In the few days before he left I hoped I wouldn't just find myself sleeping the whole time. So I deliberately avoided extra sleep, but spent time each day putting things in the house in order. I know that I have this reaction to situations when I feel a lack of control – I gain a certain amount of comfort from putting things in order. It's strange, because I don't enjoy doing housework. It's as though things can't be too bad if everything looks clean and ordered. You can often tell that I'm feeling fairly settled within myself when I don't care if the house isn't completely clean and there are things that should be done.

I managed to work fairly well, but I also enjoyed the dogs and the gardens a bit, and planned some nice times with a few girlfriends. I had been falling behind in my relationships with friends because I felt disconnected from what had been my real world. It was strange to meet up with friends and find that my main conversation revolved around dealing with a terminal illness and how far things had progressed. I didn't want to talk to my real-world friends about this constantly, and yet it felt strange to try to engage in conversations about their very real world and any problems or victories they were having. I felt I would be more able to be a 'normal' person for two whole weeks.

I got the opportunity to go for a ride on the back of a motorbike on the second weekend and was excited as I hadn't had time to go out riding and knew that I may not get time for this much in the near future, possibly for quite a long time. I didn't realise just how tired I really was. Even though I knew I was exhausted, for some reason I was not paying this enough attention. It seemed I was carefully avoiding thinking much about my own needs.

At the end of a great day out riding, I started feeling sleepy and nearly fell asleep on the back of the bike just as we were returning to my car. I was keen to get home as I was going to meet a girlfriend for dinner that night.

As I drove home, I knew that I should stop and get a coffee in town and stretch for a minute. But, I thought, I'm only twenty minutes from home; I will have a nap when I get back. I was driving through some back hills, and down a very windy road into a valley. Coming out of the last bend I went into a micro-sleep and woke up just as I was running off the road and into a ditch.

It was surreal. I woke to see myself going off the road, and there was the loud noise of coming to an abrupt stop. I must have closed my eyes at the moment of impact, when the air bags went off. With an air bag in my face and the car on an angle in the ditch, my brain was trying to come to terms with the fact that I had just crashed my car. Shouldn't I get out and clear of it? What if it caught fire? I struggled out of the car, which was quite difficult with it being on the angle it was and air bags around me, and wandered onto the small country road looking about as though this was going to just be a dream and all would return to rights any moment. I knew of course that it wouldn't but I was in shock and even vaguely knew that too. I really didn't know what to do. I kept thinking, if only Chris was just at home and I could call him, he would come and make it all right.

A car appeared in the distance and I just stood where I was until it got close. I explained to the driver and his daughter that I was okay, apart from being dazed and shaky, and that my husband was currently away. He bustled me into his car and took me to his home close by, gave me a drink of water and called a towtruck. I was so grateful – someone was taking charge and I was sitting down. It is law in Australia that if a car has to be towed from an accident, the towtruck driver calls the police. So we then had to wait for them to arrive.

They asked about what had happened, and I said I didn't quite know. I didn't admit I had fallen asleep, just that I had been coming down the hill, had lost control of the car. The towtruck pulled the car out of the ditch and took it off and the lovely Samaritan drove me home. I will be forever grateful that this unknown man kindly helped out. He admitted that he had nearly fallen asleep at the wheel at times over the years, and didn't say anything judgemental to me. I was certainly telling myself what an absolute idiot I was often enough by this time; I didn't need anyone else pointing it out to me.

I still had Chris's car at home, but I opted out of the dinner with my girlfriend and settled down to an evening of completing the process of being in shock and feeling right sorry for myself, as well as increasingly angry. I played the game of 'if only'; unable to believe I had so stupidly driven, knowing I was so tired. If only I had stopped and had a cup of tea with everyone before leaving after the bike ride; if only I had stopped and got a caffeine drink and had a little walk around in town; if only I hadn't even gone on the bike ride! We play these games, but the fact was I had now written off my car and given myself a solid shake-up.

It was awful phoning Chris and telling him what had happened. I felt so stupid and I hated that he would now be worried about me. I considered not telling him until he came home, but part of me wanted my husband to know and support me. By now his speech was so poor that phone conversations were really difficult. It was one thing to sit with him and look at him as he spoke, but quite another to try to decipher what he was saying on a phone. Of course he was upset and worried for me, but it hit home yet again how much this disease interfered with every single thing about our relationship. The further the conversation went, the more I just wanted to tell him I was okay, and get off the phone.

I did the insurance claim and organised a hire car through my insurance until the car would either be fixed or replaced. I was informed within a few days that the car was written off and it would be a full payout for a new car. Well new car is nice, but I was more devastated to think there had been that much damage, and shaken up yet again to think I could have seriously injured or even killed myself. Not so much for my poor sake, but how would we have coped with Chris's illness if I were seriously injured and in a hospital? What would he have done if I were not there to look after him? I realised that something was seriously wrong with me. I was not coping anywhere near as well as I wanted to believe and project to the world. Sure it was only a car accident but, the more I looked back at it, the more I realised I had been ignoring warning signs of my own stress levels. This had been a true wake-up call.

The day after Chris came home, we had to drive up to his second MND clinic appointment three hours away. We set off in the hire car with plenty of driving time to make it there comfortably. I drove the first two hours and stopped for coffee and a break. Back in the car and off again, all was going fine. We were about five minutes away from the clinic and I was feeling fine, when suddenly I had what I can only describe as this wave of the strangest feeling wash over me, almost like that lightheaded feeling you get just as you are about to faint. We were about to drive through an underground section that would come out at the hospital. I wasn't thinking anything in particular when it hit, but it put me in a panic and I began to shake. Somehow I managed to get across three lanes of traffic to the side of the road and stop the car, and sat there shaking.

Chris was very concerned and I told him he would have to drive. For some time I had been worried about his ability to drive, but I was a mess. We were only like five minutes from the clinic, but I was shaking still. We swapped over and he drove the last five minutes while I felt upset, angry and concerned about what had happened all at the same time.

The second clinic visit was just awful. A different neurologist saw us, so even though she had the notes from our first visit, she had no way to look at Chris and assess changes in him. Because of my concerns with his new fixation on invasive ventilation I had emailed the clinic and requested that they speak with him about this.

They brought in a palliative doctor, who walked in while text messaging, sat and ignored us for a couple of minutes, continuing to text, then basically started talking about end-of-life options. She asked him if he'd like to talk about this and he said no. Instead of accepting his answer she simply launched into the discussion anyway.

I was confused, and I know that Chris was more confused, and I started to realise that this was their response to my email. She brought up the subject of ventilation, and noted that it isn't done in Australia, but she was being vague and indirect. Neither this doctor nor the neurologist showed any interest in attempting to understand Chris. They would let him speak and then simply turn to me to interpret for him. I was embarrassed when I had to say, 'He says he knows they don't ventilate MND patients in Australia because they don't care if we just die.'

Now on top of my panic attack driving there, the fact we were being seen by a bunch of people we had not seen on the previous visit, and having this conversation caused further distress for me. The neurologist ended up saying that she was more concerned about me, and whether or not I was receiving help or counselling. I began to cry and told her that I was okay but was terribly worried about my husband. During the entire time he sat calmly and gave the impression of being someone coping brilliantly with the diagnosis and what was happening to him, while I looked a total wreck, and felt like one. The driving panic had shaken me up and I was wondering how the hell I was going to get us home again.

The neurologist began to discuss driving and Chris stated that he believed he was perfectly safe to drive. I was miserable sitting there, unable to express my concerns about his driving, when I had just had this panic attack. The entire appointment left me feeling worse than I had before we started. We went to a café after the appointment but I was still shaking and was terrified that I would have another attack while driving home. Chris was concerned for me and said that he was honestly fine to drive us home. I had to agree that he was in better shape to drive than I was.

It was peak hour when we left and the drive that had taken three hours took a gruelling five hours to get home again. I admit he drove really well the whole way, better than I had seen him driving in months.

Over the next two weeks I began to have anxiety attacks every time I had to drive. They would start around an hour before leaving. I would get a sick feeling in the pit of my stomach, worrying that I would panic again. I told myself that this was a perfectly normal reaction and I would get over it. We needed me to be capable of driving – and I had been driving for thirty-four years.

Fortunately I did not have to drive every day, but just the twenty-minute drive into town became an ordeal. I would leave up to thirty minutes early so I could drive slowly. If I felt I was going to panic I had plenty of time to stop, get out of the car and settle down. I drove with the air conditioner blowing at full fan and at the coldest temperature and my window wound fully down. Somehow the cold air and blowing sensation was a kind of distraction against the feelings of panic. When I did begin to panic I had flashbacks of that moment I had woken to see the car going off the road and would get a dizzy sensation.

Chris had to see the doctor for some routine checks and prescriptions, and I made an appointment for myself as well.

I told her what had been happening since the accident and asked if she could prescribe anything for anxiety. She said that anxiety medications were likely to make me drowsy. The last thing I needed was to add drowsiness to my level of exhaustion. She suggested an antidepressant, but I had been hoping for something I could take at the time of feeling anxiety build. She recommended I see a counsellor but I was already seeing a counsellor regularly.

I started the appointment feeling calm about explaining what was happening, but now worried that she was going to pat my hand and send me off without any help. I am normally considered a capable person but I felt so vulnerable that when she suggested an antidepressant again I softly cried and agreed.

And so it was that my relationship with Zoloft began. I knew it would take several weeks to start having an effect and firmly told myself that I could manage another few weeks. I continued driving with lots of cold blowing air and became one of those annoying people who drive way below the speed limit. I found the anxiety far less at lower speeds; anything over eighty kilometres per hour would start an immediate feeling of dizziness.

The pharmacist advised that most people take the medication of a morning, but that there is the possibility that it could make me a little sleepy, especially at the beginning as I adjusted to it, and if that was the case I could switch to taking it at night. Again I felt anxious that I might be making the situation worse by taking a medication that could make me sleepy when I was already exhausted all the time. I felt caught between that proverbial rock and hard place because I needed something to get myself functioning again in the long run. I did feel sleepiness after only two days, and switched to a night dose. Within another couple of days I realised that it was making me sleep better than I had been and was not really making me sleepy in the day. I hoped that if I began to sleep a little better I would also start to feel a little less exhausted.

After a month or so I could confidently say that I was feeling calmer in myself towards everything that was happening. I don't know whether it made all that much difference to the panic attacks when driving, or whether time was simply healing this. I used whatever tactics I felt I needed. I often used energy drinks if I was going on more than a thirty-minute drive. It took a long time until I could say with confidence that I didn't have even mild anxiety attacks driving – at least a year – but the attacks lessened in frequency and severity on a sliding scale. By three months after the accident I did not feel anxious an hour before leaving, usually just in the last five or ten minutes, for a longer drive. By four months I was no longer having panic attacks, but would sometimes have mild anxiety out of the blue. I realised finally that I didn't remember the last time I had one of these anxiety episodes and realised it was over.

7. Coping mechanisms

Thinking back on all that we both went through in those early months after diagnosis, I believe there is no right or wrong way to cope.

Well okay, there are some really wrong ways – taking your anger out on the ones you love, taking recreational drugs or drinking heavily until you can't function …

But, if you were to think about how you would cope with this situation and then find out how you actually do when the situation is forced upon you, they would likely be two very different animals.

We all like to imagine the animal is a charging white stallion and we are some valiant hero waving a sword of hope and light in the air. Or we simply can't even imagine it and put our minds to something more pleasant. I can definitely state that 'coping' is not a place that you arrive at early in the process and then stay at.

Coping is something I was challenged with day by day, some days hour by hour. Some days I realised I was not coping and had to work hard to pick myself back up off the emotional boxing ring floor and hold an icepack to my bruises.

Just when I would think I had things working okay, something changed – another part of Chris deteriorated more, or a new area began to deteriorate and everything I had in place was not enough, with more adjustments needed. This affected how I coped with routines, equipment and help services. It also had a profound effect on how I was coping emotionally.

To say I was on a rollercoaster just didn't cut it, even if it is a common description. Rollercoasters are fun – even the scary bits are fun – and at the end of the ride you get off saying wow. It was more akin to spinning like a top on the lip of a catastrophic curve.

If it is a rollercoaster, then you know that the track ends suddenly before the cliff edge. While the ride may be scary, may go up and down and around corners that are much too sharp, it is better than the end when you are going to plummet to somewhere that will hurt like all hell. It's more like a runaway train; you hang on, and you try to direct the ride as smoothly as you can by sheer force of will. The further the train progresses, the faster it goes and the less able you are to even talk to your travelling companion because of the speed and sheer terror.

Chris and I used different coping strategies at different times. We fluctuated between them and we used them in different ways. These strategies have a place, but they are not always healthy. They are best for acute or sudden short-lived situations. Situations that go on for longer (more than just a few weeks) need better, healthy coping strategies. Maybe you will cope 'better' than I did, but that's still missing the point. The point is we all cope differently and what has worked for me won't necessarily work the same way for another person. But what has and has not worked for me, may serve as some kind of help and support for you. We learn more about ourselves if we reflect on how we cope in the times of highest stress and crises. If we don't reflect we may continue through life reacting to everything around us in the same old ways.

Denial

Denial is a devious animal. It works best when you don't even realise it's at work, kind of like a termite that is hidden in the structure of your house. If you realise you are in denial, you can combat it, and so it sneaks about working on you secretly.

You might recall the customer who told Chris that his symptoms were like those a friend had experienced, and it had been MND. I went to Dr Google and checked what the classic symptoms are.

I read about limb fasciculations – check, he had that.

I read about slurred and difficult speech – check, he had that.

I read about the effect on the tongue – fasciculations and wasting. Uh-oh, he always said the speech problems were a tense jaw and feeling of looseness in the back of the nose and soft palate with a postnasal drip.

Immediately I dismissed MND as being a possible cause because what I read said it was the tongue that was the problem and the tongue would be wasting.

Now this is an okay reaction, but had I asked him that very night to stick out his tongue, I would have known that his tongue was very much involved. Instead, I sent him a text message saying I couldn't see the relationship between MND and his symptoms and he shouldn't scare himself over something so rare.

From that point, my denial filtered every piece of new information that came to light. The filter of denial draws a conclusion, and we fit every new piece of information into alignment with that conclusion.

He would say he felt it was MND; I would suggest a neurologist referral. He would say, let's wait a bit and see what the next ENT specialist says. I would think, see you don't really believe it is MND and I don't believe it either.

The more time passed, and his symptoms became worse, the more I was convinced it was not MND because he wouldn't see a neurologist. He never mentioned his tongue and I had not looked at his tongue.

Even after I finally asked him to poke out his tongue and saw the fasciculations, and in my heart knew what it was, I still didn't let myself consciously acknowledge it.

At the last visit to the ENT I requested he look at Chris's tongue, remarking that it was quite strange. The ENT seemed to think it was nothing and passed it off. Well denial then said to me, see it isn't really anything to get worried about or this specialist doctor would be worried. My denial even went so far as to berate me for having been worried about his tongue at all.

Even though I knew in my heart that this was the final symptom that confirmed why every test to date showed nothing wrong, my denial kept me calm and pretending there would still be some weird cause found that could just be fixed.

Denial received a bullet in the head when the speech pathologist listened to him talk, read some history and told him to poke out his tongue, pronouncing her belief that it was MND.

Denial can also be masked as 'focusing on the positives'. Now I believe that life is the sum of how we deal with situations, rather than what situations we find ourselves in. However, sometimes it is an evasion tactic to attempt to always be positive. There were times when I found myself in deep despair and Chris would start talking about 'living with MND' and keeping his life as normal as possible. I would feel a deeper despair because I felt that the reality was that there was nothing at all normal about how we were living, and we were barely surviving. We were just 'getting through each day', and I felt like I was pretending so much for his sake that it was ruining our relationship as a husband and wife. I wanted to be more realistic but he wanted something else, so I felt I was sacrificing to that and I was giving up part of myself in order to give him what he wanted.

Pretending things were as normal as possible was a coping strategy for him. I didn't call him out on this, but I felt us growing apart because we had different needs and different ways of coping. I did not even have my normal working life any more as I had a husband at home who needed an increasing amount of assistance on a daily basis.

He was most aware of what was happening to his speech and his body when other people were around him. He hated it when people either looked at him with pity, or looked at him like he was a 'dead man walking', as he put it. As his speech and ability to use his hands declined, he began to withdraw from people.

There was an element of denial causing him to do this. The more they had to ask him to repeat sentences or tried to guess what he was saying, the more he wanted to hide away from people. The fact that I could understand him quite well for so long, because I was with him all the time and often had lots of clues as to what the conversations were about only made this worse for him. He felt that other people just didn't care enough to bother to try to understand him. He lost the ability to realise how poor his speech was becoming, partly because of denial and partly because he knew what he was trying to say.

Withdrawing from people like this was far from normal and impacted on both of us. As he withdrew, I was being withdrawn with him. This meant I was becoming the sole focus of his life because there was little else in his life. Again, for me this was far from normal. Normal for me had been to have a full working career, wonderful family, friends that I socialised with and a very active life at home on the property. It was not normal to spend more and more time alone with Chris as he deteriorated, sacrificing my needs in order to fulfil his. Yet he would talk of being as normal as possible and I would want to scream that I didn't even know what normal was any more.

One day I was in a store and a lady in a wheelchair entered. A man, who obviously knew her well, began to talk with her. Her speech issue was very different from Chris's. He led the conversation and she mostly answered. But I found that I could not understand anything she was saying, even though he could. I had this huge breakthrough of what it must be like for people visiting Chris, trying to understand him but just not being able to get a foothold.

Using technology with text-to-speech apps would have alleviated this to a degree. He refused to use the technology, stating it would take him longer to try to speak this way. This was all part of the denial too. It's true, it could take some time, but people would just wait for him to get the text ready and then would totally understand it, rather than him trying and trying to say something that was not understood. Far less embarrassing for all concerned. If they needed to ask for more detail they would be confident his next lot of text would be easy to understand.

He knew he would reach a point where he would not be able to speak at all, and yet he refused to learn how to use the app. No matter what strategies I tried to get him practising and setting up phrases in the app, he would not put the time into doing it. Was this some form of denial also? If he could deny his speech was so hard to understand, would that make it true that everyone else was just too lazy to try to understand him? By insisting it was too hard and too slow, he never gave the technology a chance.

Even in his last months, when even I could not understand him most of the time, he wanted to attempt to speak everything. We used communication charts with letters and pictures, but it was always a last resort, and he felt I should have been able to understand him without these tools.

Distraction

Distraction can be healthy in many ways. If you use the distraction of listening to lovely music, reading uplifting books and surrounding yourself with lots of positive people, you could be well distracted and spend much of the last year of your life feeling loved and appreciated.

Distraction is not always healthy, but facing the reality of this disease is about as hard as it gets. Anyone in this situation is going to use some distractions. Distraction and denial can walk along quite happily hand in hand too. Distraction can be used to help time pass and work in concert with denial by preventing you from truly dealing with the issues.

Chris used the distraction of trying to make everything as normal as possible.

So he busied himself trying to do as many things as he could. He would decide on doing some things for the day, and then push himself through them. He would not stop to have enough fluids or calories, going on for longer than he should. Even though he would report that he felt good for doing all that stuff that evening, the next day he paid for it. I wanted him to do less, take lots of small breaks and eat lots of extra calories. Maybe he could then have had four or five days a week doing things for part of the day, and get more done in a week but not be worn out by it.

For someone with obvious muscle wastage, it simply did not make sense to spend five straight hours using a brush cutter without a break. You cannot do anything to rebuild muscles that are dying, and if you overuse those muscles and do any damage they will die faster.

A day of too much activity would then cause anything up to three days of exhaustion afterwards.

When he was out doing things on the tractor and not having to talk, he felt almost normal and could forget anything was wrong for a while. This was good for him emotionally and mentally in those early months, but it always hit him again when he came back to the house, tried to talk or couldn't do some simple task.

As he spent more time researching and making contact with others around the world, I asked if he found comfort and support by talking to others like himself. He replied that it was 'interesting'. I couldn't get him to expand on what he meant by interesting. I was saddened because I was receiving an enormous amount of online support. As the months passed, he could spend the bulk of an entire day just sitting and using the iPad. I noticed that he spent far more time reading than participating actively. Even on these days he was not eating enough, not moving about much and not even receiving support. Was he just passing time?

He would plan large activities and yet not manage to start them.

He seemed to be distracting himself by reading lots of stuff, yet doing nothing with the information. He had the intelligence to perform searches online, read complicated medical information and stories by other people, but seemed to have lost the ability to put any of it into action.

I had so many more inventive ways of using distraction!

I'm a great one for masking things with activity. I'm kind of a natural mother or carer. So being really busy doing all the stuff that two used to do, trying to make things as good for Chris as possible, and trying to work, was a great distraction from how I was really feeling about everything. It's hard to deal with such deep emotions if you are constantly battling to do everything you have convinced yourself needs doing.

Two of the things I needed to distract myself from were his loss of speech and the loss of our future. He had always been the talker in the relationship. If I was a bit quiet, he would cover that and it didn't even matter if I talked little. In the first months after diagnosis we talked constantly about the disease, what was happening, decisions we needed to make, how we felt we were coping and going to cope. As his speech and body deteriorated seriously, conversation declined in parallel. I filled in the bulk of the words, and I had to try to work out what he was saying, so talk did not flow like it once did. On top of this, conversation topics were being narrowed by the week. The loss of a future meant we could no longer sit together comfortably and work out something that we wanted to do together. I was being relied on to actually make conversation.

I offered to start reading books to him. I've always loved books, and have all my real favourites. He had never read any of them. I felt this would give us an interest together, something to do together and something we could talk about. At first he was keen on the idea and I read to him on many evenings. He began to fall asleep soon after I started to read, often within the very first page. If I tried to keep him awake he would swear he was not falling asleep, and if I just read, he would soon be fast asleep. I became distressed as I wanted us to share interests together outside the disease, but it wasn't working and eventually I gave up.

The further he declined, the more distressed I became; one of my distractions was to spend more time talking to others online than I could really afford. I was exhausted, yet once I had Chris settled for the night I would take my computer into bed, assuring myself that I would only spend half an hour and tonight I would get to sleep early. I would be amazed that once again it was 11 pm or later and I was not going to get enough sleep to be at all refreshed the next day. I needed the support, and yet I actually needed sleep as much, if not more.

I don't regret the support I received this way. I was so hyped up all the time, watching Chris like a hawk, trying to keep on top of his needs, trying to stay a step ahead, trying to work, trying to keep up with the property, trying to stay sane. The only thing there often seemed to be 'for me' was to talk with others online.

So, despite my exhaustion, once I sat down with my computer at night, I seemed to 'wake up' and hours would fly past.

And the man said
'this is mine!'

And the earth moved a little
and it was gone.

And the man understood it not.

8. Living arrangements

The day we came home from that first speech pathologist visit with MND ringing in our ears we discussed the issue of the work needed to run our small property. We agreed that Chris was not going to be able to do anything here one day. I felt that we should place it on the market straight away, rather than suddenly find ourselves unable to cope. I couldn't bear the thought of watching our beautiful paradise degrade into a neglected mess. Chris felt we would have to sell but he wanted to tell his children first, and wanted to wait to do this until after he was officially diagnosed. I agreed that we would hold off, even though I felt a sense of urgency.

Buying and selling a home is never an easy task, but doing it under the pressure of a time constraint is even worse. Our two pressures were that we needed psychologically for this to happen fast so we could cope with yet another loss, begin a new adventure while we could. It felt like we would have some kind of future to look forward to if we were going to be buying and setting up a new home.

We wanted to find a property between one and five acres, with a house with wheelchair accessibility, within ten to fifteen minutes of the major town and hospital and at least $120,000 cheaper than our current property. This dictated the price we could negotiate down to in selling. It wouldn't matter if we had to take a bit less for a quick sale if the price of what we wanted to buy was lower. On the other hand, we were limited in what highest buying price we could go to and so the juggling match began.

I applied to my bank to lend me a ridiculous amount of money that really scared me. However, I also felt that money is not the most important thing in life. If we consolidated all our debts we could still be at the same level of out of pocket mortgage payments. Well that made me feel a lot better; it was possible.

We found a property that was wonderful for our situation, negotiated the price and signed the contract. The bank procrastinated for three excruciating weeks before finally saying no. We were devastated and I was angry. Not so much because they said no, but because it took them so long to say no when we could have been working on another solution. Chris loved the new property and could see all these things he could do to make it just that bit better. He was obviously going over and over it in his mind. It was giving him something to look forward to and plan about when his future seemed taken from him. The refusal by the bank would mean smashing what he might see as the last dream he would have. He had lost all interest in our property, either because tasks were too hard for him or he saw them as a waste of time since he would be leaving.

I found an amazing mortgage broker who spent many hours of hard work putting all the financials in order and applying to another bank for the loan. She also put a much better loan structure together than my bank was considering.

Finally we would have an official decision the next day, everything was in order and the new bank was ready to say yes.

I updated the real estate agent, she spoke to the vendor and, unbelievably, the vendor said he had changed his mind because it had taken so long, and was going to rent the property out and take it off the market, so the sale was off. Next day the bank approved on the loan, but we had no property to buy. The real estate agent begged the seller once the bank had given the official green light but he said no, even though he knew my husband was terminally ill. That cost hundreds of dollars in title searches and house inspections.

The real estate agent was nearly as devastated as we were and told us that she had just been appraising a property that was about to go on the market and asked the owner if we could look at it. The property was much better than the one we had just tried to buy. We were sure fate had stepped in to shine on us.

The owner was looking to buy a new property but had not yet found it. So we had to be patient, but no one really understood that time was the one thing we did not have in abundance.

Two agonising months dragged out, with our hopes rising and being dashed, and we always seemed to be waiting one more week for something definite to happen with this property owner. She would go away for the weekend and look at some property that she would be really positive about it. We would wait another week or more to be told that she wasn't going to proceed on that one but there was another she would look at soon.

Chris continued to decline as these weeks passed, and I had to face the fact that our time was running out. What we wanted was to find a more suitable property, one that I could live on after he was gone and manage on my own easily. But even more importantly we wanted to move in there together, with us both setting it up how we wanted and enjoy that. As Chris declined, it became increasingly apparent that it was not going to be a situation where 'we' were really moving to a new start together. I would be taking a severely disabled husband to another house to care for him. Neither of us ever got used to the speed of the progression, and every month that passed I felt the need to run even harder to keep up.

We had to make the agonising decision to keep pushing for this, or to pull out and begin getting our current home ready for the next stage.

This was a hard decision because Chris was hanging all his hopes on moving to a new house, giving him something to look forward to and something to occupy his mind. He never understood that for me it became a frightening prospect to be looking after two properties and a wheelchair- or bed-bound husband. Just four months previously when we had decided to sell and move he was driving a tractor, using a brush cutter and lawnmower, was fully mobile and reasonably active. Now he was unstable on his legs, even though he was mobile, he had very little use of his hands, no more brush cutters or mowers, no screwdrivers or hammers, no walking on his own anywhere outside the house. He could just manage driving the tractor but did not attempt it often and he could not lift the drum of diesel to fill the tank.

The speed of his progression heightened my concern about the issues I could face financially. At the time of diagnosis, he seemed to be progressing at a rate that made us feel like we had some reasonable quality years ahead. Actually that statement may not be completely accurate. Our understanding of the disease and how it can progress had not fully been assimilated into our reality. It was like I could see the beginning stage, where he was around diagnosis, and I could see the awful end stage of being completely bedridden, but I hadn't really seen the process of loss from one to the other in terms of a timeline that would apply to us.

So in those early months, when it felt like it would be years, it seemed sensible to move to an easier property, even if we had to rent our current place out for six or twelve months until it sold. We had visions of coming back to our first property for a day each weekend together and doing maintenance work on it. It was obvious that he was not going to be capable of this, so how was I going to look after two properties alone?

But the whole process took around four months and, with the amount of degeneration, I no longer felt so confident in the whole idea. It now seemed to me that he possibly had only months left to live, not years. Add to that the emotional trauma of constantly being on hold awaiting the decision of this prospective seller. At one point she even suggested she may be interested in buying our property and came here and loved the place. We became so excited that it could all be solved so simply with both sales happening together. Again, we were left waiting on a final decision and after a few weeks that was quashed.

I felt that I was at someone else's mercy for everything. The number of times we would talk about how surely she would have good news for us 'this week' only to be have our hopes dashed yet again was soul crushing.

It still meant that I was going to have to find a way to manage the property on my own. The biggest fear for me was that Chris would not be able to do a thing on either property. Four months he had experienced so much progression that I was starting to realise how much of my time was needed to care for him, not in another year or more but now.

I talked it over with a friend, who shook her head and said, 'It's too messy. You need a simpler solution.' It was messy; so many things could go wrong with the messiness and could cause huge problems. I needed to put my energy into what time I had left with Chris, not clearing up a potentially huge financial mess and looking after two properties.

In all this time we had only three people come out to inspect our house with interest to buy. It was obvious that selling may not happen fast and I could find myself stuck with two properties for way too long.

Organising home modifications for disabilities is not a simple process. You need assessments, inspections, applications for funding and approvals, and then wait on tradesmen availability. We had to get this process started, rather than delaying it on a hope that something else may work out. We had not even begun the first step of an assessment to see what would be needed in this house.

One of the most important roles of the carer, besides loving the person they care for, is to try to stay one step ahead of the disease progression. We were at risk of being in a house that was not set up for a person who could not walk, so things like an accessible shower and doorways with small steps were going to be needed.

We finally agreed on a cut-off date, deciding that, if we could not get a deal together by that date, then we would stop the process and put our energy into staying where we were. The date came, and we stayed. In some ways I was a little resentful of all the time and energy I had put into trying to get loans, look at properties, be ready for people to look our home over in an instant, and now nothing was going to come of it. I had to make myself put that aside firmly, as negative feelings can take off with you when you are vulnerable. I decided to take the outlook that we had given it a good shot but it was not to be, and move on with making things work.

Chris didn't take pulling of the sale out as any kind of positive. He must have felt like his only dream had been taken from him, and I felt this too.

He felt like he was in limbo and admitted he had lost all interest in this place. It was like he was just waiting for the new place to fall in his lap. I think it was another part of that old denial and distraction tactic. At first he had distracted himself by working around the property as much as possible. Then, with the house on the market, he had distracted himself by dreaming of the new place. Now he wanted everything to happen like magic and give him a new lease on life. He would talk about how wonderful it would be to move into the new place and set it all up, and how it would be fun. Then it would be something I could manage alone. But he couldn't seem to face all that needed doing in order for that to happen. He certainly could not do all the financial side of things and talk to mortgage brokers and banks, but he could have sorted his hoarded possessions out so they were in order and ready, and we would be halfway to packing. He agreed that he needed to do these kinds of things but each day would come and go and he would promise he would do it tomorrow.

When the cut-off date arrived and I took the house off the market he became sullen and angry, as though we had never talked this through and set a date, as though I had simply made a decision and taken another something from him. From that point, we were never again able to talk about the property we lived on, so far as things that needed to be done to maintain the place. It was like he had washed his hands of everything.

It would have helped me enormously if we could have both talked openly about our disappointment. Instead the air of mean-minded resentment began to thicken like soup.

I was heartbroken. I would have done anything to give him his last dream, but I couldn't control the real estate market and we couldn't just sit in limbo forever. We weren't really even sitting in limbo, he was continuing to decline every single week and we had to get ready for this to worsen.

The occupational therapist (OT) and a home-modifications specialist came out and went through what we had and what we would need, and began to discuss the best ways to achieve this. Oh, these conversations are so difficult to have. It felt like my life had become one long difficult conversation. So many conversations with people discussing openly and frankly what was to come, and never in a way of if or maybe but simply what was to come. The only way those things may not come about would be if his breathing were to be taken suddenly and he simply died.

Fortunately we were in a ground-level house on a concrete slab, so no stairs, just some doorways to put ramps over, a bathroom that would not accommodate his needs and decisions needed on some internal doorways. The first thing the OT made us aware of was that a power wheelchair (PWC) would never make it down the hallway of the house to either the bathroom or our bedroom. The hallway was too narrow for it to turn into any doorway. It was a strange feeling to realise the impact of this. He had not been able to sleep in our bed for the last couple of months, and slept part of the night on the lounge or recliner chair. But to know that he would reach a point where he would never again even come into our bedroom was a shock that I had to hide as we talked practicalities. At this point he could walk up the hallway and I would change his clothes in our bedroom.

We looked at the first spare bedroom, beside the lounge room, and discussed having part of the wall removed. With the hospital bed in there he would be able to access the room himself in a PWC and it would open the room up as well. When looking at these renovations you want to add value to your house, not detract. I knew that in reality this modification would not add any value. Our funds to do modifications were very limited and it worried me that we may end up with a result that looked like a wall had been ripped out, rather than a great modification to this room.

The bathroom was the other major issue. I had an idea of how we could pull out the glass partitions of the shower and convert it into a roll-in shower. As the home-modifications man looked over the bathroom he shook his head and said it was not possible without it being a major job. My heart sank. What were we going to do if we couldn't even shower him? We could get him down the hallway on a rolling shower chair, but we couldn't get one into the existing shower.

He talked of a portable shower base that could do the job and would be able to be hired to us for very little money. It seemed like a poor substitute to me, but he insisted he had used them a lot and would bring one around to show us. We had little choice but to agree.

As it turned out, the portable shower base was amazing. It fitted in the space between the bathtub and hand basin, and had an idea to run a shower curtain rail across the room so that when the base went down we could screen it off to prevent water splashing. We tested the shower chair, rolling it into the base with me on it, and then I rolled the home-care worker onto the base to test again. With a few little rubber ramps, very little outlay and no actual modifications, we had a great system in place. It had already taken about three weeks.

December was approaching and they could not do the wall removal until the next year. We agreed that he wasn't in the PWC full time yet so that was no problem.

Within a short time his world revolved around moving from the lounge room to the verandah and back. In a short time he went from a vibrant man running a café and six-hectare property to someone living between two rooms and a few pieces of equipment.

Already I wondered how I would have ever fitted in moving house and running two properties, and thanked fate for preventing it.

Who can know me?
No one can see into the depths of another's soul
True freedom
is knowing myself

Why do I look without
when I carry what I seek within?

9.   Living with the monster

All the months of going to different doctors and wanting a diagnosis now seemed like the better time that was now gone. Now we had names for the things that were happening. All those months of wanting the medical profession to recognise what was happening and come up with a solution, and now we were thrown into a medical world of frightening terminology and numerous appointments, with no hope of any solution.

He was referred to a local rehabilitation day centre that had an occupational therapist and physiotherapist for assistance. He joined a weekly program designed for rehabilitation, but the true goal was to help him use what muscles he had, retaining what had not yet been affected. I soon learned the incredible importance of a physiotherapist who understood this disease.

The muscles were wasting because the nerves supplying them were dying. You cannot build up these muscles, and attempting to do so can actually cause damage, making them waste faster. The physio attempted to have him do push-ups, use putty for hand exercises and other activities that were ridiculous and dangerous. There were some good sessions he attended that concentrated on how to fall as safely as possible if you can't use your arms, and how to think about using aids, or even items around the home to complete tasks you can no longer do with your hands alone.

The socialising was good for him at first, but most people attending were aged, and as his speech declined it became difficult for him to even enjoy this side of the outing. At first I was keen for him to attend as it meant I had one morning each week alone, to work or take a break without interruption, and he had an outing that he could return from and tell me about. After a few months I became concerned that they were not meeting his needs and could potentially make matters worse.

What he really needed was personal attention focusing on stretching and retaining some range of movement (ROM) in his joints, as his muscles were wasting and shrinking. The public health system sessions were not designed to give this kind of attention and the staff had no real working knowledge of MND; neither did they have any inclination to learn. The facility and the sessions he was attending were designed to rehabilitate and the simple fact is that you cannot rehabilitate muscles without nerves supplying them.

The physiotherapist spent some time with us both after his session a couple of times to demonstrate some good massage techniques to assist with the pain he was experiencing. We were told MND does not cause pain as it is the motor neurones involved and not the sensory neurones. They did not tell us that as muscles waste, particularly when spasticity is involved, the joints are affected and become frozen. His hands were turning into claws, and his shoulders and elbows were becoming stiff, making it difficult to lift his arms. I would do passive work on his arms but I could not lift his arms up or out in the way I should have been able to because the muscles were shrinking and pulling tight. The pain became cruel, yet apart from panadol he had a fear of taking any harder pain medications and refused them.

I sometimes stared at his hands in disbelief and shock at the way they changed almost daily. I had to consciously jerk myself back out of it and pull my eyes away to focus on the person he was rather than the body he was trapped in. I had always loved his hands and arms; they had been so strong and yet so gentle and kind.

The inability to speak clearly impacts on the personality if the person cannot find a solution through technology. I had been finding his accusations towards me so distressing that one day, three months after diagnosis, I decided to record a typical evening conversation just for my own reference, to hear it as an outsider would. Listening to this conversation again two years later I was again immersed in that world as I tried to find things to talk with him about and was successful in retrieving only short answers. When he did speak in a full sentence I can now barely understand anything and marvel at how I responded to him, as though his speech was perfectly intelligible. I did a little quick maths and discovered that, even though the recorder was on for twenty-five minutes, there was less than five minutes of actual conversation, even though I attempted five different topics. He was quite happy that evening but conversation had been reduced dramatically and my ability to cover this by simply talking incessantly had not developed. I remember how I felt sitting there, racking my brain for something, anything, to talk about and coming up with nothing.

In the last minutes of the recording he said how tired he was and how hard it was to sleep and how long the nights were. Sadly, the reason I am clear on this now is through hearing my responses to what he is says.

As I realise that this recording was actually so soon after diagnosis I am stunned at how poor his speech had become so quickly and how deeply it impacted on our relationship. It has added perspective to listen to this as I was accused of so many things, but we were battling such a hideous monster blame should have been kept out of the equation, unless it was to blame the monster.

By the time he left to visit his sister for the second time, his anger and paranoia towards me had grown to an alarming level. While he was there he sent me numerous text messages saying he realised he was wasting time and that he was feeling so much better in himself. He told me that he had decided that he would not visit her again because his time with me was too precious, and how much he was missing me. He said that we had been thrown many tests in our relationship and were not going to get the amount of time together that we had wanted and planned. He said that he didn't want this illness to take centre stage or it would have victory over us; that we needed to strive together for more victories and that he loved me more than air and knew I felt the same. Then he finished the message by saying that we now had to become totally, selfishly greedy. I know I read this message over several times and, even reading it again now to write this, I have the same feeling of confusion. What were we supposed to be greedy about?

I replied that we had certainly had a lot thrown at us and that I tried to show a lot of tolerance in light of what he was going through. I told him I was in awe of how he was coping with the whole thing, and that I was struggling to cope. I told him I would do absolutely anything for him. He replied again that he agreed and felt it was time to be more selfish about our needs.

He told me that when he had got onto the plane and the engine started he had broken down and cried. He said it had really hit him what was happening to him and how depressed he had been feeling for the past few months. I wished he would break down and cry with me, instead of saying he had to hold his emotions in tightly as he did not know what would happen if he let them out.

After an absence of only two weeks I was stunned at how much muscle mass he had lost and his walking seemed off-kilter. Within twenty-four hours, I was dressing him and he was obviously struggling with many more small tasks than when he had left.

Actually, he could still dress himself. It would take him at least twenty minutes and he often fell in the attempt. By the time he had managed the task he was exhausted.

I will never forget the look on his face the first day I dressed him. It took less than two minutes and he was amazed as he had been struggling with this task for many months and had forgotten what it was like to simply pop a set of clothes on. He found that his mornings became more pleasant too, because for too long he had been starting his day exhausted from the effort of simply getting dressed.

Within days of coming home he withdrew again, responding with anger but refusing to talk about his feelings.

After a week I attempted to talk openly with him about the concerns I had of what the disease was doing to us. He responded that there was no point putting any energy into our relationship. This statement came down on me like a ton of bricks.

The law of opposites
the forces of nature
the up and the down

But who can tell me
when to push
and when to pull?

Ah that would be wisdom!

10. Facing realities

Bulbar onset is often an aggressive form of MND and, due to the way it affects the ability to swallow, quickly becomes debilitating. If the person eats and drinks less they begin to lose weight and become malnourished and/or dehydrated.

The management strategy used is to place a percutaneous endoscopic gastrostomy (PEG) feeding tube directly into the stomach. The feeding tube, or a button to attach tubes to, is just below the ribs allowing feeding directly into the stomach, removing the risk of the person aspirating food or fluids.

Aspiration – getting fluid or foods in the airways or lungs – is a huge problem as it can cause infection and pneumonia. It is one of the most common secondary causes of death in a person with MND.

Once the PEG is placed, the person can still eat or drink by mouth if they are able to, but do not have to rely on getting all their nutrition and fluids in through the mouth. It can prolong the life of the person, to some extent, and certainly makes them more comfortable, but it does not cure their problems. It is hard to say how long life is prolonged, as there are so many other factors that could be in play, such as the ability to breathe. It is true, however, that if the person is unable to swallow well and is losing weight rapidly then they are far more likely to die sooner than someone who is safely consuming lots of calories and fluids and holding their body weight.

The health professionals recommend that you get the PEG in place well before you need it, and with good reason. It can take some time to get referrals and a surgery date. You want to go into surgery in good physical condition, not malnourished and dehydrated. You need to have good lung function and breathing ability to undergo an anaesthetic. You can have the PEG in place and not use it at all, just have it ready for when it is needed. Many people take some time to slowly change over to the PEG as their swallowing becomes more difficult. Swallowing functions and lung functions can go downhill very quickly.

From the very first appointments we were told all of this but Chris was reluctant to even think about a PEG. He attended an information session on the procedure and came home saying he had no fear of having it put in and would happily accept one. He spent five months saying he wasn't going to be pushed into anything and he would know when he needed it.

No matter which health professional would broach the subject, he would say firmly that he would accept the PEG but he would tell them when he was ready.

So I watched him taking longer to eat, reducing the variety of things he could eat and losing weight. The winter turned to summer and I watched him drinking fewer fluids, while choking and aspirating frequently. Each health professional who brought up the PEG would get my hopes up, as I would think he would surely listen this time. Still he resisted and began to dehydrate.

We attended a PEG information clinic run by the team we would be working with in the hospital and he left very angry. Again he was advised to get the PEG in sooner than later and again he resisted. That evening we talked and I was surprised at how much anger he showed. He resented they had suggested that taking half an hour to eat a meal was tiring and he felt they just wanted him to fit into their routines by having it when they wanted it done.

We were the only ones at the clinic, so had the whole session to ourselves. Chris had written questions on his iPad so he would be ready and we would remember to ask everything we had in mind. But the gastroenterologist didn't show. Now I know he would have had something urgent to attend, but Chris was angry at his absence. Afterwards he kept saying that it must have been a particularly lovely day out on the golf course and it was no wonder he wouldn't bother coming and helping anyone out. Then, because the wooden model they had wasn't too terrific, he said they didn't care about anyone.

Dealing with all of these reactions from him drained me more than anything. I found myself in this awful dilemma. If I simply agreed with everything he said because it was easier, then I was not being true to myself or to him. Yet I found that in many small ways this reaction was becoming my normal. We would have conversations about issues; I would keep silent and just nod and agree with him implicitly. Then I would sit alone at night crying over my true feelings. The gap between us was widening and I couldn't tell whether I was at fault and was not approaching the whole thing well, or whether he was being unreasonable.

I ended up in trouble for sticking up for the health system when I finally said what I thought about getting the PEG placed early. I had worked in health, and I knew that they probably hated that wooden model, but were not able to order a better one because it is a public health system running on a negative budget. I knew the gastro probably had an urgent case. So I battled internally. What was the point of saying anything? But what if I found myself sucked right into his make-believe world?

His biggest question was what breathing minimums he needed to meet for the anaesthetic. A dietician, speech pathologist and stoma nurse could not answer that, so again he summed this up as meaning they didn't care. He went as far as to say that it should be common knowledge so there was no reason they shouldn't answer that.

He still held to this belief that he wanted to be as normal as possible for as long as possible and make his own decisions. They said that if his breathing was compromised now, he should get the PEG going now. But that was not what he wanted to hear, so he came home angry, saying the system was wrong, and somehow I managed to become a part of the wrong too. I could never quite figure what I was supposed to do to avoid being the one who was always in the wrong.

Maybe he expected that because I could talk I should have been saying to them all the things he was thinking. In a magical world, right! I usually could not fathom just what he was thinking until we returned home and he would start a rant over what an uncaring system it was.

I ended up making a deal with myself to try to alleviate my own feelings of guilt. We were due to see our physician again in a few weeks, so I told myself that we could talk to him about it further, then ask for a referral to a gastroenterologist and discuss the whole situation. I used to work with the gastroenterologists so I decided to suggest we go to one who I trusted would give us clear answers. It was lucky all these conversations went on silently inside my head, as I probably would have sounded like a lunatic if overheard.

Sometimes I wondered if I should just let him make poor decisions and not drag the journey out too long, as it was too heartbreaking. I began to seriously struggle with these thoughts. I wondered if he was just showing bravado in how he would talk, particularly to other people, but inside he really just wanted to let nature take its course. I was torn by the disparity between wanting to do everything possible to help him and wanting it to be over – and the guilt that went along with feeling that way.

Only one week later, after having trouble with a meal, he announced that he wanted a referral to get the PEG process started. I was stunned! I mean, really, a week earlier I had been through this awful conversation where I was accused of all this siding with an uncaring health profession and now there was no way I could say anything but, okay we would put that on our list for the next appointment. When I phoned to make the appointment I was told the gastroenterologist was not accepting new patients. The receptionist agreed to ask him if he would take Chris as I had worked with him years earlier. She phoned back to say he would, but the first available appointment was not for three months. Wow, inside I'm seething, thinking that this was just what we had been trying to explain for five months. Chris was placed at the top of the cancellation list. So we settled in to wait it out. I was not convinced that he would survive three months as he was. I watched his attitude completely changing and saw him developing a fear around the process of eating.

After another swallowing problem during a meal he announced he was no longer eating solid food but would put it through a food processor. Again I was stunned, as he had remained adamant that he enjoyed eating so much and didn't care how long it took to eat a meal – he was going to keep at it. My suggestions of softening his food in different ways had been met with total resistance. Still, I was relieved, as meals were torture for both of us. I could not enjoy anything I was eating silently, with Chris struggling, and didn't know where to look while I ate. I seemed to be eating my meals faster just so I could leave the table and clean up the kitchen while he completed his meal.

Another week later we were back for an appointment with the speech pathologist and she was very concerned that his swallowing had deteriorated further. She offered to speak to the gastroenterologist to see if we could get in faster. The magic phone call came to say they had an appointment for us. When the doctor examined Chris, he wanted to get the PEG in the following week. It was obvious that Chris was emaciated and dehydrated and that this had become an urgent case. So, suddenly, it was all happening in a whirlwind.

I was angry about how this had played out. He had hung on until he was really getting into trouble and had lost more than 20 per cent of his body weight. I know the health system is stressed to bursting, and that this should be a non-urgent procedure that is booked in advance.

But he'd won – he'd held off as long as he could, then got strings pulled because his time was running out. What made me angry was that he'd played on the system, rather than making good decisions in advance to take as much care of himself as possible. I tried to gently tell him that this was why we all wanted him to do this so much earlier and he got angry again saying, 'Oh yes, we are all geniuses in hindsight aren't we!' I seemed to be in this position too often; it had been foresight on my part.

Suddenly it was the night before the PEG placement. We were both feeling lots of things that had been building over the previous week, some were the same emotions, and yet we were both actually going through very different experiences.

For Chris the concerns were many, and he imagined so many worst-case scenarios that I was stunned when he began to lay them out for me.

Since diagnosis, when I raised concerns such as an accident while driving the car or falling and serious injury while I was out, he'd told me I shouldn't worry about all these things; whatever was going to happen will happen. Yet with this procedure coming up, his poor mind went wild with scenarios, not just about the procedure but about staying in the hospital for a couple of days and nights.

1. The anaesthetist would damage his throat while doing the endoscopic procedure.

2. They would lay him on his back in recovery and he would be unable to breathe.

3. They would try to force him to drink water or take tablets. (He was going into hospital to have a feeding tube because he can't swallow!)

4. They would put bed rails on his bed and would not allow him to sit in a chair when he was in pain.

5. They would decide he was in pain and forcefully inject him with morphine and he would stop breathing. (Nurses cannot decide to give any medications that are not ordered by the surgeon, who knows that he doesn't want morphine because of breathing issues.)

6. They would decide he is stupid because he can't speak and make him do things he doesn't want to.

7. They would pull him by his arms and damage him.

8. The night staff would be tyrants and he would be vulnerable, alone and at their mercy.

9. They would try to force-feed him through his mouth. (See point 3.)

Well that's quite a big bundle of fear and anxiety to take into a hospital procedure isn't it?

He suffered terrible arm pain in bed. His left arm would paralyse during the night, and the pain would keep him awake on and off all night. Yet he refused even panadol to attempt to ease it, as though he had a fear of taking medications.

The surgeon carefully explained that it would be critical to keep on top of pain after the procedure. The PEG is inserted as close to the top of the stomach as possible, just below the left ribs and diaphragm. In the first days following the procedure the site would be tender and painful. The most efficient way to stay on top of the pain is to take small but regular doses of pain relief. This prevents pain building and giving rise to a need for a large dose. The medication is an opioid but will not cause depression of the breathing if given in small doses. Large doses would address high pain but also depress the breathing. If he did not keep on top of the pain there were two concerns.

Because of the closeness to the diaphragm he would breathe shallowly in a natural attempt to lessen or prevent pain. With his already compromised breathing, that could lead to pneumonia.

The first feeds would be difficult if the site was painful. If he could not tolerate it he could vomit, with a high risk of aspirating, again possibly resulting in pneumonia.

Chris listened attentively, or at least he appeared to, and nodded appreciatively as each concern was explained.

And yet in the days leading up to the procedure he said he would not take pain relief if he didn't need it; he would rather put up with a bit of pain. This was totally contrary to what the surgeon had explained. He had set himself up with all this worry that the staff were going to be tyrants and incompetent, and yet was willing to place himself at high risk of pneumonia instead of taking sensible pain relief. This made no sense and I sat in stunned silence yet again.

No matter what had to be faced and decided we always seemed to be at odds with each other. But the worst of this was that in front of the health professionals he would be accepting and agreeing; alone with me he would be so different. I could not even present to him logical health information and have him listen to it, let alone accept it.

Because his hands were so wasted and weak he would not be able to use the PEG himself. He was now going to depend on me to give him most of his fluids and nutrition. And anyone who would be caring for him in future would also have to be capable of using the PEG.

It would also introduce the change of having to be organised and think for someone else, like when you have a baby. Yet this baby was going to be able to say yes or no. I couldn't just sit him down and feed him; I would need his permission. I had a sneaking feeling that the PEG was not going to make that much true difference. When I suggested he needed a meal or snack to keep a high calorie intake, he would say he wasn't hungry yet or just wanted a coffee. Would it be any different when it was delivered through a tube, or would this just become another contention for us?

The PEG was another step towards our relationship becoming one of carer and patient, rather than husband and wife. So many steps of this nature had already happened, but this felt like a major game changer. Maybe he felt this too and it was why he was approaching it so illogically. Maybe denial was prompting him to think that the longer he avoided it the more normal he could feel.

I had concerns about how well he would manage in hospital with nursing staff who may not understand his disease well and were already busy and rushed. I had some serious talks with myself around this because my natural instinct was to want to sleep there with him at night. I knew this would be detrimental in reality. If I looked after him around the clock in a hospital environment I would not sleep well and would bring him home a few days later only to find myself a total wreck. How was that going to help anyone?

Once he had talked out all his fears and I had tried to sympathise while alleviating those fears as mostly unfounded, he asked me a direct question. He asked if the situation were reversed would I have the procedure.

Oh my. I sat there in a moment of panic, as I had to very quickly weigh up and decide whether I would tell him the truth, wondering how he would react. I wanted to give an answer that would just make him happy and yet I was constantly doing this. He rarely asked directly for my opinion or feelings on anything any more. He was asking about me, I reasoned to myself, so I should answer honestly, even though I felt I would regret it. I took a deep breath to attempt to answer. Oh please let me say how I feel in a way that will be understood and accepted as being one of those choices people have a right to make for themselves without it being a judgement on what others should or shouldn't choose for themselves.

I explained that I did not believe I would choose the procedure for myself. I tried, oh honestly I tried, to be gentle and use language that clearly said I was talking purely about what I believed I would choose for myself. I explained that I would choose to attempt as long as possible to take in nutrition through the use of thickened smoothies with a very high protein and calorie content from very early on. I tried to explain my feelings for myself of where I would draw my own line on trying to simply preserve life. He did actually seem to listen and did let me complete what I wanted to say.

But his response was dismaying. He seemed to take my response not as my own choice for myself, but as a summing up of some belief about him. He replied angrily that he might as well throw himself in front of a truck in that case. I had the sinking feeling that once again I had made the wrong choice by giving my own opinion, yet another reason for him to believe very twisted things about me.

I tried to explain that, to me, there was a vast difference between accepting a disease and going with it, and giving up altogether. I told him of people I had known who had taken this approach, who had lived with quality and then gone with dignity. I tried to explain that these were choices I would make for myself, and that I would not tell anyone else they should make the same choices. I reminded him that I had totally supported his choice for the PEG, and had suggested he have the procedure months earlier.

All to no avail. He had developed a way of jumping on one thing he perceived I had said, drawing a conclusion and holding on to that conclusion fiercely, refusing to believe anything else.

I wanted to scream at him that in my view he was making a dog's breakfast of choices in nearly every area of how he was approaching the management of his disease. I wanted to scream that I would do it all totally differently if it were me, but that I loved him and accepted his choices and his right to them. I was not trying to force any of my own beliefs onto him, but I sure wanted to at times. Every time he made bad choices I was heartsick and dismayed, and wanted to take control and make him go with good choices. Yet every time I stepped back, accepted that it was his body and he was the one the disease was afflicting, and so he had the right to listen to all the same advice and yet choose differently. I even accepted the consequences that it had for me when he made those poor choices. Of course, I did not scream or even whisper any of this to him. The conversation ended with his pronouncements of my evil, and my silence at his beliefs.

Here we were, about to go to the hospital and, instead of going as a united couple we were once again in tatters. He looked at me like I was some monster and I felt guilty for my opinions, and stupid for opening my mouth.

So I dragged myself through his bedtime routine and talked to my online support group in despair, as I readied myself to face the next day.

We arrived at the hospital on time. He had been sullen all morning, yet he changed to a polite and reasonable person on arrival. We were taken through the paperwork and general check-in procedure. The nurse kindly said that it was fine for me to stay in the unit with him until his procedure. This is uncommon, but his speech issues made her realise it was going to be far easier for everyone if I were there.

All the staff proved very caring and patient, and we were to be the third cab off the rank. This meant about a two-hour wait. It was difficult as he was obviously nervous – waiting right outside the door to the theatre while others are wheeled in and out is a bit daunting.

Fortunately when the anaesthetist came to check on him and we spoke of how his eating had been dropping and particularly his fluids, he suggested he could set a drip up immediately. I was so thankful as he had been dehydrated for weeks and he had been required to fast overnight.

They explained he would be given some sedation and then they would be put a mouthguard in his mouth, and then administer the anaesthetic. The procedure is done endoscopically, which means passing an endoscope through his mouth to his stomach. The patient's mouth needs to be kept open so they can't bite on the tubing.

He had several mouth issues – his jaw could clamp when anything went in his mouth, which meant getting the mouthguard in might be difficult. He would salivate copiously when anything was done with his mouth and could choke on this saliva. If he was laid on his back, his palate would drop low, making him gag and have difficulty breathing.

I was grateful they were open to me explaining his particular bulbar issues, as I wanted them to understand that these things were normal for him in his condition. It is a credit to health professionals when they can admit they don't know everything about every medical condition. Faced with this rare condition, they accepted my explanations and were open to taking all into account. Some doctors like to give the appearance of knowing more than anyone else and don't accept this kind of information graciously. I am sure my medical background and my research helped them accept what I was saying.

Imagine if I had tried to say, 'Oh please be careful with knocking him out because he might choke.' I am sure they would have given a nice professional smile and told me it would all be okay, and then proceed as though he were any other patient.

Here's the description I gave to them: He is bulbar onset, so there are a few underlying symptoms that will need to be taken into account. He experiences jaw lock and clonus, which can happen suddenly as a result of any stimulation of his lips or tongue. If you are aware of it then you can work to avoid triggering it and know what to do if it happens. He has palsy of the palate, which has caused it to drop significantly, and it is hanging very low in his throat. If any clonus is triggered the palate will spasm and close off his trachea and cause him to panic. His diaphragm is compromised and so he is unable to breath in a prone position. I know it is very difficult to intubate a patient that is semi-erect; we have to work around this situation somehow. Because he has severe dysarthria, he cannot clearly tell you anything while you are trying to administer the anaesthetic.

It was comforting that this anaesthetist stopped and looked me in the eye while I gave this description. He considered my words and explained how he would approach working around these issues. He understood and he formulated a strategy with me. He reassured Chris that he was capable of working with his specific issues. I felt as calm about his competence as

I possibly could, considering I would not be allowed into the theatre for the anaesthetic to be administered.

When they took him in, as soon as they laid the head of his bed down a little he began to panic, and they were wonderful with him. They were able to calm him, and get enough sedation into him to get the guard into his mouth.

I gratefully headed to the cafeteria for a coffee and some food once he was wheeled through those doors. I returned to the waiting room and they were kind enough to come and get me as soon as they wheeled him out to the recovery area, so I could be with him as he woke up. This was great as he came to in spurts, opening his eyes, moaning and gagging, then going back to sleep, but I could let them know how much was normal for him and be sure he was positioned correctly and waking well.

A peaceful soul
is never harvested from
the seed of anger

It matters not
if the ground is stony or dry

Plant only the seed of love
and reap a bountiful harvest
that will fill your heart
and overflow to all around you

11. Accepting changes

Once up on the ward, the nurses were wonderful and I wrote on a whiteboard beside his bed, explaining his limitations and highlighting that he understands everything and hears well. They moved him to another part of the ward so he could have a recliner chair beside his bed and brought in a second recliner chair for me. We had more privacy and were right beside the nurses' station. This section is used as the prep area for the main theatre. It was Friday evening and theatre was closed for the weekend, so we had this spacious area to ourselves, which was a true blessing. The nurses were extremely kind and helpful and went out of their way to assist us.

Finally I left for the night. I knew he was fearful of being there alone, but I had to sleep and was returning by 7 am. He was still a little spaced out and so accepted this. I had spent around fourteen hours sitting beside his bed or tending to his needs and was exhausted. I also felt a kind of elation that I had mediated so well for him and everything had gone as smoothly as I felt it possibly could. He was in fairly good spirits and seemed to appreciate the way I had helped and cared for him all day. He even wished me a good sleep. I fell into bed that night and woke to the alarm like it had gone off five minutes later instead of five hours.

He reported next morning that his night had been terrible. They would not help him, he lost his buzzer and they wouldn't respond to him attempting to call them by moaning. He had a very red coccyx area, so hadn't really moved all night and he was very angry. The morning nurses felt that the doctor would give us oral morphine to take home so we awaited his rounds, with Chris eager to head home. We had been told in advance that he was likely to be in hospital for two nights to ensure all was healing over well, that I was confident with using the PEG and he was pain free. But he was determined he would not stay because they were going to kill him.

The gastroenterologist on weekend duty examined him and said he shouldn't really have much pain now. If he still needed morphine he would have to stay in hospital. He was concerned of if it depressing his already compromised breathing. He wanted him to stay in hospital on the low-dose morphine injections. Chris was far less than happy, but he needed the pain relief and so agreed to stay. This was a sign of how much pain he was in as he had planned on refusing pain relief.

So, no surprise that he took it out on me. I know he was in pain and frustrated, but he made it seem like I had something to do with it not working out, and now he was going to be stuck there alone at night again. I went through all the feelings of guilt again over whether I should stay the night with him to ensure he was being looked after. We told the doctor of his problems the first night and he said he would write up a report to ensure this night would be better. It was tense for the rest of the morning. I was already exhausted by mid-morning, but I completed his personal care. I was ready for a coffee break but he was too afraid to be left alone. I just couldn't bring myself to walk away. In the afternoon his daughters came to visit so I suggested I might take a break while he had his girls with him. In front of them he snapped: 'Yes you can fuck off now.' So I took a two-hour break, which meant a twenty-minute drive home, not much more than an hour trying to relax a little, and back again for the rest of the afternoon and evening.

Unbelievably, when I went to leave after his morphine at 9.15 pm he said he wouldn't let them give him any more overnight and would leave in the morning. Hang on a minute, wasn't he here because he needed the pain medication?

I told him he needed to take more through the night and get some sleep. The whole reason he was still here was to control the pain overnight so he would feel way better tomorrow. I got one of his blank looks that meant, 'Yeah whatever you want to say but I'm doing what I want.'

I just had to leave him, as I knew I needed to get some sleep and would probably bring him home in the morning, in a very demanding and angry state.

You don't get a lot of sleep when you get home at 10 pm and have to be up very early again. I wish I could have just walked in the house and fallen into bed, but in truth I needed a little time to sit quietly on my own, enjoy a good long shower and try to shake off the tension from all the sitting around anxiously in the hospital.

He did have a better night and had slept, but still said the night nurses were awful to him. He just wanted to be taken home. The nurse on duty was sympathetic and called in a doctor from another floor to see about pain relief to take home and get him discharged.

Did that satisfy him? Oh no, again he was angry, saying it would be just like yesterday, the nurse saying yes and that dickhead saying no. Finally he agreed to see the doctor on duty, but he vowed he would go home without pain relief if he would not prescribe it. The doctor allowed us to take five doses as a back-up, to take only if he really needed, but to try only taking Panadol. I was able to get him out of there.

I figured that it was Sunday so five doses were more than enough until the next day. If I had to take him in to the GP and have something sorted, that would just have to be. No wonder my exhaustion levels were dragging at me, but I could only try to imagine what it must have been like for Chris.

It was a slow drive home, trying to ensure I did not jostle him about on our pothole-strewn roads. I thought I would settle him in one of his comfortable chairs and he would rest, but instead he made a cup of coffee laboriously on the stove, but drank only two sips, leaving it to go cold. I finally got him showered, as his children were coming over, and made him a cup tea but he didn't even take one sip. He also did not want anything put through the PEG, no fluids or feeds. Right, so we were home and he was angry with me.

I wondered if I was just stupidly tired and overreacting, or if he was doing these things as some kind of punishment. I struggled to make sense of this. Now he had the PEG, getting something into him could be as simple as him sitting there – no risk of choking. But in his sullen silence he was refusing to use the very thing he needed most. When anyone is tired, sore and stressed they benefit from plenty of fluids and calories.

His children came and he was pleased to see them. It was like a switch was flipped. They got loving smiles as he lay on his sore bum and listened to them chatter on, and they listened to him complain about how bad the hospital experience had been. Everyone was sympathetic to how bad it was, and how brave he was in fighting the disease. I sure don't remember a word being said about all I had done to try to make it all work, but at least I didn't actually hear anything about how I had made it all go wrong.

When they left, the switch flipped again and he returned to being sullen and cold, refusing food, fluids and pain medications. Yet he had insisted on bringing home pain relief. In my state of exhaustion I wondered if I had gone just a bit batty, and it was I who wasn't following what was happening. Maybe I was becoming confused rather than Chris behaving erratically. I wondered if I would I know if I had gone mad, because my delusions would seem real.

Watching the man you love go through this disease is bad enough, but watching him do everything possible to make it worse, or not allow real help was nearly too much to bear.

Some time after we had been home it dawned on me that for the whole time he had been on small doses of morphine he had experienced zero arm or shoulder pain. Oh he had been angry and complaining about the PEG pain, so maybe it was just taking the front seat, or maybe the morphine was enough to address the other pain. I was too exhausted from the past few days and his attitude to say anything.

The next day was my birthday. I awoke as usual and returned to bed with a cup of tea and my computer to check emails. One of the first things I discovered was a couple of posts on Facebook. His daughter had posted: 'My dad is one of those people who will never give up. Never lets anything get him down and even though his body is failing him, he is still the same dad I love. So lucky to have such an inspiration as a dad.'

Well, I thought, that was a lovely thing to post, even if it ran contrary to the experience I was having with him.

But then I read his reply: 'Thank you. It's my children that keep me fighting, your positive thoughts and your love for me, seeing through this disease is inspiring, and not dwelling on where I'm heading and making the best of now means everything to me, thankyou, lovvvvve daddy mcbloodywellnevergivingup.'

I began the day in tears. I just couldn't shake sense out of the statement he'd made – it's his children keeping him fighting and seeing him through? He knew I would read this. It amazed me that I did everything for him every day and they visited rarely, and yet they were what kept him going and were inspiring him. But what ate at me was the statement that they were not dwelling on where he was heading and were making the best of now.

Maybe because they did not have to care for him, when they did see him briefly they could just smile and talk like everything was going well. I could understand that, and I knew that it was important for his children and anyone else who came to see him to be able to sit and have an hour of what seemed like nice conversation, telling him things about their current life. I love catching up with friends and hearing them tell me that stuff too. The point was that his children were living a normal life they so had news to tell him. It's perfectly normal that they didn't know a lot about what was to come, and when it came they would not be dealing with it, he and I would be.

As I analysed this within myself I knew that it would be a very different situation if his children were caring for him and their days were filled with tending to him, and dealing with his health and emotional issues, and having to plan in advance. But through no fault of their own they were not and so of course they could come for an hour or even a couple and make nice bright conversation and tell him how brave he was and how well he was doing and then leave.

I thought about all the times I had told him how much I respected him for the way he was dealing with the disease and how wonderful he was. It was met with a blank stare. He had lost the full use of many facial muscles and he could not use facial expressions like he used to, but the difference when he looked at his children told me clearly that he could show enough expression, or lack of, if he chose to.

I reviewed how he had treated me during the lead-up to the PEG and during the hospital stay. Reading his public applause of his children it seemed that, instead of telling me how he felt openly and honestly, he had just managed a backhand way of making some points very clear.

Now I take the whole Facebook experience with a grain of salt, but at the time it seemed clear where he was directing all his affection and gratitude. It seemed I was receiving the sharp end of the stick because I was so close to him and completely involved in everything that was happening. Perhaps he resented his dependence on me, or more specifically resented the loss of his own independence. Many health professionals advise that it is common for the loving carer to bear the brunt of all the anger the person they are caring for is experiencing. I could accept that this is probably true, but I couldn't help but wonder how a man who had displayed so much amazing love and concern for others, and particularly for me, could be so spiteful now.

I struggled hard to remember the many words, actions and promises of this man I had married only two years earlier, in the face of the way things were now unfolding daily. So I determined to put even more energy into loving him, regardless of how he changed as the disease ate him away. I have always loved stories that show how love wins out at the end of the day. I wasn't sure I was capable of showing enough of the right love the right way, with all the goblins of guilt that kept trying to grab hold of me, but I was determined to give a mighty fine try. Right, I'm good now, ready to get out of bed and face my birthday, and find the way to bring him back to me.

My only truly pleasant experience for the day was that he agreed to try sleeping in the hospital bed. It had arrived a few weeks earlier. I had convinced him to try it for a few afternoon naps, and each time I had managed to arrange myself in the bed with him. So we lay together, even if I had to lay very carefully squashed up against the rail and I had him slightly off his bum. He did accept eating a little and having PEG feeds and fluids. We never mentioned his post on Facebook.

I was amazed the next morning to find that he had slept in the hospital bed all night and announced that he liked it! I did the happy dance in the kitchen when he couldn't see me and hoped we were turning a corner for a smoother road.

As insects we crawl across the face of this world.
Thinking ourselves so far above
all other forms of life
because as we crawl and writhe
we search for meaning.

12. Palliative care

We watched a video one night of an MND conference and were both struck by the presentation given by a palliative care doctor. He spoke about the true role palliative care has in terminal diseases and the importance of registering with them early to build a relationship with the team. He explained how much more effective this was than waiting until the final stages were upon a person, who then had to work with strangers at the most sad and stressful stage of all.

Our doctor was happy to do an immediate referral. We were interviewed by the Palliative Care Unit manager and accepted into the service. Chris made a point of explaining that he knew the palliative unit well because his first wife had passed away in their hospital unit and how wonderful the unit had been for both of them. She was interested and they talked about a few details of this and the role of palliative care. We told her our end-of-life wishes and she assured us that their role was to support us in these choices.

During the course of the conversation she brought up the topic of pain and their role in relieving this. She made it very clear that Chris should not have to put up with pain; this was something that could be addressed and was one of their important roles. I believe he was aware he had experienced a lot of relief from his shoulder pain in the hospital and was finally open to a discussion.

He had mild conjunctivitis the day we were completing the registration process and were booked to see the GP that afternoon. The palliative care manager phoned our GP, discussed his pain issues and organised for a liquid morphine to be prescribed. We discussed dosages and the best way to control pain, by taking regular tiny doses and having the fewest negative side effects.

The GP talked to us further about pain management and how to use the morphine for best results and I came home feeling that we were now finally heading in the right direction. I could get nutrition and fluids into him safely, he was sleeping in a hospital bed designed to make his life so much easier, and he was accepting pain relief. It felt like a silver lining after a long period of dark clouds. Maybe even all the complications of his anger towards me would have been worthwhile if we could turn it all around now.

Within a couple of days, however, he said he did not like the effect of the morphine – it made him feel weak and sleepy. He stated he would take a small dose at night only. I tried to suggest we speak to palliative care again or to his GP, so that we could look at dosage adjustment or other strategies they may suggest. I tried to remind him that often side effects could be due to a settling in period. He wasn't having any of it, he did not want to take morphine during the day and that was the end of any discussion. His arm and shoulder pain returned within two days of stopping.

The Palliative Care Unit in our rural area has community nurses who visit the home. They phoned me every Monday morning to check how we were doing and ask if we needed a visit that week. If all was going okay I would update them and they would phone back the next week. If I had any concerns they would come and see us. If any concerns developed during the week all it took was for me to phone them and they would give advice, talk to our doctor or come over and check the concern for us.

This was a vital service because I felt totally supported medically. I didn't have to make doctor's appointments unless it was for routine checks or prescriptions, or something more serious. Often they would phone our doctor and organise something for us without us having to get in to town. This was critical as it became increasingly difficult to get Chris in and out of the car, and a twenty-minute trip to town for a doctor's appointment could mean taking over half an hour to get him ready, then one and a half hours away from home and half an hour to settle him again on return. To have someone who could make phone calls and recommendations was truly a relief for me as I was already overloaded.

It was also true that we both developed a relationship with the two nurses that came here. They got to know Chris well and could pick differences in him when there was something wrong, and I could talk to them easily as we developed a lot of trust.

As Chris lost significant hand functionality, became unsteadier on his feet and needed more assistance, I realised I would soon need to dedicate more time to care for him. For that to happen I had to complete the paid work that required me to be away from home. I was fearful of leaving him for more than an hour or two in case he couldn't do things he needed to, or had a fall and was injured or unable to get up.

I spoke to our case manager about my concerns and she organised funding to provide a series of full days of care, once or twice a week, so I could get this work completed. What an amazing service to provide. We were allocated a lovely man who was very caring and willing to do anything at all to help. I bought a huge load of ingredients and Chris worked out a lot of meal plans. While I went out working, the two men cooked large volumes and packaged meals for the freezer. The carer learned a lot about cooking from Chris, and they always had things to do together. Initially Chris had been very resistant to the idea, not wanting someone to come and sit staring at him all day. In the end, even though he did manage to complain about it all constantly, I knew he was safe. He was given meals and fluids while I was out, and he had something to do.

Caring for him in my own home was so hard, as I still had to work and generate an income. So, even when I was at home, I wasn't able to just spend all day doing things with Chris, keeping him company or occupied. He was less able to occupy himself as his activities became limited. So the days of help over those two months were great in so many ways.

There was a distressing amount of progression and injury over this two-month period. At the beginning Chris was doing a large amount of the cooking tasks himself. The carer mostly helped by setting things up in the kitchen, fetching, carrying and cleaning everything up at the end. By the last visits Chris became tired easily and needed breaks to nap, and the carer did the bulk of the cooking tasks for him.

By the time this was coming to an end I realised that I was ready for regular help at home. This man would do light housework, clean up everything he had used and take care of the washing. By the end of the two months, I was beginning to truly appreciate having these things done. You don't realise how much time and energy can be spent on the basics of running a home.

Oh proud creature
who believes so blithely
that tomorrow is a given
and will be just like today
for thousands of days yet to come

Who is there that truly
wants to know their future?

13. The falls begin

With MND, the nerves that make the muscles move, as we will them to, are dying. As the nerves die, the impulses telling the muscles to move this way or that become more erratic in their ability to get through.

That Chris's legs had begun to be affected became obvious in how he walked. He could still walk but there was a lack of coordination, and the faster he tried to walk the less coordination he had. We don't even think about it because we learned to walk way back when very young. But watch a toddler beginning to walk and you see them trying to tell their muscles what to do and not always quite succeeding. It's almost like reverting slowly back to infancy.

This becomes more apparent if you have to walk on anything other than a perfectly even surface. You not only have to make the muscles move, but you have to make sure they take other things into account in order to maintain balance.

I remember his first fall. It was like I was just waiting for it to happen, like I just knew it would have to happen. He went to pick a lemon off the tree. There are a few concrete stairs to get into the orchard and he tripped up the stairs. Because his arms were so weak, when he put a hand out to save the fall, his arm collapsed and he went down face first. He came back to the house with a lemon and minus a bit of facial bark. He laughed, saying he had been clumsy and had just tripped, that the problem was that his arms didn't work well enough to save him, that it could have happened to anyone. Now I agree, any of us can trip up some stairs if we are rushing a bit or just not taking notice. But something in the pit of my stomach grew cold and hard and I knew that it was the beginning.

I had been talking to other carers online and had heard awful stories of serious falls, even to the point of causing brain injuries or death. I told him I had a fear that he would die in a pool of blood on the floor in front of me. He shrugged and said it wouldn't happen but he was going to die anyway so it didn't really matter. I commented that he could break an arm or a hip or a leg and become even more incapacitated. He replied that he was going to lose the use of everything anyway, so it made no real difference. This fear hovered in the back of my mind all the time, and it felt like he was not going to take any kind of measure to prevent it, and would only keep putting himself in positions where it became more likely to happen.

Within the next month he had several falls that 'anyone could have'. It was a real issue that, with his weak arms, once he began to go over, there was nothing he could do about it and landing face first became the only way he could land. Each of these falls was minor, just walking along, then 'tripping' and down he would go, and each time he would have facial injuries.

He wanted to keep doing all he could as long as he could, which meant taking risks as long as he could. Every fall was laughed off as having nothing to do with MND, just a dumb thing he had done. Denial loves to rule these situations. It wasn't a pattern. He had fallen three times in four weeks, but each fall had been quite different. He just had to pay more attention. He often walked the dogs down to their day paddock of a morning. This involved negotiating a flight of eight concrete stairs leading a pup weighing more than forty kilograms. One morning he fell, and was very fortunate that he fell to one side and landed with his head downhill in the garden. For a time he could not get himself up, and the poor pup just watched him, licked his face and was uncertain about the whole situation. That was the last time he walked a dog on lead, but she never forgot it. Apparently she believed that she had pulled him over, as ever since that day she stops at the top of the stairs wanting me to go first, then very quietly follows me down.

We had different ideas of what he could continue to do safely. The disease makes a person feel so powerless, so out of control over their lives, that attempting to do more than is likely safe is a type of self-defence reaction. I so get this reaction and understand it. I also understood that any serious injury was going to allow the monster to attack him even faster, and reduce his quality of life even further. Because of this denial, he refused to use any kind of walking aids, or have anyone walk with him.

His arms were becoming so weak and his shoulder muscles so wasted that he could not lift his arms even halfway. This was partly because his arms felt like lead, and partly because the shoulder joints were freezing. His right arm and hand were far less affected than his left. He was left-handed but, as with many lefties, able to do a lot of things with both hands, so he could still do many things with his right hand and arm.

I watched the progression and knew in my heart that his denial of what was happening was going to result in a serious injury. We couldn't talk about it because his denial would rear up and say that he did not have a pattern of falling, his legs were pretty good and his balance was great.

Finally, my fears were shown to be valid. It happens so fast, so unexpectedly at the moment it happens, and yet it is life-changing all the same. We came out to the verandah to sit down; he walked out behind me and stopped behind me to give me a hug. We talked and laughed about something for a few moments; all was as good as it gets for what was happening to us. His chair was behind and to the right. He went to step sideways to put himself in front of the chair, and suddenly his leg simply did not work. I will never forget the way he went over. No arms to give any protection or buffering, just over sideways landing heavily on the ground, on his right shoulder, his good shoulder.

There was no way that I could get him up off the ground. His shoulder had awful immediate swelling and the pain was intense. I could not try to pull him up, of course, so I had to get pillows and get him as comfortable as possible and call the ambulance.

The verandah floor is hard pavers, and I felt sick to the stomach as I kept reliving the impact of him falling, hearing and feeling it. He was already emaciated and it was hurting him nearly as much to sit on the pavers as his shoulder was hurting him. I could do nothing but try to soothe and calm him, and wait for the ambulance. My mind kept racing along lines of what injuries would be found and what this was going to do to him. I admit I was also worried about what this was going to mean for me. Already he had lost so much ability and I had to do so much for him. Now he was injured and was going to need far more care. Simply as a result of one split second in which he had simply fallen over. It felt so unfair, so cruel, both for him and for me.

The ambos were amazing, and they arrived thankfully within half an hour. I had to explain to them what MND does to a person and the impact this was going to have on getting him up. They gave him a small dose of morphine to help with the pain and they lifted him gently from the ground onto the trolley.

I followed the ambulance to the hospital in my own car and noticed the time; it was already well after 10 pm. One benefit of going to an ER by ambulance is that you will be seen immediately. It is hard to give good pain relief to someone when you cannot compromise their breathing. His shoulder was terribly swollen and the bruising was already growing over a huge area. The team in the ER were fantastic and were willing to have me with him all the time as he could not speak for himself and his needs were obviously complex. The X-ray revealed that, while he had not broken any bones, he had ruptured the major tendon in his shoulder. Finally, after several hours, we arrived back home in the wee hours of the morning with his arm in a sling, both exhausted and Chris in a lot of pain that we were going to find difficult to control.

Just when I seemed to have succeeded in helping him sleep better at night by using the hospital bed and morphine, he refused to get into the bed with his injured shoulder and went back to the recliner chair. I hoped this would only be for a couple of nights, but he said that the bed had not been working out anyway and he was better off in the chair. When his shoulder was healed he was going to begin sleeping in our bed again. I was surprised, though I knew he resented the fact we no longer slept beside each other. It had been weeks since he had been in our bed at all, and his condition had progressed further in that time. I realised with a shock of guilt that I had actually been sleeping much better since he had left our bed. It wasn't that I didn't miss having my man with me, it was that I didn't miss all the constant disturbances at night and having to get up and down with him as he couldn't reposition in the bed, couldn't pull blankets up, couldn't get out of the bed on his own to move to the lounge, then to the recliner then maybe back into bed again. I didn't miss the moaning, the grinding of the teeth and the muttering as he strove through each restless night.

This injury did mean a big change in his independence. He had little of that, but now he could not feed himself, and could do almost nothing as his left arm and hand were so far progressed that he could not even get his left hand to his face. Until then at least he could lift a spoon or cup to his own mouth with his right hand, but no longer. The pain made sleeping difficult at best and, even though he did not like it, at least for a few days I would walk beside him. Even if he had wanted to accept a walker now, he could not have used it with only one arm. After a few days of me walking with him he simply dismissed me from the duty and told me that he was fine and that he walked better without someone hovering over him.

As the days passed, the bruising that came out on his shoulder was extensive and incredible. It covered the entire shoulder and halfway down his arm, and persisted for many weeks. In the centre of the bruising was an egg-sized lump, and touching any of that area caused immediate pain.

The shoulder did heal to some degree and after a week he began to move the arm a little bit; after a couple of weeks he was able to feed himself again. Of course it never healed completely, or even well. Even once it got to as good as it ever would, he could barely get his hand to his mouth and had to move his head to his hand as much as his hand towards his head. He suffered a lot of pain in that shoulder for the rest of his days, and it seized up quickly even when his hand movement came back to some degree. It was never again his good arm; it simply became an arm and hand that he could use a little bit.

For the first four days the pain was so intense, he was fairly meek and willing to accept some help and to be careful. But all too soon he wanted to again pretend that he could do as much as possible, no matter how much pain it caused. I found it difficult to watch this unfolding because I had been waiting for a serious fall to happen, and had convinced myself that if he did have an injury from a fall, this would at least bring him around to reason. As only days went by, he returned to being determined that he would go on as he had before the fall.

His weakness continued to progress, the injury meant that he was struggling with so many more things, and it was obvious that this was frustrating. It's hard to imagine what it would be like to experience your body simply refusing to perform even the simplest tasks. Sometimes he could do a certain thing one day, and the next day he simply could not do that any more.

14. Balancing the losses

Our referral to some home services was processed and I received a call to say they needed to interview us to make a care plan. Chris was fed up with having people in his home and did not want us to receive any assistance. I could understand, as I didn't really like the idea of people being in our home either, doing things I felt I should do. But the reality was that I could not do it all myself. Chris wanted me to do it all. I'm sure it was because he was frightened. Here he was watching and feeling his body wasting away, needing so much help and knowing that it was only going to become worse. It was one thing for him to accept that I would help him, but quite another to think that he would have strangers helping him. Denial kind of works this way – if I don't accept anyone in to help out, then we don't actually need anyone to help out, therefore things aren't really all that bad since we don't need help.

If I could have had someone else do my work while I still earned all the money, I would have happily done everything for Chris all day every day. This was not reality, however, and the demands on me were increasing every week, and every week I felt I was slipping a little further behind in keeping on top of anything. Even though he had agreed and signed the paperwork months earlier, when it came time to initiate regular home help, he became angry. He accused me, saying that I had been lying to him all along. That when I said I was happy to do things for him and help him, I really was not at all happy to do this; otherwise I would not now want others helping.

It was so difficult to explain to him that it wasn't a matter of my not wanting to do anything for him; it was a matter of my not being able to do every single thing every single day. He was particularly against the idea of people arriving in the mornings to do things. I tried to explain that I had to work, that we must have an income, and that I worked best and most efficiently early in the morning. If I spent my morning doing all his care, then the bulk of the work was done for him, but I was left tired and having to start my earning work late in the day. If staff arrived at this point, there was little for them to do, so they were not helping me much, and I was not going to be able to work efficiently.

Another important point was that if I were to plan to do only four hours work a day and start it in the early afternoon, there were too many things that could go awry and cause me to start late and get even less work completed. If I could have carers coming at 8 am then I could count on working for three solid hours, and on a good day might be able to continue for another two hours when they left. On an exceptional day I might still manage a further two hours during the afternoon. Losing the morning would guarantee I would rarely get even half a day's work completed and often not even a couple of hours, and I would be working when I was most tired.

In response he announced that he would do everything for himself; he didn't need my help and would not become a burden to anyone. He stated that if he stopped doing things for himself then he would only lose the ability to ever do those things. We had this kind of conversation with some regularity and I gave up trying to argue my understanding of the disease.

He was going to lose all these abilities anyway, and overusing muscles causes fatigue and actually hastens the progression. It's not a 'use it or lose it' situation as for a healthy person. I determined that instead of arguing I would let him attempt to do more than he had been, as sometimes it is better for someone to work out their limitations. However, I was not going to cancel having services begin because I knew my own limitations. I determined that I would introduce the services gradually so that we would all be able to adjust.

One night, only weeks after the first fall, he was in the kitchen and wanted to blow his nose. This was another frustration – he could not seal his mouth by pressing his lips together and could not force much air out of his lungs. So the simple act of blowing his nose was difficult. As he attempted, he couldn't get either hand up to his nose. He began to make noises in frustration and I went into the kitchen. He did not want any help and I turned to leave the room, when behind me was an almighty crash. He was on the floor and had hit his head on the stove on the way down.

I can't describe the feeling of panic at these falls – suddenly my loved one hit the floor with incredible force and noise and could not move. I raced for some pillows and got him into a partly sitting position. He began to scream that he was totally useless, that he would be better off dead and that he hated himself. I cried softly as I held him and told him how much I loved him and that he was far from useless. He was so distressed and this was worse than the fact that he had fallen again. I was able to ascertain that at least the fact he was making so much noise meant he was not so seriously hurt this time. He had a lump on his head and I knew there would be bruising, but he seemed otherwise unhurt physically, just very hurt emotionally.

It was an enormous effort to get him to his feet again. I managed finally, using a kitchen chair, and was able to prop him over it and get him up. I was nearly to the point of calling the ambulance just to get him up, when we managed some positioning that worked and with some extra hard effort I had him up.

Finally he told me what had happened some time the next day. He was so angry that he could not reach his nose, that he had opened the cupboard and thrown the tissue at the bin and missed. This made him angrier, and so he decided to give the bin a good kick to show it just what he thought about it all. What frustration he must have felt. Here was a man who was having difficulty walking, and he lifted a leg to kick a bin! As it happened, he missed the bin, overbalanced and fell onto the side of the stove on the way down to the floor.

Every time he fell there would be some reason for it other than MND. Oh no, he wasn't having balance issues, his legs were not becoming weak or showing any spasticity; oh no it could happen to anyone. The thing is that Chris had been one of these people who could walk across any kind of surface and, even if the ground started moving under him, somehow he could just shuffle his feet and stay upright when anyone else would go crashing down. So these falls were so unlike him that it was glaringly obvious to me, but he was staying firmly in denial thank you very much.

Over the next few weeks, he began to have small falls if he bent down to take something from a lower shelf. These were more like sliding to the floor but the problem was getting him to his feet again. I am not a large woman; I am 250 centimetres shorter (ten inches in the old money) than Chris, even though he didn't weigh much more than me. Each time he was angry with himself for going to the floor, but finally he agreed that he would not attempt to reach into lower cupboards. I somehow convinced him that I did not at all mind getting things from a cupboard for him, and that it was far preferable to getting him up off the floor.

Late at night, alone and reflecting on what was happening, I decided I could no longer risk injuring myself by trying to pick him up off the floor. I didn't follow through on this, however, as when he fell he was so angry at himself, yelling to be helped up, I would find myself giving it one more go, telling myself that next time I would simply call an ambulance.

I remained in a constant state of stress and fear that the worst was still to come. He still refused to use any walking aids, and was becoming obviously unstable on his feet. He did not want to discuss it, simply saying that he was all right. He would become angry if I seemed to be watching or, even worse, hovering near him. No matter how I might try to discuss safety he was adamant that I had to trust him and his judgement and that he would be careful.

Our hallway is fairly narrow and there are various paintings hanging along the way. I constantly found the paintings on an angle and realised that he was literally bouncing off the walls to get from one end to the other. He laughed about it, saying he always tried to bounce on the same ones on the way back to straighten them. In fact, watching him bounce along the hallway was funny in some ways but it only emphasised his risk of falling – and in an open space there would be no wall to catch him.

Increasingly, our physical relationship was suffering. He could barely move and was in constant pain, heightened by movement, and he could not lie down. Yet he blamed me for our relationship deteriorating, and one day told me that I made him feel unloved and undervalued.

From that day on, no matter how much physical affection I tried to show him, by touching him gently, hugging him, laying a hand on him when sitting with him, I was ignored. If I hugged him he just sat or stood limply, not attempting to return it. When I looked him in the eye and told him how much I loved him, as I did often, he never said anything back but would look at me with a blank expression. He totally withdrew from me physically and emotionally.

We had an appointment to have his shoulder checked over by the GP and Chris had decided it would be useful to have a disabled parking permit so he would not have to walk as far. After she had checked his shoulder and pronounced it was about as good as it was going to get, I asked her if she could do the forms to apply for the permit. She said of course, and as she got the form out of the filing cabinet, she looked at Chris and said, 'But you aren't still driving are you?'

There was a stillness and silence in the room as I found something desperately interesting on the floor to look at, and he glared. No one seemed to know what to do or say next, so I finally felt I had to get it moving again. I looked at him and said, 'Well you haven't driven for three weeks, so in that time have you thought about or made any decision about this?'

He started to get uptight immediately and the doctor said, 'You know you are not safe to drive.'

Oh boy, I thought, here we go; this is going to be a doozy. She proceeded to conduct a few strength and resistance tests on him and I could see he was really trying to appear strong. Her conclusion, though, was that he had little strength and would be unable to react quickly if a situation arose that required it, even if his brain was fine and would react.

He went quiet when she said she wanted him to hand his licence in. He was now fuming and went on about his rights. She made it very clear that he was not up to driving and, as his doctor, she had to tell it straight. What if he killed a child? She repeated all the things that had been said to him for months. He refused to answer and simply glared in silence. She filled out the form and told him she would say the same thing to her own father because she loved him and would not want him to drive a car unsafely.

She was upset when we left, as he was obviously furious with her. And she is such a sweetheart.

Of course, as soon as we got into my car he went right off. He went on a bit and I did a 'when ... then ...' statement: 'When you start going off at me about things like this, then I'm just not going to buy into it, and I'm definitely not going to have arguments while driving.'

I knew this was going to severely damage what little was left of our relationship. He felt he had the right to make the call on when he couldn't drive and had made it clear when we had discussed this over the past few months that he would totally resent being 'told' he can't do something. It was just so sad. I know it's a huge independence thing, but both hands were half clawed, one arm had about 20 per cent range of movement (ROM) and the other about 50 per cent. His legs were wasting and he walked without coordination. He could take ten minutes and more to get his seatbelt on and turn the key. Then getting in and out of the car was another huge struggle. How could he think he was safe to drive?

His main argument was that there were people out there driving with arthritis and other disabilities. Um, pardon me?

You can't do something dangerous just because others do. That's like saying 'Why can't I rob that store; lots of people have robbed it before?'

We went back to the sullen silence that was becoming far too much the norm in our house. I felt too wearied by everything to take the argument up again and simply put the paperwork on the kitchen bench without glancing at it. He did not bring up the topic of driving again and so it sat there for days. I finally picked it up to see what it involved and if there was anything left for us to fill out. The first page was a medical certificate of competency to drive. The certificate had been completed and signed by the doctor, saying that he was medically unfit to drive.

The second page was to do with the disabled parking permit. I brought the paperwork out and sat down with him, saying we would have to take it to the registration office to have the permit issued, and that he had to come because they would photograph him for the permit. Then I tried, oh so gently, to explain that the first part of the form was actually a certificate of medical competence to drive, which his doctor had to complete in order to request the parking permit.

The reaction was pretty much what I expected. He shrugged and said he wouldn't bother getting the permit as he wouldn't hand that certificate in. I was placed in this position yet again. Do I cop another tirade of anger and blame for what is happening to him or do I just meekly say good idea and leave it? My own feeling of responsibility for the safety of both my husband and others won out. I took a breath and joined the battle again.

I told him he was not listening to important medical advice and that I was going to have to take a stand as his carer. There were so many things involved in this safety issue. How would he feel if a child were killed in an accident that he had caused? He replied that he would feel no differently than if that had happened at any other time in his life. I explained that no insurance company would honour any claim. If someone was injured or killed, we could lose everything we owned; we could lose the property and possibly be left in deep debt. He shrugged, saying, 'It won't happen. I'm careful on the road.'

The conversation played out as it had several times previously, but the situation had changed for me now as I was witness to the doctor's examination and advice, and was given the certificate. I would feel responsible if an accident occurred, particularly if anyone was injured or killed. I felt I could not discuss it with him as his wife but only as his carer, taking the medically responsible position.

The silence hung for some time between us and finally he asked if it would be acceptable if he did not drive any more but kept his licence. The first thing that flashed through my mind was that I needed to hide his car keys because I did not believe he would definitely hold to this promise. I asked again about the parking permit and he went quiet for a bit and finally spat out, 'Oh just have it all your own way.'

I actually expected him to change his mind, but I will give him credit that he did not, though he came close. As we were nearly ready for town he repeated his idea of keeping his licence but not driving. I didn't have the heart to tell him they would take it from him when they processed the paperwork. As we were driving it dawned on him and he said, 'They're going to take it aren't they?' I quietly answered that I thought that would be the case.

The process itself was easy and they issued him with a photo identification card in place of his licence. They issued the permit immediately and he was very quiet all the way home. He wasn't even throwing anger at me and I hoped he had processed it all himself and had accepted it. It wasn't until he told people online that I had taken his licence off him that I realised it had become yet another thing that was my fault in his eyes. Never mind it was an effect of this disease, never mind it was a reality. No, it was yet another thing I had done to him.

15. Dealing with pain

As Chris's anger escalated, I wondered if it was due to higher levels of pain than he was admitting to. He resisted taking anything other than Panadol. Constant pain could be the cause of his outbursts. Anyone in pain can become unreasonable, especially if they are trying to deny the pain.

One day I was woken at 5 am by a very angry husband, demanding to be helped out of his recliner chair. I had been in a deep sleep and came out in a rush, with bleary eyes and brain-fog, startled that something was terribly wrong.

The decline in his ability to speak was doubly cruel – it was hard for him as he believed his speech wasn't as bad as it was, and hard for me to grasp what he wanted. So he was frustrated, wanting something immediately and unable to make his needs clear, and I was in a half-fog trying to figure out what he wanted and hoping I didn't have to start doing something complex and physical when neither my mind nor body were properly awake.

Despite waking up fast to jump to his needs, I was not doing well enough to assuage his anger. He kept on about how he couldn't stand all this pain; we should just put a fucking bullet in him right now; what a piece of shit the chair was; and how would I like to have to sleep in a chair every night. I got him moved out to the verandah and, distressed at his state, I asked if I could do something to help him. Did he need something or did he just need to rant in frustration? Maybe he thought I was being nasty to him, as this inflamed him more and he hotly told me to just 'go the fuck back to bed'. He was sorry he had bothered me and wouldn't do it again.

I did go back to the bedroom, but I was now fully awake and distressed at how these outbursts were occurring with increasing frequency and were becoming increasingly nasty, even abusive towards me. As I gathered myself back together that morning, I felt there was either something more going on, or he was truly in serious pain and for some reason terrified to do anything about it. Something had to give. He wasn't truly telling me what was wrong and working with me to solve it, but he was crying out for help all the same.

I had a little breakdown to our palliative nurse. She immediately agreed that the pain must be addressed and arranged a visit. He was never happy about direct confrontation that required him to explain himself. I was determined that something had to be done. His quality of life was deteriorating and he was taking it out on me, making my ability to provide a high level of care and dignity very difficult. Just before she was due to arrive he had another fall. He wasn't injured, but it was a struggle to get him up from the floor. I could feel his agitation because he wanted to be up on his feet before she arrived. Somehow I had him up and respectable on the back verandah by the time she arrived.

We discussed the pain he was having and the kinds of pain relief that palliative care can offer. I was pleased that he was able to state clearly that his main fears concerning pain relief were becoming drowsy and that it might affect his ability to stay mobile. I agreed that these two factors were of high importance and that I would like to find a solution to the pain that ensured he would stay alert and able to balance himself.

We also discussed the need to keep pain at bay, rather than letting it build and have to medicate against a higher level of pain. It was explained again that a very low dose should be given at regular intervals, regardless of whether pain seemed to be returning. This ensures that the pain does not build.

I indicated that I was very concerned that his pain levels were higher than maybe even he was aware of, because his behaviour was deteriorating and his patience was very short. I stated that he was becoming abusive when it seemed he may be experiencing pain as well as frustration. I noticed that when I made any comment on his behaviour towards me and what his anger was like, he would go very quiet, but would give an odd little half-smile. I never did ask him about this, but it seemed like he was very aware of what I was talking about.

The nurse suggested a referral to the local Palliative Care Unit so they could work with him to determine a pain management regime that would meet all his needs. At this point he began to pull back from the discussion, saying that the unit would simply 'dose him to the eyeballs' with morphine and would do him no good. It took a lot of time to attempt to persuade him that we were talking about a specific type of admission with a clear purpose and outcome in mind, and he was talking about an end-of-life admission. In the end, the nurse had to leave after more than an hour of this discussion and we had no clear commitment one way or the other from him. I know I was exhausted, so I'm sure he was probably even more so.

We discussed it again later and I asked why he felt this way about the Palliative Care Unit, when he had always spoken so highly of them. I reminded him that he had wished to sign up with palliative care, and when they had interviewed us he had in fact told them what a fantastic organisation they were. He told me that he had only said that because it was pointless to tell them otherwise. He repeated that they would simply dose him to the eyeballs. He became agitated as I attempted to speak with him and turned to verbally attack me because I had told 'that nurse' that he had behaved abusively towards me. It was one of the hardest things to have to look him in eye, and attempt with love, to tell him that his behaviour had become abusive. He said that he wasn't in pain, and that the whole situation early that morning had been frustration not pain. He had been up to the toilet and could not get comfortable again and had then dropped the chair's remote control and could not get it from the floor.

I tried to explain how it was for me to be woken by an angry man ranting and demanding, and expecting me to be awake and alert and able to understand the situation and do his bidding. He replied that this was an ugly disease and I could expect it to be ugly and that was all there was to it.

Finally after he had railed at me for some time he said he would accept going in to the Palliative Care Unit. I was grateful and told him so, but he only glowered at me.

I phoned our GP as I was hoping she would do the referral without an appointment with her. It was so much effort to get him anywhere. Her first response was that she couldn't do it as the unit is for people who are dying and they were very busy. My stomach dropped and I felt like I had just been treated like someone who was overreacting. It took a lot of control to tell her that the palliative care nurse had spent over an hour here, and it had been her recommendation that this was the wise path for us to take, and that it was exactly what the unit is there for. I was exhausted, close to tears and could not believe our own GP had spoken to me like this. Finally she agreed to see us, but I had to bring him in.

I let Chris know we were to be there at 8.30 next morning as she was coming in early especially to see us. He said the only reason he agreed to do this was to prove a point. He would prove that all they were going to do was to bomb him out on morphine just like they did to his first wife and that the whole thing would be pointless. He said that he wouldn't dare to ever be angry with me again, and from now on he would simply say that he was just fine. I could think of no useful reply.

Timing is everything – never was there a truer saying. As it happened we already had a very full day scheduled. We were to have the home care service come to see us in order to get services in place, and we had our first massage for both of us booked for the afternoon. Now on top we needed to start the day very early indeed.

It was a huge effort to have him to the doctor by 8.30. I needed a couple of hours to do his morning personal care, plus my own needs, and half an hour to get him into the car, in to town and out of the car again. He did not do well of an early morning, and he did not do well being rushed on anything. But somehow we got ourselves in there and we went over the whole discussion again about his pain and his fear of medications and the need for a pain management regime. She said she would phone palliative care and see if they would accept him. I could still see in her eyes that she was thinking we were taking advantage of the unit, and I sensed a hint in her voice that she felt they would just say no and she would have told me so.

We sat with her as she phoned and spoke to the doctor in charge of the unit. 'I have a patient here with MND, he has advanced spasticity, has had some falls, frozen joints and pain. Can he be admitted for a pain management regime to be worked out?' It was obvious that the immediate answer, without asking any further questions was 'Yes of course.' She began to talk bed vacancies with them and turned to us and said, 'Can you present to the unit at 11 am?'

I had not expected that this would all happen so fast, and felt he would suddenly back out. Instead, he nodded. I explained it would be tough to get him home and ready and back that fast. We were told we could come any time that suited us, but the bed would be ready from 11 am.

We were pretty quiet driving home to get everything ready for admission to the unit, even though it would only be for a few days. We barely had time to make a cup of tea when the home care service manager arrived and we sat down to discuss how this would work for us. Then I reorganised for Chris to have his massage in the unit and mine at the masseur's rooms.

Arriving at the unit was another of the multitude of surreal feelings I had during the whole journey of this disease. For Chris, there were memories surfacing, as his wife had died in this same unit only seven years earlier. It was my first time here and we found ourselves sitting in a waiting hall for far longer than I had expected. Why do we always expect to be ushered in and settled quickly when hospitals are notorious for delays? There really wasn't anything for us to talk about as a result of how we had reached this point. He had resisted coming, and now suddenly within less than twenty-four hours we were here.

Finally we were taken up to the ward and his room. The moment we were left alone he informed me that this was the very room his wife had occupied and died in. I had never truly thought through the impact for him of facing palliative care, intertwined with memories of having faced death with his first wife. It was a jolt and I asked him if he wanted to ask for another room but he said no.

A nurse entered with the paperwork and he told her he knew her. She looked at his name, looked him in the face and said she remembered him and Lisa. She also then suddenly remembered that this had been the room she had been in and asked if he was going to be okay in this room. He told her he already found it comforting to be in her old room and she accepted this quickly. I know that to move palliative patients to different rooms was not a simple task and figured she would have been relieved.

We had written up a careful outline for the hospital of the type of pain he experienced, the way he wanted relief and what side effects were not acceptable. We also included important things about his needs, speech issues and peg-feeding needs. There was a whiteboard in the room and I was encouraged to write about his needs to assist staff entering the room to know things at a glance. We went through the admission process, and I helped Chris settle into the room, which had its own private balcony. I felt it was going to be important to let them work with him, rather than him depend on me to be in the middle of it all from the start. He was adamant that he would not allow the staff there to assist him with his shower and dressing so I agreed that I would come each day.

We barely had these things done when the massage therapist arrived and I was able to slip down to the cafeteria, and then race downtown to have my own massage after Chris's was finished.

It was a strange feeling when I arrived home alone and it was already 6 pm! Somewhere in all of this I was supposed to be working full time, and yet here was another day that had started early, and not a moment for anything but being a carer. I did not feel angry that I was now Chris's carer; I just couldn't figure how to make it sustainable. I reminded myself that we had worked out a lot of things in the meeting with the home care service that morning, but somehow that couple of hours earlier in the day already seemed surreal. I think it hit me then just how tense everything had been for some time. As a carer I was constantly in a state of suspense and worry. What would happen next, what body part would start to fail next, what won't he be able to do tomorrow, how will we both feel as the next big losses happen, what could I do to be ready? It went on and on.

It seemed to be another sign that our relationship was failing that he was not admitting to experiencing a high level of pain. I couldn't get past feeling that although we could not cure this, there was no reason for anyone to put up with this kind of pain. Pain was the one thing we could address! I had a feeling that, no matter what I did, he was angry with me and resisting anything I felt we should do or try. The result was tension and exhaustion. Now he was finally admitted to a place that specialises in dealing with pain rather than cures, and I could rest a little from the hour-by-hour task of dealing with it all and attempting to care for him.

I was sure that we were going to get this whole thing sorted so we could have some quality of life. I was determined to get some rest and get some necessary things done here. When I spoke to him that evening I was a little less confident as the doctor had come and seen him and wanted to give him tablets and a medicated lollipop. How is it possible they can't understand that Chris had tongue and swallowing issues? Obviously the doctor did not read all the information I had put so much time and effort into preparing. Yes, he was still eating pureed food and drinking some tea but certainly not swallowing tablets and I was dubious he could cope with a lollipop in his mouth. He managed to convince them that tablets were not going to work and they prescribed a gel capsule that they could put through the peg, but still maintained they wanted him to try the lollipop.

Next morning I headed in to the Palliative Care Unit. I was concerned because he hadn't answered my earlier text messages asking how his night had been and whether he wanted anything brought in.

He had not slept well and had insisted on sleeping in the recliner chair, refusing to try the hospital bed. The lollipop, as we suspected, was not successful as it only stimulated his mouth to produce too much saliva and caused swallowing issues. I helped him with his shower and discovered that he was wearing non-slip hospital socks and he admitted they had made him wear them as he had fallen the evening before.

I talked with the doctor, who suggested a complete change in the medications. I explained it to Chris as a positive rather than a negative. Okay, so what they had tried the first night had not worked. But he was no worse off for that one night than he would have been at home having a bad night. It was exactly why he was there, so they could try different regimes and adjust them as they observed how well they worked or not. Finding out one regime that would not work must bring them closer to a regime that would work and they had not bombed him out as a first attempt at pain management.

I stayed only a couple of hours as I was determined that, as well as getting his pain under control, I needed a break and should not neglect this opportunity. I also needed to get some work done, as I was falling further behind every week. In one way it seemed stupid to use a break from caring to work, but I also knew that I would be back to caring the following week and was likely to continue to fall behind. I would feel more rested if I did get some work done as well as relaxation.

I let Chris's children know he was in the unit, hoping they would visit him so that he would have some company and a break from sitting around a hospital. I was concerned he could get a little down and lonely, especially with the fact he was in that room.

That evening, I messaged him to ask how he had gone so far with the new medication. While I was waiting for his reply,

I spoke on the phone to a carer I had met through the online support network. Her husband too had MND but I knew they were also dealing with frontotemporal degeneration (FTD), which can create behavioural changes. Chris's message finally came back to say the medication was working well and he'd had an afternoon sleep on the hospital bed, which they had sorted, and he was going to sleep in it that night also. I was stunned almost beyond belief. They were giving him a tiny one milligram of an opioid medication and planned to give him three milligrams before sleep that night. He complained that his meals were too small and wanted more stewed fruits and peg feeds. Then the message said something I had secretly hoped for, but never expected to hear.

He apologised for how he had been behaving and said he had been depressed trying to come to terms with the progression of the disease and felt it had overtaken him. He said he felt like a haze was lifting, and possibly it was the meds helping. He suggested I come in early next morning and stay only for a little while so I could have the rest of the day to myself. He agreed he should stay another night but would like to come home the following day. He said how much he loved me and was devoted to me.

I was in a bit of a daze reading his message. I was reading exactly what I had been waiting to hear from him for months. I had been right, his pain had been affecting him far more than he had realised. With excitement I explained to my friend what he had said. She warned me that he may be doing this in order to sound good so that I would get him out of there, and that he may be worse than ever on arriving home. I did not want to believe this. I was willing to accept his behaviour was linked to pain, but not to FTD.

It was hardest to deal with the emotional side of a caring situation. Chris meant the world to me and his care was my highest priority. However, it was not the only priority I had to juggle. I planned to get up super early and get stuck into my workload for four hours. I would then go to Chris, spend some time with him, then come home and relax. Now it was turned upside down as I agreed to go to him first. I knew I would not get as much quality work done, would finish later in the day and have less time to relax. But with a sigh I put that aside and agreed to myself that I could do it the way he wanted.

I arrived at seven the next morning so that I could do as he asked. But he fussed about and wanted things done in such a way that it took me until 10 am to have enough done that I could beg to leave. So much for my plan. I had cancelled the work I was booked to do away from home the following day, as he was to come home, and I doubted I would get any real work done at home. On the positive side, he had slept in the hospital bed for six hours straight. This was the longest he had slept in well over a year, so I told myself these other matters were minor. Now that he had a pain management regime things were on the upswing.

When I arrived to collect him the next morning, the nurse in charge told us they were so happy with his progress and response to the medications they wanted him to stay one more night so they could be sure they had the regime perfect. They could also organise a hospital bed exactly the same as he had here to come home with him. He was smiling. He had been so impressed with the bed, which had an alternating air mattress, he had insisted he bring one home from their loan equipment. He thought much of his problem had been the hospital bed we had at home.

They had been concerned about his mobility so an OT assessed him while I was there and he tried out a wheelie walker. What stunned me most was that he was walking far more confidently and with better balance than before the admission. The movement in his shoulder had improved and his face looked clear, the pain gone. All achieved with a tiny amount of medication regularly, whether he felt any pain or not.

He was impressed with the wheelie walker and insisted that he wanted one of them brought out with the hospital bed.

I felt like I was looking at a different man to the one I had brought in here only days earlier.

He agreed to stay one more night because he was feeling good and he wanted to have the equipment in place at home. I explained to the staff that I had to work the next day but would do it as fast as possible and collect him after lunch. The staff agreed. I completed his personal care and spent some time enjoying someone far more like my 'old husband'. I went home eager to move forward.

Just as I relaxed that afternoon, around 4 pm I got a text message from him. I will leave out the many expletives that fully set the tone of the message, but it said that they were moving him to another room, that it had no balcony and he had known he needed to get out of there today! I immediately phoned the ward and spoke to the nurse in charge. This was a new nurse, just back from days off, who had not seen Chris before. I explained his entire situation again and begged him to read the document I had put in his file explaining his needs. He assured me he would read it, then go straight in and show Chris how to get to a balcony pretty much right next to his room and that all would be well.

I repeatedly tried to phone and message Chris as the evening went on but he would not reply. My anxiety slowly built as the evening progressed. That message had regressed so quickly to the kind of tone I had experienced from him in the lead-up to this admission. The old Chris that had emerged seemed to have taken a dive again. I didn't know what to do about the next day. Should I cancel yet another day of work and pick him up early, or stick to my arrangements and pick him up after lunch? I just didn't know what to do.

He messaged me back the next morning to say he had slept a lot through the night and wanted to know when I was coming. So I left early and went straight to the hospital. They did not have him ready for discharge, but they wanted to know if I could collect him at 11 am. I explained again that I had to do some work. Could he stay here until later than 11?

Another patient was coming in but he was welcome to stay on the verandah, which is where he had been spending a lot of his time each day anyway. He was not happy about the arrangement but said little. I hurried away so I could be back as quickly as possible.

When I returned I could not believe that I was looking at the same man. He literally looked hunched again, drawn in the face, with poor colour and those dull eyes that would not meet mine. I asked immediately if he was okay and he said he was fine, he just wanted to go home. It still took them some time to complete his discharge and he became increasingly sullen. When we arrived home it was mid-afternoon already and the mattress and wheelie walker arrived as we made a cup of tea. When I placed the walker in the lounge room beside his other equipment he looked at it and said, 'I'm not going to be using that!' I quietly said it could just stay there for now. I felt I could barely move, let alone argue that he had demanded they give it to him.

We were both very tired so I settled him for a nap and lay down myself. I woke with a start half an hour later, realising I had to attend a meeting that evening and had organised his younger daughter to be here. With everything that had happened, it had completely slipped my mind and I had not mentioned it to him. I got up straight away but he was sleeping well so I left him and had a cup of tea. His daughter was to arrive around 7 pm, but I had barely finished the cup of tea when she arrived at 5.30. He woke as she walked in the door. I knew by the look on his face that he would never believe that I had forgotten about the arrangements. Suddenly I needed to organise dinner and get ready to go.

When I returned home, as expected I received an ear bashing for my behaviour. He was certain I had withheld telling him anything in advance and did not believe I had simply forgotten. He told me he did not need a babysitter, I treated him like he was useless, and should have consulted him before organising other people.

The next morning he announced he was discontinuing one of the medications. He claimed he did not like the effect it was having on him, but admitted he had not discussed this with the unit. The following morning he announced that the regime of taking the opioid regularly all day in tiny doses was stopping too and he would just take the one dose at night to help him sleep.

He was back to being sullen, had poor balance and the pinched look of pain on his face, and there was again a constant undercurrent of anger. I wondered if I had dreamed his admission to the unit and the difference I had seen in him for two days. Nothing I said would dissuade him. I wondered if this was just his reaction to being proven wrong – that the unit had not 'dosed him to the eyeballs'.

He told me very clearly that he would never agree to being admitted into the Palliative Care Unit again, for any reason. I realised my carer friend had been spot on and began to research FTD.

I had these constant running conversations inside my head and this weird ability to pause them when something had to be done or people were around. When a quiet moment came the play button would be magically hit and the conversation would pick up from wherever it was minutes or hours previously. Actually it was more complicated than that; there were several variants of these conversations, and any one of them could be paused and started again from the same spot. I think this is a sign of high stress. I called them conversations for want of a better word; they were really more like internal arguments with myself. I'm pretty good at telling myself off, consoling myself, berating myself for stupidity and assuring myself how much better I will do next time. I'm also good at holding at least two sides of an argument simultaneously. Even if I may want one particular side to win, I can argue just as hard for the other side too. Nothing is resolved, the argument just goes around in circles with both or several sides being argued endlessly.

These arguments can go on for hours, days or even months. I always seemed to have had this particular talent, but it was greatly heightened in this stressful time. I had one argument about safety that had gone for many months and it went something like this:

He is losing everything bit by bit and it is stripping him of his independence and his sense of being a valuable person who can contribute. So I have to find every way I can to uphold his feelings and let him be as independent as possible.

Yes, that is all well and fine but surely safety is a higher issue because his independence is going to get him injured and cause him to lose even more independence.

Well, maybe not, because I see so many others with this disease who have a couple of falls and then realise just how dangerous it is becoming and they have a real turnaround.

Right, so just how many falls does he need to have before I am going to see some kind of sense being put in place?

Well yeah, I know, I would have thought he would already have made that choice.

You know of at least two now who have fallen and died from head injuries, and one of them didn't even die quickly on the spot.

Why can't he see he is hastening the progression of the disease and is making life a misery for both of us? I mean I could understand it way better if he was getting some enjoyment out of life and we were having lots of happy times and all, but it's just miserable, how can he bear it? It's amazing he can walk at all because his walking is so uncoordinated and it takes him such an incredible amount of effort.

Well yes, it is amazing, but let's be totally honest here. What is so amazing about managing to walk to the toilet if it takes you fifteen minutes to get there? I mean, what does that really achieve?

Well for him it achieves having done it I think. That's how it seems anyway.

Okay he achieves it, but does it make him any happier really?

Well he sure doesn't like pissing into a urinal so maybe it makes him happy.

Well it doesn't make me happy. More than half an hour of the day spent walking at a snail's pace up and down the hallway every time he wants to go means hours of every single day are spent silently just walking up and down the damn hallway! How nice would it be to walk him out the front to the gazebo and sit there together for half an hour if he just went into a urinal twice a day?

Well he doesn't want to come and sit out there; he doesn't like looking at all the things he can't do.

He has no energy at all and he is continuing to lose weight every week because he spends all this energy just walking up and down the hallway and won't eat enough. How can this be any way of fighting a disease? It's like living a nightmare. Look I know so many with this disease who give up trying to do these basic things for themselves and they discover all these other things about life that they can enjoy, and they consume ridiculous amounts of calories. That is what I call fighting the disease, refusing to let it take over and consume you.

I wonder if he will ever find a way to start enjoying what is left because he just doesn't seem to have any enjoyment from being with me.

Well no wonder, all you do is feed him, clean him up, walk him up and down a hallway, sit him here, lay him down there. That's probably why there is nothing left to talk about once all that is done.

What can I say to help him see this?

Pffftttt – he is never going to hear anything you say.

I stared at the rising moon
please, please I whispered
In silence it continued
on up through the night sky.

I begged once more
for what I wasn't sure.
I don't think the moon heard

Oh sun that brings the warmth and light
wake me and reveal my path
bring out the flowers
bring me a new day!

16. When head meets floor

At first it was hard for me to accept help in funny little ways. I had assured Chris that the people coming in would focus on doing light housework and preparing meals, rather than his personal care. This would take a load off, and give me more time for his care as well as working. But my funny little ways in the early weeks saw me racing around tidying and cleaning up the evening before, or the morning of them arriving, so they wouldn't come into a messy or dirty house. When I realised what I was doing I laughed at myself. One day I went to sweep the back verandah and realised they were coming the next day. I stopped short and said out loud, 'I can leave this for one more day and they will clean it tomorrow.'

It was like I finally gave myself permission to really let this service help me. After that day, as the hours of help increased, I learned to plan things I wanted done and stopped doing certain tasks so they became the responsibility of these workers – another thing I could let go of in order to have more time, energy and head space for Chris.

We went back to have the PEG checked by the surgeon and discussed having the tube replaced by a button setup, which would mean no tubes dangling from him. The gastroenterologist was impressed with how well I had looked after the stoma and how clean and well healed it was. We set a date for early December to have the change done. We discussed the two different brands of buttons available, the difference in their design, and pros and cons of each type. I'm not sure if Chris understood that we decided to go for one particular type as it is slightly more robust and does not need to be changed as often as the other. The doctor and I felt that this one would last my husband out.

The doctor expressed concern that Chris was still losing weight even though he now had the PEG. Chris complained that it was because the Palliative Care Unit had not looked after him properly. I was stunned but did not argue.

We continued with the same angry and sullen behaviour. Even though the home care staff did no actual personal care for Chris, I hoped he would adjust to them coming, as it was helping me a little.

I like to have my shower just before I go to bed, and would normally put Chris into bed first, but this one night he decided that he wanted to have a last cigarette on the verandah while I had my shower, then I could put him to bed. It sounds awful, but I felt resentful because I like to have my shower just before I go to bed and he knew this. I just love that feeling of getting out of the shower all warm and relaxed and then straight into a nice snuggly bed. Well now I would have my shower, then have to spend at least thirty minutes settling him in bed. But okay, he wanted to do it this way, so I said to myself that was no problem and headed to the bathroom. As I closed the door, I heard an almighty crash. It was so loud it almost seemed like I had imagined the noise, even though that makes no sense.

I raced out of the bathroom to find him on the floor on his side, and a large pool of blood spreading across the floor from under his head. Time seemed to stand still, and all my fears came racing up through my stomach and screamed at me. All I could see was this growing pool of blood, and I had a horrible, weird, almost déjà vu feeling. Not that I had been there before, but that I had known, truly known, for many months that this very thing was going to happen and yet I had been totally unable to prevent it.

The gap closed and I raced towards him, he was alive, he was very quiet, and obviously in great pain and shock. I grabbed a pillow from his bed and carefully lifted his head and put the pillow under it, partly to try and stem the flow of blood, partly to cover the very frightening pool of blood and give him something softer than the vinyl-covered concrete floor. I phoned the ambulance. They were wonderful in helping me to check what I could of him and had me place a rolled-up towel between his head and the pillow to put better pressure on whatever wound was under there and slow the bleeding.

I propped as much of his body as I could with pillows and got a blanket over him, trying not to let his moaning sear right through me. Then I waited at his side for the ambulance to arrive. He was conscious enough to answer basic questions but was unable to do any more than that. In fact, his quietness was disturbing after the way he ranted and yelled on all his previous falls.

I came to enough sense after about fifteen minutes to work out where I would need to get the ambulance to enter the house to get access to him, and began to move furniture around so they would have plenty of room to get the trolley to him. It is one of the worst experiences I've had. Waiting for the ambulance with Chris lying on the floor with an obvious head injury, not knowing if this was going to kill him. I couldn't but wonder what horror of changes this was going to bring to our lives.

The ambulance officers were lovely, but this was going to be a far more difficult lift than for the previous fall. We did not know the extent of the head injury or if there were any broken bones, and he was so frail. I realised I had a pelican belt, which wraps around a person and has handles, to help keep someone stable as they walk. With three people and the belt, we finally managed to lift him.

He was highly distressed once we had him off the floor, and became vocal, insisting I ride in the ambulance with him. I didn't think much beyond getting him seen to and agreed. On arrival at the hospital I called my stepdaughter and stepson and asked them to come in so that one could stay with him and one take me back home to get my car. When I walked into the house I could barely look at the mess on the floor, it looked like a murder scene from some movie.

Again, by the time we got to the hospital it was well after 10 pm and after several hours of being prodded, X-rayed and poked they took me aside. He did not appear to have fractured his skull, though he had split his head open in a long gash. They would need to do a CT scan to know if there was a brain injury, but they were not sure if we should attempt it. We had to be honest about this – if there was any serious injury, there was nothing that could be done because of the underlying MND. This was beside the fact that he could not be laid flat to do a scan. I agreed that a scan would be one more trauma and what would be would be.

He had fractured ribs, a huge golfball-sized lump on his left hip and swelling and bruising of the left shoulder. The pain he was in was cruel, but we could only give so much morphine as it depresses the breathing, and you have to keep head injury patients awake.

By around 2 am they were stitching his head wound. He had a lot of swelling and a massive shiner. They said he needed to stay overnight for observation. He became agitated, wanting to be sewn up and allowed home. He progressed to furious because neither the doctor nor I would agree to this. I explained that once we had him sewn up and settled I was going to have to go home and get a couple of hours of sleep, which meant he would be alone. We all assured him that they had a very comfortable recliner chair they would put him in. The ER beds were too hard and wouldn't adjust enough for him to stay in for long. He was already in pain from being in one.

It broke my heart all over again to have to look him in the eye and insist he must stay for the night.

I cried all the way home. Entering the house was even worse on my own. I looked at the room – furniture everywhere, blood everywhere, towels, pillows and blankets strewn around with patches of red. I allowed myself another cry in the shower as I tried to come to terms with what had happened. I had known this would happen, I had told him my fears, I had begged him to use equipment and assistance to be safe and he had simply refused.

Now he was in hospital, sewn up, but injured yet again, more loss of functionality yet again, more pain yet again, and angry that I couldn't just sit up all night with him in the hospital. He had a huge fear of the hospital, he would nearly panic at the mere thought of being left there alone, yet he would not attempt to be safe. I couldn't believe that he insisted on taking all these risks, and then expected that once injured it would mean everything stopped to ensure he was going to be okay in a hospital. My mind spun around and around and I cried. I finally got to bed around 4 am and slept for a couple of hours. The moment I woke I had to get out of bed, as I knew that my mind would start spinning again if I lay there.

I just couldn't face the room. I've raised children and livestock, and worked in several kinds of nursing, but something about this scene had me completely undone. I made tea and literally closed my eyes every time I had to turn my body towards the dining room. I sat outside until our home care worker arrived. I cried again as I explained to her what had happened and that I had to get back to the hospital to pick him up. I apologised profusely that I hadn't yet been able to clean up the floor, but would do it when I returned.

I was honestly shocked when she walked me into the house, took one look and said, 'Are you okay to drive because I can take you to the hospital.' I assured her that I could drive myself, and she calmly and kindly said she would clean up. I just nodded dumbly and told her to throw out anything with blood on it. I didn't care what went. I was halfway to the hospital when I felt a sudden wave of guilt, realising that this person, who had only been here once before, was in my home cleaning up what looked like some gruesome murder scene!

The drive home was excruciatingly slow as he was in so much pain. Every little bump went through him like a jolt. He was very quiet, and I gently told him that he had to accept assistance. He could not walk about on his own as he had a concussion and would be even unsteadier. He didn't truly answer me, but I had brain overload and was driving as carefully as I could so I didn't quite absorb this at the time.

Our home care worker helped me get him from the car to his chair on the verandah, and I walked into the clean house.

Before I even made it to the kettle I turned and there he was standing in the doorway about to walk into the house. I felt what little sanity I had left was about to leap out the window and run off down the paddock, never to return. I think I made it across the room to his side in a single leap, I certainly don't remember walking or even running there. I looked him in the eye and said, 'Please, you just need to rest and you need someone with you if you are going to walk around!' He said that he was all right and didn't need assistance.

This began a series of awful disagreements between us, and huge distress for me. I thought before this fall that I was fearfully just waiting for it to happen. Now my fears were ignited even more and I was nearly frantic. He really was going to keep on this way until he died in a pool of blood in front of me, in agony and fear, with me unable to do anything about it. How could this be happening to me, to him? As if this monster of a disease was not bad enough, now that I was going to be in such constant fear how would I function at all? I kept getting flashbacks of seeing him on the floor that night, but also the whole feeling of his pain and terrible fear of being in that hospital and being left alone there. Yet none of this was enough to make him actually think this was that final warning he needed to heed.

With all the people I talked to online, I knew that many people with MND understood quickly that they had to avoid falling because of the issues a serious injury would add to their already full plate. I knew that many of them had one or two, maybe a few, minor falls, realised the peril and changed their attitude. I knew some had a major fall and this opened their eyes to the need for safety. I also knew that many of them never had a serious fall because they understood the risk. Many showed concern for their partner, by not putting them in the situation of having to deal with falls and injuries on top of everything else.

But here we were. He looked shocking – stitches all down the side of his face, black eye and all manner of facial swelling, breathing uneasily with broken ribs, an amazing huge lump

168

on his hip and bruising of many colours covering his left shoulder – and he was up and about to attempt to step through the very same doorway on his own. My head was spinning, I had not had anywhere near enough sleep, I was still upset about what that room had looked like covered in blood, the pain he had been in and the horror of being in an ER with him. I was amazed that he was alive at all and he was looking at me like he was screaming, 'Don't you dare think you are going to tell me I can't do whatever I want to.'

Somehow the care worker and I managed to turn him about and sat and talked to him about the need for safety, and how we understood what he was going through and how it was for him. He agreed that he would not walk about on his own. Then he had a coffee and a cigarette, and seemed to settle a little. He ended up napping a lot of the day in his recliner. I hoped the worst was over.

He finally told me what had happened. He had gone to step out through the doorway onto the verandah and had lost his balance, falling backwards. He had hit the dining table with his left ribs, throwing him to the side, and his head had hit the edge of the water cooler, then he had hit the floor. I only felt sicker realising what every part of the horrendous noise I had heard had meant, in the order of things that had happened. I kept getting flashes of the position he had ended up in on the floor.

The next morning I got him up as usual and started his routine. I had just made a pot of tea when he requested to be taken to the loo. He always had his shower straight after this so I sat on the verandah to have my tea while I waited for him. He made a few grunting kind of noises and I wasn't sure if he was trying to call me to say he was finished, so I called out asking if he needed me. He did not answer, so I asked again. It is so hard when MND takes away the ability to speak, but still at this time I could often understand him, even though most other people could not.

He made noises back at me that seemed negative, but I couldn't work out what he was saying, so thought I would just continue my cuppa a bit longer. He made more noises, some grunting, some that seemed like complaining, but I couldn't catch any actual words. They seemed to be increasing in intensity. He was obviously unhappy about something. I began to feel very disquieted, one of those feelings that something bad was going to happen.

After some minutes of noises on and off, I called again and asked if he needed me and this time I could clearly hear the f-word being said among flurries of unhappy mutterings.

The usual routine was that I would undress him, and help him into the recess. He would shower himself using a lambswool washer on a long handled stick that he sloshed around himself. I would help him out, then dry and dress him. Before this fall I had said a few times, carefully, that it was becoming unsafe to stand in a glass shower recess. The home care staff and OT had all tried to tell him the same thing. These conversations never went well.

He insisted that he was fine, and careful, and we did have non-slip mats. The home care staff would only accept this as long as it was done before they came on shift. The longer I sat out there, the more fearful I became of his ability to safely shower today. He had a concussion and broken ribs and was becoming quite upset. Was he just upset or did he have a more serious head injury? Was he in pain, was something wrong or was it, as it sounded, that he was just angry with me for some perceived wrong? There were obvious barbs, despite my inability to understand each word, and I felt myself waiting for him to strike.

His agitation increased and he told me to just get him out, so I opened the door. His face was livid and he started to yell at me that I wouldn't even allow him to go to the toilet, sitting on top of him like that, listening to his every move and it was all my fault. I was stunned. I didn't argue. I assisted him to stand and brought him out of the room. He was still ranting, and was shaking and angry. I became frightened. How could I get him into that shower and leave him standing in a wet area surrounded by glass in the condition he was in?

As I got him to the bathroom I expressed my concern. This agitated him further: he wanted a shower and he was doing it and he was just fine. I explained that he did not seem just fine at all, and that he had a head injury and was not looking good. Standing up, his face turned from red with anger to a sickly pale colour. I suggested that it would be far safer if, for today, I were to get the shower base down and sit him on the shower commode.

He became as close to violent as was possible for his physical condition and as close to violent as I had ever seen him before. He tried to push me away, hit me, yelling as much as he could manage that he was having a shower and I was not stopping him. He was becoming seriously unstable on his feet and I was scared for both his and my safety. We were in a small bathroom, with glass and tiles and sharp edges and he was trying to physically fight me and push past me. It took everything in me to remain calm, keep him upright and insist that I could not, in all conscience, put him in the shower in the state he was in. I refused to move, or budge on my position. Finally he wound down a little and agreed; he would sit on the effing commode chair and be showered.

Now I had a new issue. The chair and the shower base were out in the garage as he had until this time refused to use them. I told him carefully that I would have to retrieve the equipment, and could sit him in the hallway on the regular shower chair for a moment, but needed him to agree that he would not attempt to stand up from that chair while I was out of the house. This began a whole new barrage about how I had planned this all out and yet hadn't even bothered to have the equipment ready. Silently I got him seated on the chair, and said I would be as fast as possible.

I got nearly to the end of the hallway when very clearly he began to speak and I turned. He looked me directly in the eye and with loathing in his voice said, 'I hate you.'

I would never have believed, even in my worst fears, even with everything we had been going through, that I would hear anything like that come from him. I couldn't answer. I fled the house, trying to stop myself from shaking, got the equipment organised and in silence I showered him, ensuring that I made it as good a shower as I possibly could. Lots of hot water over his back and shoulders, lots of attention to all the parts of him that weren't too badly battered.

He would barely speak to or even acknowledge me, for the rest of the day. He was rubbing it in like I had somehow caused all his problems and wanted to make them worse. I was shattered, reliving the moment of his face, his eyes and his voice saying words that to me were the worst thing he could ever have said. This was interspersed with reliving the sound of his fall and seeing him on the floor with a pool of blood seeping from his head. I somehow staggered through the day of silent treatment.

The next day he woke seeming far calmer and was steadier on his feet. As it began to approach shower time, he asked me a little sheepishly if I was going to shower him on 'that' chair again. I said that if he were able to remain calm he would be far safer today. Of course, inside I was thinking that it hadn't been safe for him to shower that way for a long time. In an instant he was a different man. Suddenly he behaved as if all was right with the world again and I was his loving wife. This was nearly as hurtful as the vehemence of his words the day before. I wondered if I was supposed to magically forget what he had said.

He had his shower, and all was pleasant all day and the next. I felt myself sinking into a new level of despair. It was like I had imagined that whole scene, like it hadn't really happened, because now he was happy again and saying please and thank you and even smiling. Finally that evening I tried to sort out what had really happened. It took all my courage to bring the conversation up.

When I asked him how he felt about how he had treated me, and the things he had said that morning, he made it very clear that he felt totally justified. I had treated him poorly by sitting right outside the toilet and pestering him as to whether or not he was finished. I had tricked him into using the shower chair. I had planned it all and was never going to let him shower himself again.

I explained the reality of my concern for him, how badly he had been shaking and how unsteady he had been on his feet. I then told him as carefully as I could that he had been very hurtful and asked if he realised this.

He looked at me as though I had said something like, 'What's so bad about genocide?' He stated that my behaviour had been totally unforgivable.

I had believed before this that things could not have become any worse than for my husband to say he hated me. But indeed it could.

A critical part of me died in that moment, and indeed 'us' died in that moment. I realised that never again would we be an entity. The monster had already taken him; now we just had to find a way to live with this until it took his body as well.

The most significant moments in our lives
come upon us unexpectedly

If they were announced ahead of time
we would dismiss them
and their significance would be lost

17. Escalating anger

He had been set to have the original PEG tubing changed to a button that Friday. I realised he was probably not fit for an anaesthetic. I checked with the surgeon and he postponed the surgery a week.

Chris met this with a new burst of anger.

To make matters worse, the hospital called early the following week. There had been a mistake as there was no surgery scheduled for the coming Friday. He would be done the next one, two weeks later than our original date. They then informed me, as though it was inconsequential, that our surgeon would be on leave and we would have another surgeon. Of course, as luck would have it, this was the surgeon who had failed to come to the PEG clinic and refused to send Chris home with opioid medications after the first surgery.

So I let Chris know and said I would prefer him to be done by our surgeon, but he would be away for some weeks, until after the New Year. Again he was angry with me and decided that he wanted the button put in and would take the other surgeon.

Chris became slower and increasingly uncoordinated. Just three days after the head injury, friends and family were coming by prior arrangement to give some help around the property.

My son had come to help for the weekend, two friends came for the morning to do outside work, and Chris's son came for the day. Chris was beside himself the night before that he couldn't contribute and said he was getting on the tractor to do some slashing.

As crazy as this seemed I dressed him in his work clothes and told his son the plan. His son told him off quite soundly. Chris instructed me to put his work boots on him, which I did. Then the arguments really started and I left them to it. I joined my friends and we got stuck into some gardening.

After about twenty minutes of arguing, I heard the tractor start up and guessed that his son had given in. The two men lifted him onto the tractor and the agreement was that he was to only work on a flat area up the top of the property. He took off and had a grand old time zigzagging up and down every hill. There were some very strange slashing patterns.

The good bit for me was that his son turned to me and said, 'I have *no idea* how you are doing this. He is a fucking lunatic!' He was deeply distressed at his father's behaviour and again this was some relief for me. I needed others to see what was happening, as nearly everything that was distressing me was going on privately, without witness.

I'm glad he didn't roll the tractor. His son would never have gotten over that as he had put him on it. I realised this was another consequence he would not even attempt to consider – how his behaviour might impact on the people who loved him most. Any attempt to talk to him about safety, in relation to how the ones who loved him felt, was simply met with 'Well it's my body and my disease and I will do what I want.'

After two hours, his son went off across the property to talk him back for some water and calories. I know his son was distressed about him being way off at the bottom of the property on his own. I knew what his son was going through; I'd been living this way for months.

When he came back in I asked if he was happy and had enjoyed the tractor, and he snapped at me, 'No I am *not*. My own wife thinks I am a total write-off.'

He'd had a half-hour argument with his son, who was immediately forgiven because his son gave in, yet I was the awful one, because I left them to make the decision together. I presume he expected me to have stayed and stuck up for him so he didn't have to do the arguing. The plain truth was I did not have the energy to argue a point I disagreed with. I really needed someone else to deal with his behaviour.

That evening saw him in a lot of pain as his injured ribs did not appreciate two hours on a tractor. He was in pain all over. His hands were very tight and he was grunting with every step. I knew he would be even worse the following day, and told myself sharply to stop and let tomorrow deal with tomorrow. As I helped him with his personal care that evening it was very hard not to give my opinion that he had just aggravated his injuries and helped to move his progression along even faster. I understood that he loved using that tractor, but couldn't understand why everything had to be done in anger, and to a point that caused him even more pain and progression.

The next morning I did something rare and slept in, without any intention, and woke to the sound of the electric recliner chair. I raced down the hall to find that he was about to get up and go to the toilet on his own. He was most upset that I did not think this a good idea, even though we had agreed he would not walk around the house on his own. As my son was staying the weekend he witnessed this, for which I was grateful.

That afternoon his son returned and I brought up my concerns regarding his safety. I called him out by asking if we still had the agreement we made on Wednesday that he would not walk anywhere unassisted. It is was hard to do this with our children witnessing, but I was becoming so frustrated that he could constantly behave and talk one way in front of others and then turn completely when we were alone. This time he showed his angry side, insisting he had the right to do whatever he wanted, no matter the consequences.

I stated that if he wanted the right to fall again, and injure or possibly kill himself, then I wanted his three children here and for him to tell them to their faces that this was his wish. I was not willing to explain to them why I had allowed him to fall.

He felt it was totally invalid that he should have to take anyone else's feelings into consideration. He stated that he

177

was going to die anyway, so what difference would it make when and how I had to tell his kids. He stated this in front of his own son. He then accused me that all I wanted to do was make him sit in a corner until his legs rotted away.

I knew I had to get a meeting with his children organised quickly to keep the momentum. I felt constantly concerned that we were going to have yet more injuries. I knew from what had happened so far that we couldn't solve this alone because we were finding no real middle ground. This happens with two people – they have one vote each, so the situation is tied. I kept wondering how I would feel if I ever had to face his children and explain that, even though he had already had two serious falls, I just left him wandering about doing stuff on his own: 'I'm sorry he fell and hit his head and died last night.'

At the very least I felt he needed to explain his reasoning to them himself. This way, if something did happen, they would know that this was how their father insisted it would be. I approached his three children and arranged the meeting.

One daughter became unwell on the day so she attended via speakerphone.

I stated my reason for the meeting – my concerns for Chris's safety – and made it clear that we were disagreeing. I explained that with five opinions, an odd number, we could arrive at a majority opinion rather than a stalemate.

I explained that I wanted to let him continue to do as much as possible, within safe boundaries. I expressed my fears of him being seriously injured again or even killed. I kept it brief, then asked Chris to give his side.

Chris explained what he wanted and remained quite calm and lucid. I was proud of him, as this was a very difficult meeting for all of us. He spoke without the level of anger I had been receiving from him, and I interpreted his words.

His son then responded that he understood both positions and reminded everyone that they had watched their mother 'rot in a bed and die of cancer over six months'. He didn't like to think of his vibrant father going like that. He didn't want him falling again and injuring himself, but he acknowledged that his stubborn father would not want to just lie down and rot.

Chris's eldest daughter said she felt the opposite, that she had been distraught to arrive the morning after his last fall and see him injured and wanted him to take safety seriously.

His younger daughter had been the least involved in seeing her father or talking about the disease. We hadn't seen her for weeks and she said little, basically that she understood he would take risks that I couldn't control.

His son stated that I am now their mother, and said some amazing things about his opinion of me as a person and of my care for their father. It was quite an experience really because we all had the chance to say how we felt, and there was no blaming anyone or being nasty, when so much had been so heated here for many months.

The outcome was that we all acknowledged that Chris could fall again and it could even be fatal. Chris agreed that he would not walk about unassisted. We agreed that if his son visited and was willing to put Chris on the tractor then that was fine, but I was not confident to do this on my own.

It was the first 'real' conversation we'd had as a family. I was thrilled because we had reached some compromise. I felt we had taken the first steps on the road to enlightenment.

The next day, as though it had suddenly occurred to him, he announced that he felt he might be better off going into a nursing home as his care needs increased.

I asked why he felt this would be better and he gave his reasons:

1. I wouldn't have to care for him as a high-needs person and he didn't believe I was up to the task.

2. He would have a regimented personal care routine.

3. He would be fed regularly.

4. He would have the company of other patients.

My immediate responding thoughts, which swamped me with guilt, were:

1. I knew I could take care of him and he was already high needs, but I had help coming in. Nurses work eight-hour shifts, then go off to their presumably normal lives for the other sixteen hours of the day, and have days off as well. So his care would be split across a host of people he didn't know, rather than primarily being carried out by his wife with some casual hours of help. Strange for him to say this, considering he constantly wanted me to do all his care and was against having staff in here at all.

2. We had deliberately set everything up so that he had as much choice as possible in his day. He could say yes or no to pretty much anything at any time. Of course, if there were appointments to attend this would influence choices. But if he wanted coffee, then breakfast then a shower he could have it that way. If the next day he wanted shower then breakfast and coffee afterwards that was fine too. If he was offered a meal or a PEG feed he could say no, same with medications. If he wanted a clear routine every day, or wanted to fit into a routine like a nursing home, he could opt for that as well. Actually it would have been much easier for us all to just make a routine and stick to it.

3. Very much the same as the second point because he was offered meals and PEG feeds regularly, and refused them more often than he accepted them.

4. One only had to sit with Chris for five minutes to realise that his speech was extremely poor. By this point I could only understand half his words, and only if I already had a grasp of the concept or subject being discussed. I had developed the ability to understand him because I knew him well and spent every day with him. I had also developed a way of grabbing keywords I could comprehend in a sentence, fixing them to the context, and somehow filling in the words I didn't understand. I got

pretty good at this, especially as I'd been through the process as his speech gradually declined. I tried to imagine Chris in a typical nursing home lounge room, sitting beside someone who may be thirty years or more older than him, with poor hearing and sight, and expecting to be understood. For months he had resisted people coming to visit, as he was embarrassed about his speech. He had isolated us both progressively when I would have said yes to nearly every offer we received from people to visit.

I decided to take the bull by the horns and discuss this fully, but not overlay it with any of what flashed through my mind. I did not want him to become defensive.

So I talked about his needs and how he saw a nursing home meeting them and suggested I would find out about homes in the area. If they had a respite bed becoming available we could check the facilities out. If he thought one looked okay we could book him in for a week. If he liked the place, he would know it was an option for him. He stated there was only one nursing home in the area he would be comfortable with and gave me the name.

I emailed our case manager, who replied that the nursing home Chris wanted only took people over sixty-five. She found a couple of places that took people under that age and when beds were available for respite.

He took the news fairly well and agreed we would visit one of the places. I organised the visit and made a booking for one week of respite starting just before New Year. I must say I was a little excited to think I would get a week of rest!

We went to the facility and the staff showed us around very pleasantly and answered all our questions. I noticed they did not really attempt to speak directly to Chris but through me. If they wouldn't try now, how might it be when he was there alone? The place had a lovely layout, a nice little garden, a large outdoor verandah and a patients' lounge room and kitchen. I tested that he could get in and out of the chairs.

He said very little until we were out on the verandah and I noted that it would be good if we had somewhere he felt he could go if there was any kind of emergency for me. We needed a contingency plan in case something happened to one of my children and I needed to take off for a few days, or if I injured myself and could not manage his care for some time. He quietly replied that the place looked okay, but if there were ever a situation like that he would rather go into the Palliative Care Unit. Totally stunned silence from me – he had said he would never go back there for any reason only the previous month.

Still, my reasons for raising this were to force him to face the reality of going into a nursing home, rather than let him throw it at me in anger like some threat. I had hoped he would do the respite there and that this would make up his mind, but of course this meant that I had to cancel the respite week as well. He never again brought up the topic of being placed somewhere else for any stage of the disease.

18. Starvation

The day came for the PEG button so I was up early. Chris was asleep and seemed comfortable. I decided to leave him sleeping, as he was fasting, and do all I needed to do. When I got him up and started to get him ready, he realised that we were going to be leaving soon and became angry with me. I should have tended to him earlier and allowed him time to wake up properly before carting him off. I apologised that I had made the wrong choice. So off we went to the hospital in silence, with him glowering because again I'd done wrong.

We were second on the list this time so were happy that we would get through faster. It was a different anaesthetist so I again explained the specific issues for Chris and how well the previous procedure had gone. He listened well and assured me all would be fine.

The surgeon was running late and I was watching the clock and wondering when he would arrive. Normally he would be there well before the first case and talk directly with each patient before the procedure to ensure we all knew what was being done. He rushed in late, and went directly into the theatre without a word to anyone. Once the first procedure was done, Chris was simply wheeled into the theatre without me even laying eyes on this doctor again.

Once again I raced down for a coffee and back up in time to be there as he came out to recovery. As he woke up and I made him comfortable, I noticed a box on the bed at his feet. I saw it was for the other brand of button, not the one we had all agreed on. I showed Chris and called a nurse over and asked if we could talk to the surgeon. The surgeon was already doing the next procedure so we knew we would have to wait. Chris was furious and stated adamantly that I was to insist he be taken straight back in and have the correct one inserted. I told him that I would advocate for whatever he wanted.

It was well over an hour before the surgeon was available and I quickly asked Chris if he still wanted me to advocate this way. He emphatically said yes. So I put on my best negotiator's voice and told the surgeon we were dismayed because we had made specific decisions with our original surgeon for the other button. I explained that Chris was upset that the wrong one had been inserted and wanted it fixed.

The surgeon was quite abrupt and obviously felt we were making a fuss over nothing, saying that this type was nearly always used and it made no difference. But, with a sigh, he said if we really wanted it then he would change it. He turned to Chris and said that if that was what he truly wanted then he would do it, but he also suggested that he maybe give this one a go. Chris smiled and nodded in agreement that he would just accept what he had.

I felt like the biggest fool and just wanted a hole in the floor to open up so I could disappear. I had asked him repeatedly what he wanted, gone over what he wanted me to say and how, and then I had done it all only to have him say the opposite.

All right, I thought, get over it, put your big girl panties on and let's go home. They showed me how to use the new setup and I was glad to get out of there.

A few days later we had an appointment with a physician we now saw instead of going to the MND clinic. He was nearly two hours closer and had a wide range of experience, but just as importantly was knowledgeable and compassionate.

By the end of the appointment Chris was furious with me. Chris had turned the regular half-hour appointment we got every two months into a big whine about all the stuff that had gone wrong. The doctor tried to address the important issues, such as why he was still losing weight and wouldn't take in enough calories. Oh dear, I answered that I gave him what he wanted and would accept.

Chris wanted to talk only about how bad the Palliative Care Unit had been and repeat the long story of their supposed mistreatment. It was excruciatingly difficult for me to interpret this story as I did not agree with him, and it was not relevant to what we could achieve in the time we had. I could barely understand him, so of course the doctor couldn't at all. He was speaking four or five sentences at a time, and I couldn't repeat them all verbatim. By the end of the fourth sentence I realised I had lost half the first and probably the second sentence. I became distressed as our time slot ticked away, wasted on complaints that were not the real issues and were not producing strategies or solutions.

I finally said I felt he was depressed so I was yelled at for about ten minutes straight from the moment we stepped out the door, and while driving, until I got through to him that I couldn't understand him! Well, he got his point across to me, over and over, once we were home. My job was to interpret for him. It was his appointment and it was not my job to inject over his words what I think or feel. If I wanted to give my point of view to his doctor, I could make my own appointment!

The only thing that sustained me was that he had agreed to take the antidepressants. What convinced him was that the doctor said it might help him sleep and reduce his pain. I was incredulous that for all the resistance to pain medications, and all his insistence that he was not depressed, he had accepted these grounds. Still, I wasn't planning on arguing, I was going to fill that prescription fast and get him started.

We had a follow-up visit with the dietician two weeks later. Chris was weighed at 54.9 kilograms; last visit he had weighed 55.5 kilograms.

The dietician talked seriously about starvation and asked him directly, 'What is your barrier to getting enough nutrition?' His response was that he couldn't give the meals to himself. The dietician looked him in the eye and said, 'So she is not giving you enough to eat?' I started laughing at this, and the dietician joined in, but Chris looked far less than amused.

There was an upside because, after some stern remonstrations from the dietician, Chris actually agreed that I would be in charge of his intake. He would accept whatever

I put in front of him to eat or whatever I said needed to go through the PEG. The dietician drew out a detailed intake plan, and a selection of ways we could increase calories from there. We worked on ensuring we could space meals and PEG feeds out enough to get all the calories he needed during the space of a day. We all agreed he would eat two meals and a high-calorie, high-protein special dessert each day, as well as five PEG feeds. We discussed the nausea he experienced and planned that he would eat a little yoghurt or anything he wanted by mouth before each PEG feed as it reduced the nausea well. I noticed how health professionals were now repeating everything several times to ensure he had understood.

That very night he attempted to refuse the last PEG feed and I had to remind him of the plan we had made only that day, and of his agreement. Reluctantly he accepted the feed. For the next three days he accepted taking what I gave him and I started a chart to record his intake, which the home care workers filled in as well.

On the fourth day he refused a banana, ice cream and Ensure shake but accepted a straight Ensure through the PEG. After dinner he refused the dessert, but soon after requested a PEG feed. He looked quite bloated and uncomfortable and I was worried he would lose the meal. He refused the feed just before bed. The dietician had been so detailed and clear in his explanation of the plan and how it would work. Now, only four days in, he was bucking and changing the plan.

The next day he complained that he was feeling full all the time, uncomfortable and sleepy. I knew from talking to others online that this was common when first starting to take in a lot of calories regularly, and advised that it should settle. Starvation does not mean someone is thin; it means that their digestive system is shutting down. I suggested his system needed to adjust to being used again and if that meant feeling a bit full and sleeping more, then that was probably no big deal as his body was using the calories well while he slept.

I took a deep breath and said, 'If you had continued losing weight at the rate you were losing it, you were not going to live much longer.'

He gave one of his funny little smiles that were always hard to interpret and said, 'Yeah, well no one knows how little time I've got left.'

I was frustrated that he chose the PEG and told everyone how he was fighting the disease, yet would not manage his calories well, either before or after the PEG. The need to manage his diet properly appeared to be too complex for him to now understand. I remembered how this man ran cafés and restaurants of his own for years, and had always been a believer in eating a good and varied diet. You could say his life had revolved around eating. Yet now he couldn't get a nutrition plan in place and stick to it, even if someone else was delivering the portions directly into his stomach.

I hated it but I felt it was 'all or nothing' – either we pumped him with calories and got his weight up a little, or stopped nutrition so he could starve quickly and it would be over. I felt guilty and disloyal for thinking this, even in the privacy of my own mind, but he was crying every day and was so down, I couldn't understand why he chose to 'live' this way. I couldn't understand why he would take in only half the calories he needed and thereby 'just' keep himself going a little bit longer, but always in a state of starvation. I wanted him to take in all the calories he needed to keep himself at the best he could be. It wasn't that I wanted him to stop eating. To me, his choices were not fighting the disease, were not even accepting the disease. Instead they were actively assisting the disease to do its worst.

As the days progressed he asserted that he wanted to lower the amount of calories he would take in. It started with refusing the last PEG feed of the day, stating it made him need to get up to the toilet through the night, as it was too much fluid. He stated that I wouldn't like him getting up at night as it wasn't safe, and that he then often had trouble getting back to sleep afterwards. I couldn't find any way to add that lost feed into the day's routine as he was already having something every two hours and complaining of feeling full all the time and nauseous for at least half an hour after.

When I considered whether I would have to argue with him about it every single day, I realised that I wouldn't win, no matter what I did, so I let it go. If prolonging his life just a little more would make it better, I would have argued, but it was far more likely he would resent me because I had made him consume more.

By the second week he was refusing one of the daytime feeds on some days. It felt like he was testing me out to see what he could get away with. So we had progressed from starting with five PEG feeds a day, two meals and a dessert, to four PEG feeds on a good day, but three on others. He felt it was no problem, but if you do the maths, he was still barely taking in enough to maintain his weight. He was possibly going to slow down the weight loss slightly, but was not going achieve any increase. Taking in more calories than he was previously was not the same as taking in the amount he needed.

19. Family events

I received a distraught phone call from Chris's mother to say that his sister had been found dead in her bed that morning. She had been suffering many health issues for years but had seemed like one of those people who would live a fairly long life despite them. She had been quite unwell when Chris had last visited her in August, but she had phoned me often over the past couple of weeks trying to organise to visit. He had always rolled his eyes at the thought of her coming. All of a sudden she was just gone.

When I told him what had happened, he appeared to accept it as a matter of fact. He did not seem to want to talk about it and I felt that I should let him absorb it in his own way.

I asked if he would like me to book plane tickets so that we could go to her funeral and he very quickly said he did not want to go. I asked if he was okay and he said he was fine.

Later that afternoon I noticed that he was walking worse than usual. He said his entire lower half was hurting. I asked if he knew the cause, and he snapped: 'Well my sister did just die you know. How do you expect I would be feeling?' As I dressed him for bed he glowered at me like I was the most insensitive person in the world. I tried to hug him and offer support but he remained stiff and cold and we never spoke of his sister again.

He wrote a lovely eulogy piece for her funeral, which I sent to his mother, and the priest read it. His mother posted us a CD with a recording of the service but he refused to listen to it.

As Christmas approached, he began to have increasing trouble using his hands and arms at all. He had needed me to light his cigarettes for him for months. He used a cigarette holder that he could clamp hold of with his teeth. However, at times the cigarette would drop into his lap and he could no longer pick it up.

His first power wheelchair (PWC) arrived and I wanted him to spend as much time in it as possible, to both give him some

189

freedom moving around and reduce the amount of assisted transfers needed. He could move around areas of the house more frequently because each move was not dependent on him doing a standing transfer, let alone attempting to walk. It had a tilt-in-space function, which allowed him to tilt the chair back rather like a recliner so he could change position a little and change where the pressure was on his bum. These are expensive pieces of equipment, loaned to us at no charge, and the chair included a ROHO cushion to sit on. These cushions alone are worth over $800 and would not be cigarette resistant. I felt that we needed to devise a safe way for him to smoke in the PWC. He was less than happy again. I felt we had a responsibility to look after it but he did not see this as being his problem because he would be dead when I would have to give the equipment back. What was it to him if I had to explain how it was now damaged?

I put it to my online support group and began devising a contraption to allow him to smoke safely in the chair. I tried to involve him in thinking of designs, but he treated it all like a silly idea of mine to be tolerated at best, but not to be engaged with. Several of my children were arriving in the days before Christmas – this could be a fun project to get into together, and I hoped it would get Chris involved.

Two days before Christmas I tipped a bag of items onto the verandah table, gave my design idea and set them to it. My kids enthusiastically opened packets and started sorting the bits – headphones with microphone, harmonica brace and lightweight ashtrays.

Indeed, it turned into a bit of a game and a challenge. Having a bunch of young men take an active interest got Chris to stop rolling his eyes and get inventive. He had always been the kind of man who could make something amazing from any bundle of junk and could fix anything with a four-inch nail. It's all about attitude and imagination really, and these were things he used to have in abundance. Once this was no longer just my idea, he got creative again for the first time in months and decided on how it would work. The kids were sent off to the shed to trawl for all kinds of clamps, bits of metal and tools.

It took many hours, lots of laughs and a few failed attempts, but they put together a contraption that Chris agreed would work. It was such an achievement for everyone. One of the things that really had me smiling was that they had spent the better part of the day together and been involved in something together. In the long run, he only used it three more times – there was always some aspect he did not like. I wondered if it had any bearing on the total dislike he had for the PWC or if his dislike of the PWC stemmed from not wanting to use the smoking contraption. One of those chicken or egg mysteries I will never solve.

I always had to ask him if he would like to get in it, and most time he refused. He would have left it sitting totally unused if I had not asked as frequently as I dared. I had hoped it would give him a little freedom and allow him to move away from the house, even come outside to the gardens with me. He had no interest in seeing all the things he could no longer do, preferring to sit and smoke cigarettes that dropped in his lap on the verandah. I will never regret trying to make any improvement for him, even the ones that didn't really amount to success.

During the week leading up to Christmas Chris had became increasingly depressed and morose. He had ordered presents for family online and I had helped by typing up some words he wanted printed to go with their gifts. I had not managed any gift shopping and frantically realised that it was going to be vouchers for everyone, if I could even get to the shops to buy some. He organised for his three children to take him out shopping the weekend before, and I thought this was wonderful. This would be the very first time his children had taken him out alone since his diagnosis, apart from his son taking him fishing very early after diagnosis. An outing for them all sounded like a wonderful idea.

And it was a good outing for them. It backfired for me, however, with Chris angrily pointing out that it hadn't been me taking him shopping. That I had helped him shop online and hadn't done any of my own shopping was disregarded.

Christmas was approaching so fast it was going to bowl me over. Even though I didn't feel well prepared for it all, I had been really looking forward to having some time with family around to share laughter and company. With people around and lots of distraction we would have some respite from being so isolated and focusing on the disease. Instead, he became clearly more irritated each day closer to the first of the children arriving. Just a few days before, I asked him how he was feeling about it. He told me he was dreading it. I was dismayed and a little shocked, as he had raised no objection during the months of planning for the day and how long different people would be staying. Now, when it was far too late to think of any other arrangements he told me this was how he felt about it. Much as I tried not to, I began to worry, looking at the day itself and the week of visitors with apprehension.

Christmas morning arrived whether we were ready or not. Once the early things were done I began to organise the layout of furniture on the back verandah for lunch. He became even more agitated and told me to put the PWC away, as he had no intention of using it. He insisted on a particular position for his chair and I knew he was going to be fairly hemmed in. It would be difficult to transfer him to get him to the toilet or inside. He barely moved from the chair all day and I believe he did not want to be seen having difficulty with transfers. As a result, in just one day he had developed a very red area on his bum. I've seen pressure sores and ulcers, and know the pain they can cause and how hard they are to heal if they take hold. I know what one looks like in the very first stage of development, and this is exactly what I was looking at.

The entire day was incredibly difficult for everyone, as the monster and the way it was taking our beloved man from us overshadowed us all. The gift he had purchased for each of us was a beautiful tealight candleholder and candles. To go with it was what he had written: how much he loved each of us and that he would like us to light the candle every Christmas Eve, or any time we wanted to remember him. To me the gift was beautiful but macabre, highlighting his coming death.

When it came time to open presents, the kids were instructed to open their gift from him at the same time. It was a very emotional time. Everyone had tears in their eyes, including Chris, and when he started to cry one of the kids shrieked and ran from the room. It was so hard to move past this to truly enjoy opening presents from each other and become smiling and happy.

His mood continued declining through the day, and he cried often. This caused saliva and swallowing issues and became quite frightening. Recovering, he then switched from nearly hilarious laughing back to crying. So distressing for him, and for everyone else. Someone sat with him all day, but we each felt the need to have times away from him due to the high level of emotion. By the end of the day I felt this had probably indeed been his last Christmas, and it had been a most awful day, and would be the last Christmas memory of him for each one of us.

Boxing day was a far better day for him emotionally. From the start he was a bit lighter in spirit. I wondered if he had shed a bit of his heavy load. The red area on his bum was still angry looking and he reluctantly let me rub a little cream into it and asked me to get the pressure pillow. I had purchased it weeks previously but he had refused to use it. He complained of a lot of nausea through the day, and the stoma looked red and slightly swollen. By evening his hands were also red and swollen. The previous day he had started with none of these issues but had been so down all day; now, with all these issues starting up, he was far brighter in himself.

His spirits continued to rise for the rest of the week, in contrast to how they had sunk before Christmas, yet the stoma continued to worsen and became painful. His hands swelled each day and went down again at night, and the red area on his bum persisted in much the same state. Having guests staying most of the week helped me a lot. They were distractions for me and someone could always be around Chris. He still refused to use the PWC and refused to use his new smoking contraption but was fairly bright with anyone who made conversation with him. They were all so good at trying to find things to talk with him about and include him in everything. I was grateful, as I knew how dull his life had become and how hard it was to make conversation. It's hard to talk excitedly about something coming up in the future or something you may think sounds great, when the person you are talking to has no future.

I felt emotional when the last of my children were leaving. It felt like the walls of isolation were about to close in on us again. There was a desperate feeling that we were about to go back to the previous behaviours, and his attitude towards me would be my only real source of sensory input once again.

He had not used the hospital bed for six weeks, so it had become yet another highly expensive piece of loan equipment sitting idle. I had organised to have most of the wall to the spare bedroom removed to open the room and perhaps make it more pleasant to be in.

I could get him to use the bed in the afternoon if I lay down with him. We would usually be in it for an hour or so, and he always seemed comfortable even with me squashed in on one side. After a nap in there one afternoon early in the New Year he said, 'If you brought this out into the lounge room I would use it.'

Don't you love those 'lightbulb' moments?

It was one of those flashes that come in an instant, but you process it later. He wasn't really resisting the bed; he was feeling that he was going to be 'shut away' in a room. Even with the plan to cut the wall out, I could see that he had a fear concerning the room more than the bed itself. Maybe it was a fear that I was going to put him in there to rot.

I had his son here the next day and we moved the lounge into the spare bedroom and the hospital bed into the lounge room. The excitement I felt when I had him bedded down in it for the night is hard to describe. I went to bed wondering if I would be woken by a screaming man in a few hours.

As it turned out we actually both slept all night, well I did and he didn't call through the monitor. I went out to the lounge room to find he was awake and I smiled, kissed him and said a cheery, loving good morning. He started ranting that the bed was a fucking piece of shit. Ho hum here we go again. No, don't let the despair drown you; hold your head up, breathe, smile. There doesn't that feel better? You can do this girl.

His hands continued to swell on and off and were red, and soon skin began peeling all over the palm and fingers. My lovely pharmacist looked at photos I took and gave me some cream for them. Sitting still all Christmas Day had left him with some new issues. It had been a very hot day, so sitting still in one place sweating, had now given him a fungal infection around the stoma, fungal hands and a pressure area.

It seemed so odd to me that he had worked himself into so much distress about Christmas Day and our visitors that he caused these issues for himself. Any other day he wanted to be up and down often, moving to here or there, using the toilet, cooling down parts of his body, keeping the circulation going a little. All the times he accused me of wanting him to just sit in a corner so his legs would rot, and now he had sat himself there for that day and these new physical issues, reminiscent of rotting, were the result. He didn't do these things deliberately. I don't think he had enough comprehension of consequences to think his decisions through.

The red area on his bum soon developed a small skin break and the palliative care nurse came every second day to check it and apply dressings. We tried to convince him that he must accept lying in the hospital bed on his side for at least one hour, if not longer, every afternoon. He couldn't lay flat, so the head of the bed was always inclined to at least a half-sitting position. So even in bed he was not actually off his bum. We both tried to impress on him the seriousness of a pressure sore developing, and that if it did develop into an open sore he would not be able to be on his bum at all.

The stoma was constantly irritated, oozing, and proud flesh developed around it. The nurses used silver nitrate to try to burn away the proud flesh. Nothing seemed to help enough and it became increasingly painful. The entire area would spasm regularly.

The next week or so seemed to just roll along. I was having a break from work due to the festive season, and my days were pretty much consumed with doing his personal care and trying to spend quality time with him. This comprised of massage, long showers, hair, nail and skin care, trying to encourage him to use the PWC and come to other pleasant areas of the property to sit for a while, and trying desperately to find topics of conversation. The gardens and flowers had been one of our biggest joys together. His complete disinterest in them meant not only that I couldn't enjoy them with him any more, but also that I could barely get time to work in and enjoy them myself. When I did I felt guilty about his inability to work out there with me.

For the most part he seemed to have responded to the antidepressants because he was becoming less flammable, though he was more often sullen and withdrawn. I'm not sure if that was related to his continuing speech decline. It was hard to tell anything for sure when the situation was so complex.

His care needs were increasing weekly, and the workers were taking on more care tasks and the hours of help were increasing every few weeks. He still resisted giving over any personal tasks to them, and I tried to get him to help me by being ready for tasks he needed, in timeframes that were helpful. Too often he would resist, as though it gave him some kind of stress relief or feeling of control to do things in a way that would make my day harder. I could never quite shake this feeling that he was in some way sabotaging deliberately, as much as I desperately hoped he was not.

His birthday was in mid-January and I organised something for each of his children to do so that together we could try to give him as nice a day as possible. I was dismayed at how difficult Christmas Day had been, and how depressed he had been. I was striving to make his birthday pleasant. One daughter suggested she could come over and cook dinner here for us and his son said he would bring ice cream cake. We discussed the menu several times until she was really happy that she had worked out a dish that he could eat as well, so it would feel somewhat normal for him.

Our speech pathologist secured an appointment for us to see another gastroenterologist about the stoma, but it was for the morning of his birthday. We needed to get this tended to, and I figured his birthday would go by a bit faster if we had to go out for a while.

On the day before his birthday, we were suddenly informed that his electric transfer hoist was arriving the next day and the OT would be at our home to train me at 10.30. We needed to get this done too, and again it would make the day go faster. I knew also that it was going to be exhausting for us both, but dinner would be lovely.

The new gastroenterologist gave the button and stoma a good examination. He felt the best thing to do was change it for the type of button we should have received. As much as we didn't want him to undergo another procedure, we agreed. He suggested we have the original surgeon do the procedure and placed us on the list for his first operating day of the year. We were so pleased with this outcome.

The OT was brilliant at training me with the electric hoist. I was surprised at how easy it was to use, and I think Chris was too. He was very amenable in allowing us to put him in and out of the bed several times. He could feel the huge difference in being able to place him correctly into bed and make him comfortable.

I tried to make the day as nice and lighthearted as possible despite being scheduled for another surgical procedure and using yet another piece of equipment to cope with the progression. Still, I think the day went far better than it would have if we had just been at home all day. I settled him in bed mid-afternoon and cuddled up beside him for a nap, hoping he would at least enjoy the physical contact.

His daughter made a wonderful curry dinner and the ice-cream cake was a hit. All up it was a far more pleasant evening together than we'd all had in a long time. The only real issue was the reminder of how pleasant mealtimes used to be, filled with conversation and laughs. Chris needed every bit of concentration to prevent choking on his food, and laughter at a mealtime was something I couldn't remember us doing for a very long time.

The next morning he knew I was going out for work at 9.30, and yet he wouldn't agree to his care tasks being done early, but still wanted me to do them all. As I got him out of the shower at 9.55 I explained that I was running really late, dried him and asked if the home care worker could finish his care so I could leave. Sullenly he agreed and I raced out the door.

The carer reported that it went well and he had been really happy and chatty all day. He'd been easy to get along with and hadn't seemed at all bothered by her dressing him.

I arrived home to discover his daughter was visiting. His hands were very swollen and blue, and he had been in one chair on his sore bum all day. I was dismayed as we were supposed to be regularly repositioning him to prevent this pressure sore worsening. I got him organised and was about to put him in bed on his side, when he told me that he was 'just a routine' not a person. I tried to start a conversation but he refused to engage. I ended up leaving the room after finally getting him settled right and had a little cry.

It seemed to me that he was lovely to all these other people, because they just pandered to his wishes and smiled brightly, though they hadn't done the thing that was so essential for his care. To him, my immediate attention to this side of his care indicated that I saw him as 'a routine', and those who neglected his care saw him as a person. Somehow I just didn't 'do' enough 'with' him.

I tried to explain that if he would allow home care to 'do' his care, I could work properly and then have time 'with' him. He said he didn't see it happening, inferring that I didn't mean it. I tried to explain how I felt exhausted doing all his care and would rather have time with him. To that he replied, 'Don't worry, I won't be here much longer. You will have choices and all the time to do what you want soon.'

So once again our communication had totally misfired. I found, as the months dragged along, the more I tried to explain how I felt to him, the further from my reality his comprehension became, and the more caustic the reactions towards me.

I believe he was experiencing a high level of fear, which had a powerful impact on how he reacted, interpreted and lashed out.

The ability to talk with others who understood was incredibly powerful for me. I would have been a complete emotional wreck otherwise. The support of my online peers was constantly a lifeline for me.

So I took another approach to talking with him about both our needs, and we agreed to try a new strategy. We would start rising earlier and go to bed earlier. This way we would have his shower completed before 8 am and the home care worker would take the morning from there. I would then be free to begin my day of work. I felt good that we had found a strategy we could agree on.

In all the nastiness when I had arrived home that day, I had forgotten, until late in the evening, that I had bought him some new clothes. We arose early the next morning and he was quite pleasant and willing to cooperate. We had his care done in good time. As I was doing up his shirt he suddenly asked if this was a new shirt. I smiled and said yes, I had bought him some new things yesterday. He told me it was so soft and it felt so nice on. I kissed him and told him how much I loved him and he sat and cried. That was the closest I got to an apology from him, but I took it as one, graciously and gratefully.

20. Unrelenting progression

Finally the day arrived for the second PEG button change with the good surgeon. I was sure to get him up a little earlier this time and we went to the hospital without me being in trouble for anything.

It was a relief to have our original surgeon back as he had a way of making you feel important, and that your needs will all be taken into account. One look at the stoma and he agreed that this needed to be changed and that he would be very gentle.

Chris was becoming so used to this procedure, it felt almost easy by the third time. As soon as he was awake, and I had checked that the correct button box was on the bed, he demanded to go home.

The surgeon spoke to us after a while and gave us the all-clear. I pulled the privacy curtains and began to dress him and he was quite smug. One of the nurses, with lovely intentions, came to the curtains and asked if I needed help. He looked at me with wide eyes and began shaking his head furiously. So I poked my head out of the curtain and thanked her sincerely but said that I was fine doing this.

A few minutes later she was back at the curtain asking again if she could help me dress him. I politely answered, quietly saying things like I was fine, thank you for offering, but I do this at home on my own all the time and it's no bother.

Amazingly she came back a third time when we were nearly finished and tried to come through the curtains offering to help. I guess she thought if I couldn't dress him in a minute flat I must need help. Dressing him was a slow process with frozen joints. So again I quietly explained that I was fine and thanked her again. I suggested it would be most helpful if she got a wheelchair for us.

As she left I noticed he had that glowering look back in his eyes. As we waited for them to allocate someone to take us to the car, as was their policy, he refused to make eye contact with me or talk to me. With a sinking feeling, I wondered what I'd possibly done this time, knowing that I'd rather not know but would have it made clear soon enough.

A nurse was allocated and, as she wheeled him out, we chatted and he gave a few grunts. I leaned forward and asked if he was okay as I thought he may have some pain. He gave his curt 'I'm fine' reply.

It was a very quiet drive home as I would not attempt to talk these things out in the car. I was relishing the quiet like the calm before a storm.

Once I had him settled at home he exploded that I was just such a martyr in all I did for him, how awful it was that I had to look after him and other such rubbish. Once again my actions, in thwarting the nurse's attempts to assist, in line with Chris's wishes, had backfired.

I went to give him some water through his new button and discovered that it was nothing like the previous one and we had no instructions. Oh dear, I wasn't sure how to use it properly and looked at it in dismay as Chris asked why I hadn't asked to be shown before we left. I cried in the kitchen as I frantically fumbled with the pieces and worked out how they should work together.

Chris began to develop language problems. If I could not understand him, we had to play a bit of a guessing game. I would repeat what I thought he said, and he would let me know if I was right. We had developed strategies that had been working, but they began to fail in his last few months.

I would give my guess and he would say no. I would try again and, after four or five different guesses, I would go back to the first thing in desperation and he would say yes. The first couple of times we both laughed.

I spoke to our main home care worker about it; it hadn't happened with her but over the past week she noticed he had spelled a few easy words incorrectly when using the communication chart.

Chris liked me to give him a lot of notice of events coming up, such as me going out for a day or someone coming over. So I made a real effort to keep him informed in advance and give him full details. This worked for a while, but he started to forget details. A couple of days later I'd go to do whatever it was and he would question what I was doing. This happened with increasing frequency and it appeared that he was beginning to lose the ability to comprehend anything complex.

Because Chris could not speak easily and found using the communication chart became increasingly time consuming, we often communicated through a series of questions that required a yes or no response. It often needed several levels of questioning to get to what was needed. For example, if I started with 'Are you cold?' A yes would then lead to questions such as 'Do you want to come inside?' or 'Do you want a cardigan?' If no I would continue – something for his feet, a blanket, close some blinds, windows or doors, or whatever until I got to what would solve the situation.

He began to give mixed signals. It became nearly impossible to tell a verbal yes from no, and he could not grasp a concept such as one sound for yes, two for no. So usually a nod or shake would help me differentiate the sound he made. But now he was frequently shaking his head as if to say no while actually saying yes, or vice versa.

The strangest part was that he didn't seem to understand it was happening, obviously leading to further problems between us. There was absolutely no point in becoming angry with him over this. Communication was so difficult that, if he became at all angry or frustrated, he would simply stop trying and then refuse anything to be done for him for hours. It put me in a difficult situation as I became fatigued and frustrated, but I could not show this in any way, without completely cutting communication off. He also became fatigued and frustrated and expect me to patiently get him through it. Somehow I did meet this expectation, no matter how I felt inwardly.

I finally received the call from our case manager that we had made it to the top of the list for the attendant care package we had been awaiting for five months. She had been updating them nearly weekly as Chris declined. I was informed that the department would phone me and do an assessment in the next couple of weeks. Once we got through that, we would get up to thirty-five hours of fully funded help a week. I remember how I felt about this when I had the very first meeting with the case manager, back when we were newly diagnosed and Chris was fairly independent.

It doesn't seem to matter that you are told what the disease is, and what progression means, and what it would do to him. At the time, thirty-five hours of help a week seemed something I couldn't possibly imagine needing, and I saw it as something that would be years away, not just five months. Now, with the level of care he needed, and the level of exhaustion I was feeling, it seemed like it just couldn't be put in place fast enough. It now took around eight hours each day to do his basic personal care.

In the interim, I had been receiving home help through another source of government funding, and our case manager had been funding a few extra hours. She said she could keep funding that extra time until the package kicked in. On average we were having help at home from Monday to Friday for around eighteen hours a week. We had someone in at 8 am every weekday for between two and three hours. We had six hours on one day so that I could go out for the day, run errands, work, see my counsellor or do the shopping.

I was elated, but when I went out to tell Chris the good news, his reaction was less than pleased. He immediately complained that he did not want people here anywhere near that number of hours and there was no need. I could see we were heading back to the same old argument of him accusing me that I did not want to do any of his care. I tried to suggest that, with his care needs only increasing, maybe he would consider seeing his care as the new equivalent of having a full-time job. That he was employing people to assist him and he could consider making the very most of those hours, so that when his job was over for the day and my job was over, we would be able to be together. He actually let me talk that one all the way through, but he didn't make any kind of assent to the idea. He still did not feel his care was any big deal. He did not understand he was already a high-care-needs person, and was still deteriorating every week. So the waiting game for the big phone call began.

I constantly had to work hard to keep myself in a positive frame of mind, especially after any conversation where Chris was resisting what I felt was needed. The guilt was like some hungry wolf waiting just behind the door and I had to keep vigilant to prevent that wolf from consuming me.

There was a huge difference between talking to health professionals, care services and my peers about what was happening and talking to Chris. With the former I was told I should be trying to get more help than I had, should allow the staff do even more than they did, and that I was providing a level of care for my husband that few truly achieve. The staff would often tell me quietly that working in our home was so different from anywhere else they worked, because the tasks were so clearly defined and they were so welcomed and appreciated. Then in one foul swoop Chris would shoot it all down in flames, and I would feel like I was barely doing a single thing right.

In the quiet of the late nights when I was alone in my room, seeking peer support online and reflecting on the day, I would feel I was doing all I could to look after him in such a hopeless situation. I never felt like I was better than anyone or that I was all that clever. I knew where my heart lay and I knew why I was aiming for every little thing I worked towards. Every hour of help, every piece of equipment, every change to the home environment and every strategy to make his care the highest quality was examined over and over, and improved at every opportunity. Unfortunately he was progressing so fast, I felt like I was barely keeping up and often felt like it was going to overtake me any day. I refused to allow this to stop me constantly aiming for the best I could do for him.

Many times I had to pull myself up and refuse to become bogged down in despair at what was happening in front of my eyes, and focus on solutions to make the best of a bad situation. I often felt that sinking into total despair would be easier, but that is a trap of course; it would have meant he would not receive quality care at all.

I could never seem to find my way through to the heart I had fallen in love with. It seemed that he was gone, eaten away like his wasted hands and arms. I would have given anything to have the man he was back, even if we had to live with the physical challenges of the disease. One can wish and hope for many things in this life and I had achieved many dreams in my time, but this was one I would never be able to wish into existence.

Chris's mother and stepfather had organised to come and visit for a few days. As she is elderly they had elected, thankfully, to stay in a motel in town and visit during the daytime. With the hours needed for his personal care, and the amount of space needed to move him about, having visitors staying would have been very uncomfortable for everyone. I realised that it had only been weeks since my children had stayed over the Christmas break, and already things had changed significantly as he could now only walk a few steps.

Chris became less happy about the visit as it approached. I was nervous, as I had never met either of them before, only spoken to them by phone. I knew his progression would shock them. Oh, if only he could have been supportive; after all this was his mother coming to see him and I had never met her before. I was just the one who had to make the whole thing come together and work.

I had come up with a design in my head for a new contraption for Chris to drink a cup of coffee on his own. He could no longer hold a cup, let alone raise his hand to his face. It is very difficult to give someone sips of coffee, even when it is thickened, when they have poor lip seal, mouth control and swallowing ability. I suggested this could be a good project to work on while they were here. His stepfather is a handy kind of person and he would probably feel good to be able to do something practical. Chris agreed, though he wasn't convinced the contraption would work.

Sometimes I did receive positive responses, such as when the coffee-drinking contraption turned into such a success. We had a project to tackle together and the result gave Chris back some independence. It was not achieved easily, and we had to trawl through Bunnings and work hard to get communication straight. Once Chris was engaged with the project we had to do it all his way. I was happy to leave them to work on it together, but would often be called back as communication broke down and Chris's frustration levels soared.

The result allowed Chris to use his one functioning finger to pull a string and tilt his coffee cup to his mouth. We added an ashtray and discovered a place that the PEG syringe would fit into perfectly. So it became the multifunctional contraption and I was rather proud of it. Chris appreciated being able to sip a cup of coffee at his own pace again.

The rest of the visit was a success in general and I know they were glad they'd made the trip. Yet Chris was relieved when it was over, as he preferred isolation to the energy needed to communicate.

The attendant care package assessor conducted our assessment the following week. She was compassionate, and understood enough that he was going to continue declining rapidly. Her assessment still had to be submitted and approved and he would be even worse in the intervening weeks. She discussed how the thirty-five hours a week could be spread to give best advantage, and recommended that care staff came in three times per day to assist. She submitted a recommendation for someone to come morning, noon and evening on weekdays, and then morning and evening each weekend. She also informed me that she had the authority to say the package could begin immediately, even though it would take weeks for the administration to be completed. Although Chris had declined be in the conversation, and I knew he would not be at all pleased about the result, I was elated and felt lucky to live in a country that supports ill people so well.

I contacted our home care provider to organise a meeting to get the new hours instigated. They were short-staffed and she was about to go on two weeks' leave. They were in the process of advertising and hiring more staff, and would be able to fill the extra hours within a few more weeks. We set a meeting date for when she would return.

I had a premonition of things going awry at this time. It was hard to articulate to anyone as it all sounded so reasonable. I felt a sense of urgency as the next week wore on. A strange feeling that we had to get this sorted and in place or he would not even be here for it to happen. I tried to shake this feeling, but the reality was that he was weaker, losing weight and his breathing was noticeably declining.

Not long into the New Year, as I watched him sleeping, I saw he was having episodes of apnoea. His breathing had been shallow for a long time. He needed to use his upper chest and shoulders rather than his diaphragm. When asleep he used his diaphragm more, but now he could stop breathing for up to ten seconds at a time every couple of minutes. I found myself transfixed, watching him, counting and holding my own breath with a feeling of impending doom.

One would think that my life was stressful enough and that I was barely coping with all I could manage. Somehow life has a strange way of finding even more to throw onto an already full plate.

21. Double trouble

It was my day to have a carer here for six hours, until 2 pm, my respite day. Normally this day was spent racing from one appointment or errand to another, barely getting home in time. My plan was to visit one client early then spend a day hiding in public. This meant doing whatever I felt like in town – buy some new bras, something yum for lunch at a café with an audiobook, anything but being at home having to think about and care for Chris, so my brain could have a little time out. I was truly looking forward to the day.

As I was about to leave I received a phone call from my brother. He had been having rapid eyesight deterioration since just before Christmas. He'd finally had a CT scan that showed a mass above his pituitary gland that was putting pressure on the optic nerve. He was to be admitted to hospital immediately. He was in a state; he had been on medical disability a long time and lived alone. The next thing I knew I was madly phoning for emergency care for Chris while driving the two and a half hours to my brother, to then take him to hospital.

The service provider was having trouble finding someone on short notice with PEG experience, and as I was driving phone calls were going back and forth. I was trying not to panic that there would be no one to look after Chris. It was just too much to think of while doing this mercy dash; I had to trust it was going to be worked out. Chris's older daughter was down visiting and I tried to call her to see if she could help look after him, but she forgot to call me back and went on home. Finally, after I got my brother to hospital, several hours after all the drama had started, it was confirmed that the service had someone for Chris.

Fortunately Chris handled it well that a total stranger had turned up to look after him. Chris's younger daughter was able to come after work and also be there with him. I was supposed to be back at 8 pm for this emergency carer to finish, but with his younger daughter there I knew I would be covered. That turned out to be fortunate as there was so much traffic, the two-hour trip took over three hours and of course it was pelting rain and I didn't get home until 9 pm.

So far as his evening care went Chris had only been fed. He had become an expert at 'laying low' when I was not there; the dogs hadn't even been brought up to the house. So I still had all his evening care to do. So much for my lovely planned day of respite. I wanted to collapse and have someone hug me and give me a little care, but when you are the only able-bodied person on the floor, you just suck it up and keep doing what you have to do.

The hospital had no real idea when they would begin further testing to work out exactly what was going on in my brother's head and what his options were. I felt awful having to leave him there but, of course, I had no choice. At least I had been able to get him there.

Our mother came the following day and stayed nearby so he would have someone with him.

It took a couple of weeks to conduct all the tests needed to diagnose him with a giant carotid artery aneurysm. They decided to do stent surgery but the chances of him surviving were not high, particularly as he was frail and underweight. As it was a public hospital with an emergency department, booking surgery is only ever tentative, emergency cases taking precedence over some booked procedures. So we had to wait for a surgery date to be set. I was just grateful my brother was in the care of a hospital while this was being worked out.

My case manager secured some extra funding to have someone come of an evening while we waited for the home care service to provide the hours the attendant care package would fund.

Before this was in place I would finally finish my work for the day, then sit with Chris for ten minutes, remember something that needed to be done and jump up do it. I would sit with him for ten minutes again, realise another task and so on until I had him in bed and feel like a totally washed-out rag that had barely been thrown over a line in the wind.

The lady provided to us, from another service, was lovely and very happy to help out in any way. When she left I couldn't believe how many tasks had been completed and it was only 6.30 pm! I was so pleased to sit and relax with Chris without constantly getting up to do all these things. I started getting him ready for bed a little early so I could spend extra time with him, massaging his shoulders with magnesium and doing lots of little extras. It was like a luxury to have this time and energy to enjoy such a simple but intimate thing, rather than trying to fit some massage into the overfull hectic day.

As my hands were sticky I pushed the wheelchair up to the toilet door and dashed into the bathroom to give my hands a rinse. I kicked the chair in front of the basin knowing immediately that my toe was broken. I pretty much ignored the pain after giving a gasp, and washed my hands and finished his care, including hoisting him into bed and getting every pillow settled in place just so.

I remember walking – well, hobbling – out of the room to a dining room chair and sitting down. The pain finally hit me in a huge rush and I began to cry as I looked down at my injured toe. When it first happened and he asked what the noise had been, I did say, 'I just broke my toe.' I don't know if he thought I was being dramatic or something, but he just glanced at my toe and didn't say another word. Maybe he expected that had I really broken my toe I would not have been able to walk, let alone do all his care. I'm still not sure how I managed it; I guess the adrenaline rush took over. As I got into bed that night, I couldn't believe that, just when things were turning upwards a little with the extra care, I had set myself back all over again.

The only silver lining to this injury was that the next morning he could see that I truly was in pain, and he said the home care worker could do his shower for me. Valentine's Day – and that was as close to a present as I received. In fact, neither of us acknowledged the day to each other at all.

That evening I was back in the bad books because I phoned his son and younger daughter, who lived nearby, and asked if they could possibly give me some help over the weekend due to my toe. I could not bear weight with the foot flat, and used his wheelie walker by either walking with it or, mostly, sitting on the seat and scooting backwards up and down the house. I still had to assist him with standing transfers and it was excruciating if I accidentally put some weight on the side of that foot while moving him. If I gave any sign of the pain he became angry and sullen. So I tried to bravely soldier along when doing anything with him, and would then go to another room and cry. He did not believe that I needed to 'put his children out' by having any help from them. He started suggesting all the things that didn't need to be done, and said we would just manage. Happy Valentine's Day indeed; thanks for caring.

His son was a hero and came both mornings to help with the early tasks for Chris and the dogs. I was happy to let some things be left undone over the weekend but I doubt Chris meant that I could just leave him in bed all weekend.

I let some things slide, trying to keep off the foot as much as I could. It also gave an opportunity for some of my girlfriends, who had been offering help to me for months, to lend a hand. I had been resisting because Chris did not like anyone helping me out. The laughs I had with one girlfriend who went grocery shopping for me, about what a treasure hunt it had been to follow my list, were heart warming. It was an enormous help.

Any little thing a friend was able to do for me was often small to them, but to give someone even a small task and just have it done was huge to me. Having this injury of my own finally allowed me to receive some help from others without a big scene from Chris.

I had previously had offers of help from people that they failed to follow through on. These people probably didn't truly realise that letting down someone with the huge responsibilities I had could cause complete despair. To anyone who wants to help someone caring for an ill person, please remember that the most important thing is to simply be reliable.

We planned to visit my brother for the day so that my mother could have a day off as she had been spending every day with him for the past three weeks while he awaited surgery. The visit went really well. Even with my broken toe, I was able to get my blind brother out of the hospital on my arm while pushing Chris in a wheelchair, and we went to a lovely park and had lunch and coffee together. The only hitch was when I managed to get the wheelchair stuck in some sandy soil – we all rolled about laughing at the dilemma. I spotted three young men not too far away. They were not the kind of lads, by their looks, who I would normally talk to, a bit unkempt and looking like they probably spent a lot of time avoiding doing much.

Well sometimes you just have to do what you have to do, and I asked if they could give me a little help. There was a moment of hesitation, as we probably looked an odd little group – more like the three stooges than three wise monkeys. They sauntered over and I explained our situation. They got the chair out of the sand and grinned, asking where we needed to get to, then brought Chris right over to the car. I have always hoped they had a really nice day after putting themselves out a little to help someone.

The whole day was exhausting but, all in all, Chris had one of the most enjoyable days out with me in a very long time, and my brother truly appreciated being with us for the day. Chris even suggested that we should be up there for the day of his surgery in case anything went wrong. I had mixed feelings as I knew what a huge day it would be. Yet I also knew that, if I wasn't there and something did go wrong, I would always regret it.

We also talked about the enormity of my brother's diagnosis, surgery and recovery. I was very surprised – in fact, extremely surprised – when Chris suggested that my brother couldn't possibly go home on his own, as he had talked of doing. Chris felt we could cope with having him come here for a few weeks or a month to recover and become adjusted to whatever the vision prognosis may or may not be after surgery. I honestly don't know where my head was, but I actually agreed that it might well work for everyone.

We envisioned a quiet man recovering from major surgery, needing lots of rest, but providing some company to Chris. They had both been friendly with each other, but had also not spent much time together, particularly in a 24-7 sense. Before I really knew what I was doing, I had agreed to the whole idea.

Surgery was set and there was a flurry of legal paperwork nominating me as Enduring Power of Attorney. His Advance Health Care Plan and will were also drawn up.

On the day of the surgery, our case manager had booked an assessment of our home and how the services were working out for us. Chris and I discussed the appointment a couple of days beforehand so he knew it was happening.

I showed her around the house, the equipment and systems in place with Chris and one of our workers. I raved about how well the care workers were doing in general, and how they needed more hours to get through everything. We discussed how great it was that the new funded hours would start soon. We talked about how to access more help if needed when my brother arrived. I felt the assessment went smoothly and we were all in agreement on where everything was at, and where we were heading in terms of looking after Chris's needs.

After the appointment we had planned to drive the two and a half hours to the hospital so we could be there during my brother's surgery. So off we set. Just as we were pulling into the parking lot, the floor nurse phoned to say the surgery had been postponed, as they had an emergency.

We met my mother and sister at the cafeteria, as Chris wanted coffee. I settled him at a table and hobbled over, returning with the coffee without even spilling it. But there it sat, untouched on the table, as he wouldn't let me hold and tip it for him. His bags of food and drink were still in the car, as I couldn't manage them and the wheelchair with my toe. So I left him at the café with my mother, and went to retrieve the bags with my sister. I got lost, thinking the car was on a different parking level, and walked way too far for my poor toe.

On returning with all the gear, Chris then refused the high-calorie pudding I had brought, refused a PEG feed and even refused water. I could have just left them all in the car and relaxed with a coffee myself.

We completed the legal documents, spent some time with my brother and headed off for the long drive home.

Just as we walked outside the building, my sister phoned me from upstairs and asked us to wait while she came down to talk to us. A minute after we'd left, the doctors rescheduled the surgery for the following Thursday, and said he could go home until then. Hang on – huge brain aneurism, almost no sight and he lived alone.

We went back up to the ward to sort out with the doctors that he couldn't go home, unless I took him home. I explained our situation and that I was willing to care for my brother after he had recovered enough to be released after surgery, but no way was I taking the risk of someone with a giant aneurysm that could rupture at any moment.

The answer was that the registrar was in theatre and that I would have to wait for, say, two hours to talk to him myself. I can't believe how calmly I answered, as I was so distressed. Chris had completely refused fluids or nutrition and I just wanted to get him home. I explained that we were exhausted, Chris needed care and we were leaving – and they had no one to discharge him to. And leave we did.

By the time we got home, eight hours later, Chris was irritable and exhausted, and refusing to take anything but a half-feed with his meds before bed. I was barely holding back tears. Chris's refusal to allow me to give him any kind of care, from my experience over the past few months, meant he was angry with me about something, and attempting to make me feel bad by forcing himself to be neglected. I couldn't imagine what I was supposed to have done this time.

As I was getting him ready for bed, two hours later than normal, he told me, seemingly right out of left field, that I was putting him in the hands of incompetent staff. I could not believe what I was hearing, let alone exactly what he meant. He complained at great length about the quality of care being given to him by the staff, and their general incompetence at even the smallest tasks.

I asked why he'd said nothing before this, especially when we'd just had an assessment. He said it was because he couldn't talk over the top of me. So why had he not said anything before the meeting, to me alone? I asked him to clarify that he even meant the staff member he seemed to particularly like, and who was here the longest each week. Yes, he meant all the staff, though some were worse than others; he wouldn't say why he'd not said this previously.

These were such difficult conversations as he could barely speak, and it involved much repeating and spelling of words. If he was reluctant to talk it was impossible to try to force it. So to start this conversation late at night, after the day we had just been through, was more than I could manage.

I wondered if the morning appointment had been why he had become so withdrawn and refused all care. Was it some kind of revenge on me for speaking highly of the staff and asking for more hours of help? I had certainly felt his behaviour had smacked of revenge at the time.

The following week my brother was set for surgery again and I did manage to speak to Chris about the need for him to allow me to at least hydrate him properly, if we were going up to the hospital again. He agreed he would allow it, as I made it clear I wasn't willing to do the trip otherwise.

One of the biggest issues with the swallowing problems is the risk of accidentally aspirating fluid or food into the lungs, resulting in pneumonia. Because the breathing muscles are affected, the ability to cough is reduced, which means the ability to cough out anything accidentally breathed in becomes nearly impossible.

We were both fearful about choking episodes. Chris was afraid he would choke and die, unable to clear his throat. On the other hand, my research had shown this was extremely rare, but the incidence of aspiration pneumonia was very high.

Even after the PEG placement, he continued to take in some food by mouth, though he could only eat pureed food. The most he could manage was eating a half a teaspoon at a time very carefully. He was very prone to choking and had difficulty clearing his throat.

As the months passed I was amazed he had not developed any chest infections, let alone pneumonia. However, I knew in my heart that it was only a matter of time. We were rolling the dice every time he took a meal, and we were going to lose the toss at some point. Choking or coughing episodes during meals progressed from taking several coughs, to several minutes of coughing, to twenty or thirty minutes to clear something from his throat. Each episode became more frightening, yet he learned that he had to stay very calm in order to clear his throat at all. Watching your husband unable to clear his throat for twenty minutes or more, and wondering if this would be the time that would kill him was cruel beyond words. It reached the point where every meal involved a choking episode to some degree.

The day before my brother's surgery, Chris was quieter than usual. Within five minutes of the carer arriving, she took me aside and said his colour did not look right. I asked him if anything was wrong but he said he was all right, just a bit tired. Apart from being tired much of the day he did not seem to worsen. The next day he was the same, but no elevated temperature. He wanted us to go to the hospital for my brother and promised to behave.

The surgery was done but it took far longer than anticipated. We found out the next day that he had suffered a major bleed, which had complicated the procedure, but he did pull through and was placed in the ICU, which is normal practice. Before the surgery he was expected to be in the ICU for around twenty-four hours. He would be on a ventilator for at least twelve hours and completely sedated, as it was critical that he did not move at all. We spent the entire afternoon waiting for some news of him, and we didn't leave until he was settled in the ICU and my mother was allowed in for a quick look at him.

The next day he was awake, with a terrible headache, disoriented but responsive. They kept him in the ICU for several days. He was kept medicated and received blood transfusions until his symptoms resolved.

That morning Chris announced that 'it' seems to be moving to his lungs. So a doctor's appointment and antibiotics were first on my agenda. I started another day in near despair, wearily wondering how I would get through all that was happening to both my husband and my brother, and ignore all that was happening to me. I'd reached the point with my broken toe where I could walk on the side of my foot, going slowly, and ignore it as much as possible. I didn't have the time or the energy to do anything more, and told myself firmly that it would heal and there was no sense dwelling on it, as it only made the pain worse.

No matter what research I had done, no matter what my health and peer support had told me, it didn't make it any easier when it happened. We had so far avoided any infections, but I knew that in the past three weeks or so his breathing had seriously declined. My mind worked in paradoxical circles. I had expected aspiration for so long, and wondered at how he'd managed to avoid it, and now that it was happening it seemed to have happened too fast.

With rest, lots of care and attention, giving every antibiotic on time and lots of fluids, his colour began to improve after a few days. His breathing returned to about how it had been the previous week. I knew that we had to be vigilant now, and watch him closely as pneumonia was such a danger.

I also knew he was going to continue eating, choking and telling me he was fine. Even if he stopped eating, his breathing was declining. It was only a matter of time. Yet time seemed to have been the one thing we had been robbed of from the day that fatal diagnosis was uttered. I felt the understanding sinking deeply into me. No matter how vigilant I was, no matter how closely I observed and cared for him, the monster was wreaking its havoc.

Every evening I went through this ritual of reflecting on where we were at, allowing my fears to bubble and roil for a little bit, then talking myself through the reality of what was happening and steeling myself for whatever the next new days would throw at us.

My brother spent four days in the ICU but became oriented to his surroundings again; the headaches were dealt with and he was considered stable. He was sent back to the surgical ward and they announced he could be discharged immediately. I was dismayed, and tried to convince them that he could be transferred to our local hospital. They could then send him here with some services, as he had almost no vision. They were adamant that their task was done and he was being released.

True compassion
does not repay evil for evil
harm for harm
violence for violence

Compassion says
who is without fault and can judge?

Compassion is not pity
Compassion is not weakness
Compassion is the healing river that flows
out of understanding

22. Full house

So my brother came to our home for what was to be a few weeks of recovering and for me to get services in place for him to be able to live in his own home alone again. He had been adamant that he wished to live in his own place, so a plan was made to help him recover and start adjusting to whatever was going to happen with his eyesight. Chris was happy that he was going to have some company, and I was feeling that I could cope and maybe, even with his own health issues, it would be pleasant to have my brother here. It's funny how I thought things at the beginning of a situation, and wondered later what could have possessed me to think that way! I guess that is the wisdom of hindsight. The old retro-spect-o-scope has twenty–twenty vision.

He was so grateful when he arrived. I got his things unpacked and oriented him to his room and the layout of the house. I took his vision issues very seriously. I walked him carefully through the house, helping him concentrate on what he needed to remember to help navigate. His vision was certainly very poor – he could see no detail, just basic shapes in light and dark patches.

I had put a lot of thought into the way I had the house set up, and rearranged some things so that it would be most convenient for everyone. I set up the back verandah so that my brother could walk out of the house and down the wheelchair ramp in a straight line to a chair at the table. This was designated as his chair and the entire end of the table would be kept clear so he could arrange any of his own things there. From the right side it was clear walking to the door that opened out of the screened verandah area, if he wished to go outside. I sat on the left, and then Chris. Behind his chair we stored any equipment not currently in use, such as the PWC, manual wheelchair, walker, roll-in table and drinking contraption. My brother was told clearly that he was only to walk straight to his chair, or turn right and go out the screen door, but never attempt to go left as it was so cluttered.

Since I had broken my toe, all equipment in the bathroom was now stored in the other spare bedroom when not in use, making the bathroom area safe. I showed him how to walk straight through the lounge room, which was really Chris's room now, and out the front door. He was not to attempt to move into this room unaided, as it had equipment stored in it.

I felt this meant we had all Chris's equipment easily stored and in reach when not in use, and also had all pathways clear for a vision-impaired person. We all enjoyed eating dinner together that night, listening attentively to my brother break down all his experiences in hospital during the previous month, and we settled in bed easily. Well, so far so good, I mused as I fell asleep. This had been the right thing to do.

The second day was nearly as good, as my brother settled himself into being here and enjoying the freedom of not being in a hospital ward, even if the house looked quite hospital-like if he could have seen it. He was being extremely polite, patient and respectful. I felt like a week would see us all settled in quite a comfortable way and it would not prove to be much extra on me at all.

That evening we were talking on the verandah and again listened to my brother's repeated stories of hospital. I let him know that I had to organise Chris into bed. I suggested he might like to sit in Chris's recliner once we were done, and watch some TV with him. Of course, I meant more like listen to some TV but the thought is what counts.

So I began our usual evening routine and my brother came in a few minutes later and took up the hospital story again. Chris and I grinned at each other, as we knew that he had been lonely for some time. I made the appropriate noises of response in the right places, as I tended to Chris's needs. I only really needed to give a little acknowledgement, as he seemed to have a lot of stored-up need for talking but little for listening. We were really grinning by the time my brother followed us up the hallway and continued while Chris went to the loo, and then followed us back again to the lounge room.

He stood at the door, talking away, and I wondered if he really had no idea that I was now putting Chris to bed with an electric hoist right in front of him. I hoisted Chris into the bed and began to organise his many pillows. This took all my attention as he could not reposition himself. I had to get every single thing right for him and I took this task seriously. The next thing I realised my brother had wandered into the room, and was coming down to go around the foot of the bed. He tripped over some equipment and I only just managed to grab and steady him in time. My heart was in my throat and Chris's eyes were so wide I didn't know whether to laugh or be angry.

I steered my brother out and explained carefully that the lounge room was a dangerous place when I was tending to Chris, because I had equipment and electric leads and things everywhere. Because I had to concentrate closely, it may be wisest if I did this on my own of an evening. Of course, my brother was very apologetic and went out to wait for me on the verandah while I finished Chris's care, with us quietly giggling.

In the evenings I would light at least a half-dozen candles on the table on the verandah, just as the sun was going down, and arrange them among a collection of exquisite orchids. I played around each evening making a slightly different arrangement of them. We enjoyed looking at these rather than having lights on. We both had a love of flowers, particularly orchids, so any time I saw a lovely new orchid, I would have to buy it and bring it home for us to enjoy together.

From the kitchen, I saw my brother pick up one of the glass candle holders and reach forward, right in front of Chris's chair, and let it go. It smashed into what seemed a million tiny slivers. I raced out and led my brother inside, insisting I needed to clean it up. He kept saying he didn't mean to, and would buy me a new one.

I felt sick to the pit of my stomach. Chris could not wear shoes, and he lived in non-slip socks. The glass had hit the floor right where Chris's feet would be when he was sitting. But worse,

Chris was still doing standing transfers, and this was where he stood from his wheelchair to laboriously turn himself to sit in his chair. Now the whole area was covered in tiny slivers of glass. The pavers were not one smooth surface, so there was a myriad of places for the slivers of glass to hide. I barely held back my tears. I wanted to wail and scream as I kept envisioning Chris in mid-transfer, suddenly having glass in his foot and falling, and me falling with him. I kept telling myself I was overreacting. I was going to clean this up, but I couldn't get some truly awful scenarios out of my head.

I spent a long time cleaning up laboriously, and my brother would pipe up every now and then, saying he was so sorry and he would buy me a new candle. When I finally felt I had myself together, I gently told him that I knew it had been an accident and I wasn't the least bit worried about the candle. I took a breath and explained my real concern for Chris. From my brother's look he seemed to not see this was such a big problem.

Finally I had my shower, made my brother a coffee and took him to the lounge room to settle him in the recliner. Once Chris was in his bed, all his equipment was put away and the bed pulled out diagonally across the room. It was safe enough for my brother to be shown to the recliner. I sat him in the chair then put his hands on the remote control and showed him how to operate the chair. He was very happy, so I went off to bed exhausted, but thinking all was fine.

Just as I was going off to sleep, I realised my brother was in the doorway talking to me. He said something about having spilt his coffee in Chris's chair but he'd cleaned it all up. I could not have cared less at this point and told him not to worry. As I fell asleep I wondered why he had gone outside to the verandah and sat on Chris's outside chair.

Chris was in hysterics the next morning as he got the story across to me. My brother had sat in the recliner with his coffee and decided to get up, but instead had reclined back further until he was laying back with the coffee all over him. I was looking at the recliner, which was laid right back still, and trying to figure how he had managed to climb out of it in that position. We all needed a bit of time to adjust and my brother had just lost his sight, so we needed to be a bit forgiving and patient. At least it gave Chris a good laugh.

My brother complained that he had not slept well that night and he was less settled in himself all day. I noticed that if I were doing something for Chris, my brother would ask if I could do something for him. I also noticed that while my brother could sit and talk constantly to Chris, they could not actually have a conversation. Chris's speech was so deteriorated that, without any visual clues, it was difficult for my brother to understand anything. My brother was not very patient. He had not seen Chris more than once since the illness had begun and that had been prior to his diagnosis.

Part of the speech issues was the obvious extreme difficulty to form clear sounds, but he was becoming very slow at attempting to speak. Watching him, I could see clearly he was about to say something, and wait for him. My brother could not see this, so he would talk over the top. If Chris did speak a sentence, my brother could not understand it and so would often just carry on talking. If the three of us were together my brother would speak, then Chris would go to answer and I would have to halt my brother and indicate he needed to wait, and then I would have to interpret. Often my brother would presume he had understood and half-repeat what he thought Chris had said but, instead of waiting for confirmation, would just race on with the conversation anyway. A lot of eye rolling and grinning developed between Chris and myself, but it started to drop after a few days. It is hard enough when you can't speak, without having to feel stuck as a captive audience.

My brother showed no interest in watching the TV with Chris, as it was quickly apparent that they had very different tastes. So my brother took to bringing his CD player out to the verandah and listening to a lot of music. As the first week wore on, he began staying up later at night and refused to take a nap during the day, even though his lower legs were hideously swollen as a result of the surgery. He wanted to play music late into the night. I tried to explain that he needed to try to stay in the pattern he had established in the hospital, because Chris needed to sleep and he was right in the middle of the house.

By the end of the first week my brother became agitated, as he wanted to be up all hours of the night. I couldn't seem to get through to him that coming in and out of the house, into the kitchen to make cups of coffee at 2 am and playing music all through the night was not working for any of us. I had to talk to him gently, as I realised that he had his own huge health issues and fears, as he was trying to adjust to possibly being blind the rest of his life, at only fifty-seven years old. But I had to impress on him that we had brought him into our home, where Chris was battling a terminal illness. I explained that Chris did not sleep well and could not reposition himself in bed at all, not even a little bit. If he was asleep and my brother came out turning on lights and banging about in the kitchen, it woke him up. If he were now at all uncomfortable, he would have to put up with it and be awake the rest of the night or wake me to spend half an hour fixing him. He solemnly said he would try not to disturb Chris at night, but I really got the feeling that he did not understand the impact this was having on either Chris or me.

We had organised, prior to my brother coming, for my two sons and their girlfriends to visit for a weekend, both to see us and help out around the property. I felt it would be nice to have Chris's two children, who lived locally, come for lunch as well and he was actually looking forward to it. When I told my brother what was happening I stressed that, if it was too much for him at any point, he was welcome to take breaks in his room or simply go and sit under the gazebo in the front. He was happy about the whole idea, as he had always been on good terms with my children.

A couple of days before the weekend, he said he was concerned about the coming weekend and asked if I had explained clearly to all the children about his state of health and that they understood. 'Of course I have,' I said, reminding him he didn't have to sit among us all the time. He said he needed me to talk to my sons because, although he'd never mentioned it, they were always very loud and he just wouldn't handle it. He began to voice several concerns, and I told him again that he could do what was comfortable for him. I stressed that Chris was terminally ill, and our children wanted to spend time with him and do things for us. He very seriously told me to remember that he was also very ill. Oh dear, I did know he was ill, but I also knew I had allowed him into our home and he could not rule what could happen in our home or limit Chris, who had been so isolated for so long.

He actually made a point of being around everyone nearly all the time they were here. He talked over the top of everyone, and talked on and on about when he was young and his plans for a trip to Amsterdam with me. It was the strangest time. Everyone was stunned at his odd behaviour and we would all have been happier if he had spent much of the time doing his own thing. He brought his radio out during the afternoon and sat in the middle of everyone with it on loud, listening to sport as though there were not people having a social gathering right around him. I didn't quite realise at the time that his behaviour was as erratic as it was. It's hard to explain my level of exhaustion but I was pretty much just trying to get through each hour of each day without everything falling to pieces. I was willing to ignore as much as I could in order to get through a day.

The more the situation worsened, the more upset he became that he was doing this, and therefore the more agitated and unsettled, and the more out of control his behaviour.

He became disruptive when home care staff came to look after Chris. I had made it clear that they were here for Chris, but that of course if he needed something, they would always assist him. By the second week he began attention-seeking behaviour by hovering around them, waiting for them to start a task, such as feeding Chris, and then asking for them to do things for him.

One day I came home from a day out and he confronted me, asking the name of that day's worker. He had thought it had been one of the others, and said that probably explained why she hadn't answered him, as he was calling her by the wrong name. Then he said, 'I don't think she is doing her job; she sat and watched TV for nearly two hours today when I needed things!' I gently told him that she was the one staff member with nursing training. On the one day a week she was here, she massaged Chris's hands and arms in his recliner chair and it usually took close to two hours as she did a thorough job. I suggested this was likely what had been happening. He replied that since he couldn't see, he wouldn't know anything about that.

Chris now began showing signs of jealousy that there was someone else in the house with needs, even though it had been his idea for my brother to come here. His reasoning was that it would be good for him to have company, so possibly he was reacting to that not becoming reality. Maybe he was just getting fed up because he was being disturbed at night too. This concerned me greatly, as MND causes such huge fatigue and now we finally had him sleeping at night; to disturb this was terribly cruel.

I don't know if I was doing a poor job or if it was just one of those times when nothing works, but one night it took me two full hours to get Chris settled correctly in bed. I knew this was the norm for some carers, and a fear was building in me as the time wore on that this was the beginning of a new pattern. Usually I could settle him correctly in about twenty minutes or so. The longer it took, the more wound up Chris became, making the entire task harder, and I was fatiguing. After two hours of doing what I called 'the pillow dance', he still didn't seem happy. I was nearly in tears because my broken toe was throbbing and sending shooting pains up my leg. I didn't think I could stand on my feet any longer and Chris appeared to be positioned correctly. I asked if he was good now but he said his shorts were cutting into his balls and demanded that I start again.

With tears in my eyes I said I would be happy to but I just needed to take a break for minute, as I couldn't stand any longer because of my toe. My heart broke every time I saw this person, who used to be such a lovely man, look at me in disgust as though I was the most selfish and unreasonable person he had ever encountered. How did this disease just waltz in and steal him away like this?

When I had hoisted him back into bed and all his positioning was done I asked him if he was okay now. All I could get in reply was the usual 'I'm fine.' This always meant he was anything but fine.

The following morning I woke early to Chris calling, demanding to get out of the bed. Most mornings I had a moment of mental peace on waking, before reality hit like a shovel. This morning I didn't even get that one moment. I sorted him out, got him settled on the verandah and spent all the time needed to do what he wanted done. It was now close to 6 am, so I decided to stay up and put on the kettle. My brother came out and announced he was also up now, and so I made us both a cup and told him I was taking mine back to bed.

I love having my first morning cup of tea in bed and this had been my routine for many years. I heard some strange noises coming from the verandah and went out to ask Chris if he needed something. He turned to me with one of his wide-eyed stares that usually indicated I was about to cop a tirade. He seemed to be saying something about me treating him like he didn't exist. As I tried to decipher his words exactly, he shut down, saying adamantly, 'I'm fine!'

So I trudged back to bed with my cup of tea to start the day with a good hearty cry and pour out my misery to my online peers.

When I came out a little later, he refused to attempt to use the toilet, refused a shower, refused to eat any breakfast, but did accept a PEG feed. Oh the sorrow this disease brought to our lives. What suffering he was going through inside to make things so miserable for us both – and I couldn't do a damned thing about it. No matter what I did, he saw me as the enemy. No matter how much time I spent searching my soul for how I could fill his life with love and caring, it seemed I was thwarted at every turn.

That evening, as I was doing his teeth, he was still completely cut off and refusing to make eye contact. I cried and begged him to look me in the eye and talk to me because I hated us being opposed like this, and feeling like I was just going through the motions with him. He finally responded that it made no difference because I did not want to spend any time with him.

The next day, when Chris finally did deign to speak to me, he confided, quite seriously, that my brother was dangerous. He stated that he was unsteady and at risk of falling. He needed a walking cane and should be wearing his neck brace. He could break an arm you know! He could set the house on fire!

Poor man, I couldn't help it. I burst out laughing, which did not impress him.

For this to be said by Chris, who had insisted for so long that it was his disease, that he would rather die trying to do something than lay down and rot. Who had all those falls, rupturing tendons, splitting his head open, breaking ribs, multiple soft-tissue injuries, all of which sped up his progression. Said by Chris, who still sat and smoked, refusing the safe ashtray set-up, and had holes in nearly every piece of clothing he owned. He had burn marks, and laughed himself stupid if I got burned pulling live cigarettes off his lap. He thought the image of setting himself alight was hilarious! In fact, only that week I had stood him in the lounge room for a transfer, and all this black ash dropped into the pale carpet and he nearly fell over laughing.

Chris could not control his head because his neck was so weak, yet refused to wear the neck brace that was ordered for him by an OT.

I could not even begin to get across to him how ludicrous his comments were in reality. I asked him if he felt that because my brother had vision impairment he should be sat in a corner to rot. Or did he feel that my brother should also have some kind of a right to decide to take risks? I gently told him that it was very hard to watch someone when they do not look safe, and that I hoped it gave him some appreciation of how it had been for me all this time watching him. The only real reply I received was, 'So you are not going to intervene, are you?'

My brother was waiting for me the next day when I came home, and as soon as the carer left, he informed me that someone had been through his room. I was stunned and asked what he meant. He dragged me down there and started saying how everything had been moved, even inside his wardrobe. He did not care what anyone said; he knew someone had been through his things. I asked him who would do this and why. He said if it hadn't been me, then it had to be one of the care staff. I assured him it had not been me and that I could not see why any of the care staff would do this. He became highly agitated and I felt myself reach a breaking point.

I emailed our case manager and told her we could not keep my brother here any longer. I requested a respite facility and explained what had been going on. She was amazing and replied the next day that she had a bed in the same facility Chris and I had looked at some months previously. We would have to wait four days for the bed to become vacant, but I thought we could manage if I knew we had something in place.

I then sat my brother down and explained to him that I did not feel it was working out, that I was concerned for him because he was becoming agitated. He was not sleeping at night therefore we were not. I felt he was not settled here, and needed more care than I had been able to provide so far. We had hoped some home help would be put in place for him, but there had been all sorts of complications. I was still working frantically to solve this. He responded as though he were totally surprised that I would say these things and that he had truly been trying to fit in with us. I made it clear that no one was to blame, that I felt terrible I could not be 'all things to all people' and we needed to get this sorted. I explained that I had found a respite bed for him for two weeks and that I intended to spend that time sorting out his needs for help in the home. He was not at all happy but it seemed he would accept it.

That afternoon he began to complain of a headache. He took a lot of medications for this, as he had a history of headaches and had prescription medications for when they happened. Nothing was working and he became morose and highly agitated in tandem. I was very concerned for his health and asked if I should call an ambulance. He also had a fear of going to an ER department with a headache, but I explained that he was barely two weeks out of major brain surgery and if his headache was this bad, it needed to be seen to, and he agreed.

He had dozed off after I had sat and comforted him for a while, so he woke he disoriented when the ambulance arrived. It took a lot to convince him to go with them as he suddenly became very fearful of being taken away.

Actually it was a little funny when the ambulance arrived. It was late evening so I had Chris in bed in the lounge room. The ambulance officers entered looking at Chris. 'Oh he's fine,' I said. 'It's my brother down the hall who is the really sick one tonight!' The look on their faces was priceless. I've often wondered what raced through their minds as to what they were going to encounter down the hallway, if the emaciated man in the hospital bed was the good one of my patients.

The hospital found nothing had gone amiss from the surgery and his headache subsided through the next morning. I told my case manager that he could not come back here for the weekend because Chris and I were totally exhausted. I remembered what the previous weekend had been like, with Chris not talking to me for most of it, and complaining about my brother for the rest. I could not face another weekend like that. The case manager was brilliant and the nursing facility agreed to take him straight in for respite.

When pressed very flat
one person can be made to stretch
over many miles.

A wafer thin person
risks being broken with the lightest touch.

23. Bureaucratic frustration

I was determined to get some relaxation that weekend, and give Chris a lot of my time and attention. I needed to try to mend some bridges and regain some stamina.

On the Friday night, the night after my brother left, Chris ate his dinner well. About ten minutes later he tried to clear something from his throat. He relied on each mouthful to clear any food left in his throat from the previous mouthful. So that very last mouthful of the meal often left something behind that he would have to clear through coughing, which he was unable to do easily. Fluids were no good as they posed an even greater risk.

This coughing and choking episode went on for one and a half hours before he was able to finally settle. I could do little for him. He was always left so incredibly exhausted; this time he was a wreck, and I wasn't much better.

The next day he was tired, as was I. After all the escapades with my brother, and the awful, long coughing the night before, we were at last able to settle down to have a fairly quiet weekend. I wouldn't say we had a lovely weekend, but we did have a quiet one, and I caught up on a little rest. I didn't even wonder if Chris was feeling okay, as he was so quiet and easy. I took it as a blessed contrast from the madness we had been living through.

I received the official paperwork for the care package approval. Unbelievably, in between the assessment date and the contract being issued, the government had replaced the attendant care package with a new community support package. We were one of the very first people awarded the new package. Instead of being allocated thirty-five hours per week assistance, we were allocated a budget for the year. I could then elect to either spend that money on care in the home or on equipment or other services such as physiotherapy, occupational therapy or even taxi fares. Looking over the paperwork it seemed that this was a great improvement on the previous package, and I began working out how that money could be best spent, using the hourly rate the home care provider had given me.

My case manager was providing interim assistance and we were receiving around twenty-five hours of help each week. I had no help on weekends and they were exhausting; carers never actually get a day off. A lot of people thought weekends were days off for me because it was just the two of us together. Chris saw weekends as being his days off from staff coming in to help.

For me, of course, it was at least eight hours of daily personal care to deliver without any help at all. I tried to spend of the rest of the time making a nice weekend with him. We actually did have many nice weekends doing things together, but it was always me doing for him. I was always exhausted by the end of the weekend and felt that Monday would give me a little break. This was nonsense, as I would be back to scrabbling to try to keep up with my workload again, alongside a constant stream of phone calls and emails to make or receive, communicating with the network of people and services involved in Chris's care.

It took home care far longer than expected to hire new staff. The manager visited after her leave and we discussed how the hours would be spread out during each week. We agreed on everything. I was told they would not charge me any extra fees if I nominated them to administer the package. I had to complete a detailed care plan for Chris that would be submitted both to the funding body and the care provider. So amid all I was doing I worked diligently on the care plan while trying to patiently wait for the provider to have enough staff to fill the hours.

Once I had submitted the care plan, I received a phone call to say I would need to adjust the hours and days, reducing the hours of care by twelve to fifteen hours per week. Twenty hours a week was less than the interim funding would have provided! I was shattered and had a sick feeling in the pit of my stomach.

I was told they had quoted the hourly rate incorrectly. I asked what the correct rate was and she began to hedge and only gave a vague answer. Oh, don't you hate it when people put on that very correct tone of voice, to sound so concerned for you, as they deliver news that is totally devastating? I had felt a premonition of something going awry weeks earlier and it was trying to rush back and flood me. I tried desperately to set that aside and attend carefully to what was being said and work out a solution.

It turned into three weeks of heart-sickening arguing back and forth between the home care provider, the funding body and me, the meat in the sandwich. But it wasn't just this. I was becoming seriously concerned that I was fighting a losing battle as Chris was rapidly declining. Each time I spoke with the funding body they insisted that the care provider must be completely transparent concerning every detail of their fees. Each time I spoke with the care provider they became increasingly vague about their fees. They complained that ours was the first of these new packages they had dealt with, and they were trying to work out how to put it in place.

I told both parties my main concern was that my husband was declining rapidly, and if we did not get this sorted and in place he may not be alive to receive the care. The care provider became annoyed that I spoke this way, and kept saying they would get back to me. The funding body told me to leave it in their hands and they would investigate.

In my professional life I have applied for and received government funding to run projects, and I hold qualifications in project management. Even though the subject matter of this funding was very different, and I had an emotional connection to it since it was for the wellbeing of my own husband, the processes are the same. You make a clear detailed plan, with measurable outcomes and milestones, conduct risk assessments and set a budget that maps against the plan. These documents are detailed, but they are very familiar. I began to feel that someone was not being open with me. Maybe they thought I was not smart enough to see through what was happening. I had clear paperwork prepared and a far more detailed budget, yet on submitting it I never once received my budget layout back with amendments. I received phone calls saying I had to change it.

To add insult to injury, I couldn't even vent my frustration and anger to Chris because he would have just said to not even bother with the funding, that he didn't need any of that help anyway. People talk of hitting their head against a brick wall, and my understanding is that means you need to assess your strategies and find new ones. Continuing to hit your head against a brick wall and being surprised it hurts just the same each time is sheer stupidity.

Okay, rack your brain then girl – what strategies can you change here? The brick wall looked exactly the same; I drove myself up that wall and simply slipped back down the same side in a heap. I went to everyone I could go to and everyone was oh so sympathetic, but no one could do a thing about the situation. How long could I fight this, when Chris was deteriorating every single week?

The care provider complained that I wanted hours of help on a weekend, which were expensive. She had the hide to suggest I should be able to get family or friends to help me on a weekend. Oh yeah, right, what a great idea. I wonder why I had never thought to simply roster up friends and family for weekend care. Chris would just love to have friends doing all this very personal care for him, and would love his children showering him or dressing him or toileting him too, I'm quite sure. Of course I was simply short-sighted not to have realised what a simple thing it would be to enlist people for these duties. Yep, I was becoming a little sarcastic when arguing with myself by this point, but it did give moments of relief, even if it did nothing at all to help the situation in reality.

Our case manager informed me that she could not continue paying for extra hours as the package had been awarded. She had guidelines that she had to work to and a higher manager to report to. I was stuck between a rock and a hard place.

238

All this time I had believed that when his needs became high we would be awarded thirty-five hours per week. Now with the new package in place, I was going to receive around twenty-five hours help per week and he was now high care and worsening.

I was beyond distressed, as I was going to receive less assistance than I had been receiving before the package, but the care provider was going to receive a much higher hourly rate for providing it. How could this possibly be called patient-centred care, which is what the new package structure boasted?

My case manager worked in the background and secured me a separate package, under different funding, purely for respite. It was substantial, so I planned to take a true break in a holiday house in a seaside village only twenty minutes' drive from home. Carer burnout is a real threat and I was fast running down. Chris's three children agreed that they would all come here and be with him. The respite money would cover paid staff being with him all day and his evening care. His children would share nights.

I doubt that any of them ever thought about the irony of this situation. I looked after him with some casual help each week. I also worked what should have been a full-time job, organised and coordinated all his care and appointments, and looked after the property. Now for me to have five days off, it was going to take forty hours of paid care and three family members rotating so that two of them were always there the entire time. No one would do property work or any coordinating, and would take leave from their jobs to do this. It was going to take all of this just to fill one of the roles I was filling.

Chris was devastated at the prospect. He suggested, if I wanted to, I could go away for one night, or maybe two at the most. He could see that I needed a break but he felt it was totally selfish of me to think I could go away for five nights and leave him alone.

I explained I would only be twenty minutes away and if there was any true need I could be back home quickly. I explained that I needed an actual break, and this funding recognised this. I knew if I went away for two nights I would only just feel I was beginning to relax and it would be over.

Other carers I knew made the real point for me as I could see a definite pattern. Those who seemed to be coping the best were those who took regular respite breaks, seven days every three to four months. They planned their respite well, from how the care was coordinated while they were away, to what they would do to relax and recharge. I was determined to do this, and knew it would be good both for him and his children to be without me for a few days, and spend some true time together. It was nearly nine months since I'd had a break from his care.

Tomorrow
I told myself
faced with so many things
yet to be done,
yet to be experienced, enjoyed

Why do we presume so much
and deceive ourselves
when today is all we ever have?

24. Rolling the dice

The second chest infection hit fast.

We had been through the terrible hours on the Friday night when he'd been unable to clear his throat. Even as it was happening, I knew he would likely have some aspiration. I went to bed that night feeling sick. I knew he had rolled that toss of the dice we had dreaded.

He was far more unwell than with the infection three weeks previously, and the rattle in his chest was easy to hear every time he tried weakly to cough. It sounded like it was fairly high in his lungs, but the fact it was constant was a concern, as it could easily move down to become pneumonia.

The doctor told him that he might have to consider no longer eating or drinking even thickened fluids.

I can't imagine being completely robbed of the ability to taste any food, coffee, anything at all. Though he took in little by mouth, for a man who ran restaurants and cafés, it just had to feel even worse. We were sent home with a new round of antibiotics and strict instructions to rest, take in lots of fluids through the PEG and call an ambulance if he worsened.

I had to work the next day, and left with him assuring me that he felt okay. I was still very worried about him. No message or calls at morning break, but when I checked my phone at the end of the class I was teaching, just after midday, a message from the carer asked me to call. She said he was very aggressive and distressed and I was needed back home. He wouldn't let her attempt to do anything for him. When I arrived I knew immediately that he was very unwell. The carer had asked him several times if she should call an ambulance and he had said he was fine. She certainly looked relieved to get out of there. As soon as she left he admitted he did not feel well at all and asked me to call an ambulance.

He was promptly checked, given a chest X-ray and diagnosed with aspiration pneumonia. They started him on intravenous antibiotics and admitted him to a ward. Having a person with MND in a hospital ward is an absolute nightmare. The nurses do not understand the disease at all, and Chris had very high-care needs. With pneumonia on top of this he was incredibly fragile. I was able to get his son to come and sit with him after work. I went home, quickly ate and gathered some things we would both need and returned to sleep the night on a recliner chair beside his bed. He had absolutely no speech by now, and we made some new charts to help him quickly tell me his needs in relation to the hospital setting.

It is so much harder to care for your husband in a hospital setting. We had to ring a buzzer for anything he needed and it could take up to half an hour to be answered. I was not allowed to use their electric hoist, and so had to buzz and wait for them to page a wardsman to operate it. Yet I had to be there to explain and direct how he needed to be placed in it and positioned into the bed.

Sleeping in a recliner chair beside a hospital bed on a busy and noisy ward is not actually sleep. It's more like fading in and out of strange dreams and semi-consciousness. I have no idea what I must have looked like by the morning after the second night, and I would rather never know. He started sprouting fungal infections everywhere, far worse than any he had experienced after Christmas. They were so red, angry and sore. The more time we spent there, the more withdrawn and depressed he became, and his weakness increased by the day.

As I went to leave the hospital that afternoon to bring the dogs in for the night and have some dinner, a lady identifying herself as a social worker stopped me in the hallway. She wanted to know if I was all right and if there was anything she could do. My body betrayed me as tears began to spill from my eyes just as I was going to say I was okay. She quickly ushered me aside. She started asking lots of questions that were reasonable, but I began to cry more, saying I just needed to go home for a little while and I didn't have long. She wasn't hearing me, asking more questions, which made the tears flow faster and seemed to make her even more determined that

I needed her help. She pretty much dragged me into a private room, and I only went because I was crying in the middle of a public ward. She sat me down and started again with her questions until I desperately interrupted her to say, 'Please, I would love you to come and get me any time tomorrow to talk; it would be so helpful. But for now, I just want to go home. I need some quiet, I want to organise my animals, I want to be alone and I don't have long. I have to go now!'

Reluctantly she let me go. As I headed out of town I wondered what in the world would possess her to treat me that way. Who in their right mind starts in on twenty questions when someone is in obvious distress and exhaustion? I never saw her again. We were still on the ward for some days but she didn't come near me. I wasn't exactly waiting for her to return, or even wanting her to, but I did feel it made her cornering me even more insensitive, because she didn't follow up. Ah well, in truth it was the least of my problems.

On the third night he insisted he wanted to sleep in the recliner chair and it took until 10.30 pm for me to do the pillow dance correctly. Finally I collapsed on his bed, hoping we could get a little sleep, or at least just stop and be still in the dark for a while. He announced that his bum would become very sore if he stayed on the chair all night!

'Right, of course, yes, okay, no problem. I will fix that. How about I put you into the bed instead?'

So, again waiting for the buzzer, then an hour of rearranging and settling him and I was beside myself. I didn't even have the privacy to cry, let alone scream the way I wanted to scream, and I was far too exhausted to wander off to a toilet cubicle. What little was left of him was literally wasting away in this hospital. I was beyond exhaustion and despaired at how little control either of us had regarding his care.

His daughter had organised to arrive at 6.30 the following morning so I could go home and get some things done. I had been awake since 5.00 am, so I left the hospital at 6.15, figuring that, if I stayed to wait for her and she was late,

I would not be able to leave him alone until she arrived. I had completed Chris's needs for the early morning and he said he would be fine for fifteen minutes until his daughter arrived.

I came back after a couple of hours and did his personal care. His daughter agreed to stay the night with him this fourth night so I could actually get some sleep. I was becoming worried about how exhausted I was, and how I would cope when I could bring him home. I felt like a walking zombie and found myself just staring blankly at people talking to me or stopping in mid-sentence, forgetting what I was saying.

I had to go to the nursing home my brother had been placed in, with our case manager, to do an assessment on him that afternoon. I explained to him that we were coming and why, and that Chris was very ill in hospital, so I was travelling with the case manager and we could not stay long. The drive from one hospital to the other alone took forty-five minutes each way.

When we arrived he had his bags packed and said he wanted to leave, as he hated it there. It was stressful trying to focus him to answer questions on what he wanted in the long term. We kept explaining that we were there to try to help get him what he wanted if he could be clear about it. All the time I was only aware that I wanted to be back with Chris and that my brother just absolutely had to stay in the nursing home because I was at my wits' end.

When we finished, he had accepted that he would stay there for now, but he wanted us to come for a walk to the common kitchen, make us a cup of tea and have a nice chat and visit. I could barely get him to comprehend that I had to get back to the other hospital to Chris.

When I returned, I stayed with Chris until I had him completely settled for the night and went home wearily, tearily, and slept the sound sleep of exhaustion, despite how worried I was for him. I had my phone beside the bed and knew they would not hesitate to call me, even if it was only because he was scared and wanted me back. I couldn't quite figure how I would respond if I received a call like this but I was prepared that it could happen.

We had experienced solid rain for several days, after a lot of dry weather. I had barely noticed, with my focus on Chris in hospital and sleeping there each night. Typically around March and April the area is prone to floods and we can get cut off from all towns. The rain was unceasing, the river levels rising. I had two dogs that needed at least a little basic attention and feeding.

When I arose the next morning the forecast was for rain all day, with thunderstorms and rain again for the next five days. I began to worry seeing two main options if it flooded. Either I would be stuck in town with my husband in hospital, with the dogs at home alone. Or I would get stuck at home with the dogs, and my husband in hospital alone. Neither of them were comforting!

So I drove in looking at the water levels rising in the places where the roads usually go under, thinking I might need to phone a girlfriend (who lives 700 kilometres away) and see if I can put the dogs on a truck and send them to her. That way if it flooded I could just stay in town. But what if they send him home over the weekend and it is pouring rain, dismal, and everything is damp? I ponder on how bad this would be for recovering from pneumonia and wondered what would happen if he worsened once home and we could not get him back into town.

The doctors did their morning rounds and announced that he was much improved and could soon go home. My immediate response was to ask of we could go today. Chris's eyes sparked up for the first time in days. I began to argue the case, saying I had all the equipment at home and a dedicated care team. In my head I was certain Chris would not now say the care team were incompetent. The doctor conceded he was probably far better at home if we really thought we could do it. I wondered what the hell he thought had been happening with his care up until now.

By this point Chris was drooling, grinning and nodding his head vigorously. I asked if he could be transported, as he was so weak. They said it could be arranged and we were elated. Chris actually looked much better just for the fact he had been told he could go home.

One very strange thing that was discussed during this doctor visit was that that they wanted to organise a pump for his PEG, so he could be fed slowly overnight, rather than in meal amounts during the day. Chris had been adamant he would not accept overnight pump feeding and I explained this to them. But they were very concerned that if we didn't he would have another aspiration. I was incredulous. Somehow they had mixed up the story on admission and thought that he had been given too large a PEG feed and it had come back up out of his stomach, causing the aspiration. We finally got that sorted and they were off to do the paperwork.

Two hours later there was still no word on transport, so we decided I could get him out of the car at home like I'd always done, even if he was weaker. When we got out to the car, the sun was shining and there were almost no clouds in sight. The rain had completely cleared up and I laughed aloud as I remembered my fears just that morning. It seemed like that morning had been weeks ago, not hours.

When we arrived home, our home care worker, who had dropped in for an hour to do a little cleaning, was still there. Thankfully I had help getting him out of the car and into the house. The massage I had booked for that afternoon, which had been cancelled and rebooked twice, still managed to happen, and he arrived just as I settled Chris in his recliner.

The day went on to become glorious, the evening perfect, all stars across the sky that night. Chris looked as well as the previous week before any of this started and we got to sleep at home. So many parts of this journey took on an incredibly surreal state; days could feel like they took weeks, and weeks could feel like they passed in a few hours.

25. The final slope

I still had no resolution regarding the fees for the care package; there was just no transparency in the information I was given. I spent many hours on the phone, sending and reading emails and reworking the care plan. I am sure I would be horrified if I actually counted up how many hours I put into this task, simply because someone else kept changing the rules. I finally decided I was going to be better off agreeing to fewer hours and had managed, through numerous negotiations, to increase the hours to twenty-six and a half. I was able to add six hours respite on top. This meant that I would only receive weekend assistance of one and a half hours on a Saturday and one hour on a Sunday.

I was nearly at the end of the extra hours our case manager had funded, and so was in a desperate situation. If I did not take this offer, I would be reduced to only twenty-two hours of assistance per week. I was so heart weary from the whole process and concerned that Chris was declining rapidly now. If I did not get this all started I was going to be in crisis. So I agreed, and the services under the new funding arrangement would start on Monday 28 April. I was then going to take my five days' respite, starting Tuesday 29 April.

Over the next couple of days Chris's general health improved just for the fact of being home, but he was far weaker and barely able to stand. He agreed he was not up to walking any more. I knew this was huge, because he had always been adamant about walking no matter how long it took him or how much energy it consumed. I was purely exhausted from worrying about him, advocating for him constantly in the hospital and getting very little sleep in an uncomfortable place. I could barely imagine how he felt after his side of the ordeal.

I also knew that to stop walking was a fundamental internal change in Chris. I knew in my heart, from the moment the word 'pneumonia' had been spoken, that we had reached a true turning point. In those first days at home, I knew we

249

had reached the beginning of the end. I didn't know what that truly meant; he could possibly last for months, but I knew that we were on a steady last downhill run that was more likely to be only weeks. He amazed me in his recovery and yet I knew he had been affected by what he had been through. He refused to eat anything by mouth, but had a few sips of thickened coffee a couple of times a day. He was barely able to take any of it in but I am sure just getting a taste of it was some comfort to him.

It was plain to my eye that he was more scared than he had been letting on. I had known he had been very scared for a long time but for the most part had tried to hide the fear from me, mostly only letting it out in angry, nasty statements. Now he became quieter, but not in the sullen, angry way, just quieter like his energy was drained. His breathing was shallow and laboured, and his fear was heightened at night. I knew from things he had said at different times over the previous months that he feared he would stop breathing in his sleep. I hoped it would be that simple for him, as the experience we had just been through in hospital had only impressed even more deeply on me that there were far worse ways for the end to come.

He began to get me up every few hours during the night to transfer him from bed to recliner and back to the bed again. I am sure most of this was fear, but he had fungal infections everywhere and they were causing him pain and discomfort. We had been battling little fungal infections since Christmas day, but now they spread to his mouth, his groin and the stoma, which was looking very nasty.

A few nights after we got home he said plainly that he did not wish to go back to the hospital as he did not want to die there. This was the first time since the month after his diagnosis that he had been willing to have any real conversation about end of life. I could see he had been putting on a brave face and he actually wasn't healing well after the pneumonia, at least not like he tried to make it seem when we first got home.

250

He started to build up fluid in parts of his body, particularly the hands and legs, and experienced headaches. On any exertion he became short of breath quickly. We had an appointment with our specialist coming up, and he started talking about wanting things in place for end-of-life palliative care in the home. I suggested we put together a list of what he wanted, so we could make the most of the appointment, and he agreed. He seemed more able to see things plainly and work with me than he had for such a very long time.

I agreed that he should not die in a hospital. I would rather care for him calmly in loving and peaceful surroundings here at home. We needed a plan so we could be sure we weren't suddenly sucked into the medical system and things taken from our control. I also suggested that it was exhausting and incredibly stressful for me to be in the hospital with him, as I just couldn't do his care easily or even well there.

The appointment with the doctor went very well, especially considering how some of our previous appointments had ended with him angry with me for trying to tell my side of any situation. For the first time we were on the same page and, with the list of what he wanted addressed, we had an organised and productive meeting.

Chris asked for a bipap machine to assist his breathing. A prescription was sent to the equipment provider. We discussed end-of-life needs and how we wanted to handle this. We were given a prescription for anti-anxiety medications that would help him cope when things got really tough. We already had the morphine and knew how to use it when more would be needed. The doctor totally supported our desire to do everything at home and not return to hospital.

The doctor let me know the next day that we needed to see a pulmonologist to work out the correct settings for the bipap. He had already spoken to one he highly recommended, and referred us. On the same day I received a call offering us an appointment within days.

The night before the appointment, I asked Chris if he was certain he wanted this machine and he said he was. I gently talked to him about the experiences I knew of others who found it difficult to adjust to. There are different mask set-ups, and sometimes it took weeks to get things working correctly. I hated having this conversation with him, and hoped he did not think I was against him getting the machine. In reality, I knew he should have been using the machine for months. The best result is obtained by starting early to prevent fatiguing the breathing muscles. I didn't bring this into the conversation, but it was whirling through my head as I talked to him.

I had a new fear building in me. I knew we were at the beginning of the end. I knew what we had been through so many times, with him demanding equipment, only to refuse to use it when it arrived. I did not have the energy to go through that again.

I asked him clearly if he would work with me to find the right mask and settings, so we could make this work for him, and he agreed.

The appointment with the new specialist was not quite what I had imagined. He was thorough, blunt and honest. To get the settings right Chris would have to spend two nights in hospital for a sleep study. Unfortunately the sleep laboratory at the local hospital did not have the facilities Chris required, for an electric hospital bed with alternating air mattress and a hoist. The specialist offered to find out if the Palliative Care Unit could have him there for the study. Otherwise he might have to go to the Gold Coast.

Chris immediately said that wherever he went he must have me stay with him. I don't know if the shock registered on my face or not, but I was stunned because I had made it clear I couldn't stay full time in a hospital with him. Of course, at the same time I knew I could not leave him alone either, so why should I be shocked?

The next day were told the only option was the Gold Coast Hospital, over two hours' drive away. I would not even be able to come home for an hour. I was nearly beside myself. I would have done anything for Chris if it would help him. But thinking about the track record, I could well be facing two nights in hospital with him angry and me exhausted. Then we would come home with a piece of equipment he might refuse to use. I would have felt totally different if we had been heading there months earlier. If he refused it at first, he might have started using it after some time. Now I feared we were looking at another waste of time that was going to use up energy neither of us possessed.

So I gave the details to Chris, remaining as neutral as possible, and he said wanted to go there for the sleep study. The following day, he decided that he did not want the machine after all, as he did not want to spend two nights in hospital. There was so much energy I could waste on worrying in advance. We had spent five days in this process and I had been worried about all the extra stress it would be, and he cancelled it. I did not bother to phone and let anyone know. I figured they would call me with an appointment and I would remember to tell them then.

The fungal issues in his mouth and groin worsened despite treatment. His mouth began to cause him a lot of pain and it was sapping what little energy he had left. I think it was starting to make breathing harder too. He requested morphine during the day for the first time.

Chris had always said he was fighting the disease and was fine. Now he told me he was dying. I hugged him and we talked a little and I cried. It had been so long since I had cried with him, cried in front of him about what was happening, and I was relieved that he did not criticise me for doing so.

We went to his doctor for morphine prescriptions and a general check-over of his chest. The doctor was concerned about the fungal infections, particularly his mouth. We had been battling different fungal outbreaks for nearly four months, and only ever having partial success. He suggested a liquid oral treatment that we could put through the PEG. It works as a systemic antifungal and is rarely used as it is very strong but, with so much widespread fungal activity, it is often the only thing that works. We all agreed he was in high distress and he wanted to try this treatment.

It was to be given for five days straight, three times per day. I was also giving him probiotics to try to keep some balance in his body after all the antibiotics and antifungals. I've always had a particular dislike of fungal infections and now I found myself battling the mother of all fungal attacks.

A couple of days later we had a meeting with the palliative nurse about how we wanted his end of life to be, and how they would work with us. She gave us every assurance that they were there to meet our express needs and desires in this.

Some months earlier I had chosen a funeral home but had not put any actual arrangements in place. It was not an easy thing to do. All discussions with Chris, either alone or with our MND adviser or health professionals, had resulted in him stating he didn't care what happened after he was gone. He was clear that I could make whatever arrangements I wished and he didn't have any interest in knowing what they might be. This only made it harder for me to focus on a decision.

His care needs were so high it had been easier to put this matter aside. However, I realised it would be difficult if he were to go suddenly. So I had made an appointment for the Tuesday following Easter to meet a funeral director in town to make the decisions, do the paperwork and have both of us clear on what the process would be. I was adamant that I wanted to meet him away from home.

Before the palliative nurse left she took me aside and asked me a very direct question. She asked me how I would cope afterwards, if it turned out that I had given him his last dose of morphine. I knew by the way she asked, her body language and tone of voice, that she wasn't talking about me giving him too much or a fatal dose. I could soon be in the situation where I would be caring for him alone, and may give him a dose and he may pass away soon after.

I looked her in the eye and said that I had absolutely no problem with this because I understood that my purpose in looking after him was to provide him comfort, and that he was terminal. She strongly suggested I sit down and write out how I was feeling right at that point, how Chris's condition was and how I felt about his end of life. I told her I would, but I didn't actually feel it was a priority for me, or that I really needed to do this. That night before I went to sleep, however, I suddenly felt I would give it a go. Before I knew it, I was writing and writing and writing, and I wasn't even really thinking. It was just all pouring out of me.

By the fourth day on the antifungal treatment he developed diarrhoea and was exhausted and distressed. The palliative nurse came and we spoke to the doctor by phone together. He advised to stop the antifungal, as it was most probably the cause. I was distressed to think that he was now less than fifty kilograms and this seemed to be sucking the very last little bit was left in him. He was very weak, tired and taking morphine for fear more than anything. I could see his body was shutting down and refusing to respond to anything we tried to do.

The palliative nurse returned the next day and spoke about placing him in the Palliative Care Unit to get everything under control. His doctor suggested some treatments we could try to relieve the pain and get him better rested and coping. Chris wanted to try the treatments at home, but the doctor insisted he would have to spend at least a full day and night in the unit, particularly because the next day would be Good Friday and no community services would be available for four days. They organised a bed in the unit but at the last minute Chris refused. He just wanted to stay at home. I had been in two minds about trying anything new on him and being back in a hospital setting. I felt this was a far better decision from him, than if he had elected to go, and had ended up angry with me because it wasn't working out for him.

To live this life is a wonderful thing

Life is a gift tis true
but the gift of being loved
is the greatest we can receive

The gift of loving
is the highest honour we can achieve.

26. End of life

Easter Friday dawned a beautiful autumn day. I had been planning for weeks that over Easter I would tackle cleaning out a storage room in the shed. It was piled with boxes of stuff belonging to Chris and his two daughters, and I knew the room had been infested with rats. I had not been game to walk in there for a couple of years. But I didn't want to have to clean it out after he died. To be honest, weeks earlier when I had decided to do this, as far as I knew he had months yet. The pneumonia and continuing decline only made me more determined that I would feel so much better if that room was dealt with.

So I completed Chris's morning care. After that, normally he would either sit in his recliner chair with the TV on or sit out on the verandah, but he asked to be put back into bed. This hit me immediately as it was the very first time he had wanted to go back to bed. I asked if he was all right and he assured me that he was just tired and if I was going to clean out that room he would be more comfortable in the bed. He also asked for a dose of morphine. As I went out to start cleaning I felt a true foreboding that he was seriously unwell again. Every half an hour I came back to the house to check on him. Each time he was happy to stay in bed watching TV and sleeping on and off. He got up for a little while in the afternoon when I had a break, and he was extremely weak and tired.

He was quiet during the evening and I spent extra time on each of his personal care tasks, taking care not to rush. I felt a deep sorrow that our time was nearly at an end. I went to bed with the storage room half cleaned out and sorted, which meant all the contents were now covering the floor of the main building. But all the rat leavings were removed. I had decided I would be best scrubbing down the wooden shelves and throwing a coat of fresh paint over them. With four days off I figured that if I could finish the cleaning and sorting the next day, I could do a coat on each of the next two days and the room would be clean and useful. I would have a full load of rubbish on the trailer by the end, as I was not prepared to pull apart boxes that had been rat infested, as they stank.

Once I had decided on these details I could no longer distract myself from thinking about what was happening with Chris. I sat very still for a while and allowed myself to go over how he had been all day, and all the previous week. I considered how unwell he must have been as he had been so very tired and uncomplaining all day. I knew we were heading to a stage that we were not both going to emerge from. This conviction began to settle over me like a slow fog coming into a valley. I actually felt calm as I contemplated what I could see happening. I couldn't explain it to myself and didn't actually question the feeling at the time. I let the fog of calm roll over me, and prepared myself to sleep, knowing I was going to need all my energy charged.

Saturday arrived and he did not want to bother with a shower. I knew by how he looked, how shallow his breathing was, how quiet he was and the fact that his shower was one of the few things left that gave him pleasure that we were indeed close to the end. The only other times he had refused a shower was when he was angry with me. That slow fog of calm settled over me again, allowing me to accept and not push him into anything he wasn't feeling capable of. I can only describe it as some kind of letting go for me. After all the tension of trying so hard to make things right for Chris, we didn't have to pretend any more that he was fighting. I could just concentrate on his care, dignity and comfort.

He sat up for a little while, and then asked for the new anti-anxiety drops that had been prescribed for him. The fact that he asked for this medication told me the last of what I needed to know, even though I had felt sure the night before. He had no appetite but I gave him half his normal quantity of PEG feeds at the times he would normally have one with lots of water. His temperature was normal, but with only a look it was obvious he was very unwell and his systems were beginning to shut down.

His whole attitude towards me had even softened. I took his hand, looked him in the eye and told him how much I loved him, and was so glad we had found each other when we did. I had told him these things many times since diagnosis, but his response generally had been to look at me sceptically and not return the sentiment. Today he looked at me, and his eyes were soft, and he accepted that what I said was truth.

As it was Easter there were no home services, but palliative care had a twenty-four-hour hotline. I phoned the nurse and told her the situation, what I felt was happening and what I had been doing since the previous day. She was amazing in her support. She talked calmly and assured me that I had everything well under control and informed me of our options. I let her know that we definitely wanted him to die at home and so she lent me every kind of advice and support that was possible over a phone. I was to call her at any time of the day or night if I needed anything. She asked me to call back at least the next morning with an update on how we were doing.

I spent my time sitting with him, doing little things for him, massaging his hands and feet, wiping cool cloths on his face and just being with him. We watched some episodes of *Breaking Bad* as we had just begun to watch this together recently. I asked if I should let his children know he was unwell, as they may want to visit. He said he did not want to worry them at this point.

I remembered at some point that evening that I was supposed to meet the funeral director on Tuesday and that, no matter what happened, I would not be going out and leaving him with anyone in a few days. So I emailed and asked if he would be able to come here for the meeting instead, and let him know that Chris was very unwell and I did not think he would recover. He assured me he was more than happy to come here, and that if anything happened before then to simply phone him.

I went to go to bed that night very concerned that he may be closer to the end than he seemed and his children may not get to say goodbye. It then hit me that I wanted to be with him and made up a bed on the recliner where he had slept for so long.

I had to get up to him several times through the night and he requested morphine. I realised that it was only with the use of morphine and Clonazepam that he was settling at all.

The second phone call to palliative care was even more helpful. Because it was the same nurse, I didn't have to tell the whole story again. She advised me on what levels and frequencies the medications should work well for him, and how much I could consider increasing them by. She told me again that she was there for anything I needed and I agreed that if all were well I would update her that evening. I would not have felt as calm and in control of the situation without professional support like this, and the reassurance of how well I was caring for him. I was able to nurse him by my own gut instinct because of the way she gave me guidelines.

I was advised maximum doses and frequencies; however, it was stressed that it was better to give a little often, than wait too long. With this information I could simply look at Chris and give his medications accordingly. They might be a little closer for one dose or left a little longer for the next dose if he was sleeping peacefully. But I didn't allow the pain or distress to break through.

Having my online peers was amazing for my emotional support. I let my two support groups know what was happening and had my laptop on the kitchen bench, where I could see Chris in the next room. The messages that were flooding in were so special, and my online family held my hand all through the next few days.

The next morning he was far weaker and, although alert, he did not want to get out of bed at all and needed both his medications together. Once his morning personal care was complete, I asked him to please let me call his children and he agreed. He did not want any nutrition so I only gave him a bit of water with each dose of morphine. There was no point giving any nutrition or even extra fluids, as the system shutdown he was experiencing was obvious.

I called each of his children in turn and told them gently that their father was very unwell and that I felt it would be good if they came to see him. None of them asked for details but I think they knew by my voice that it was serious.

I called each of my own children and let them know as well, and asked if I could just update them by text message, as I didn't want to take the time away from him to make multiple calls. I kept my phone on silent and messages of support came in frequently. With one update I could let all our children and his mother know what his condition was.

Updating twice daily with palliative care became like talking to someone I knew and trusted. I was fortunate that one single nurse had been put on the twenty-four-hour line for the entire Easter weekend, so I had just one support person all through. This made things much easier, but also I felt sure of her advice, as I didn't have different staff who might have different views. I had known this to happen to others in my situation, even to the point of being told on a second call that everything the previous nurse had said was wrong.

We actually spent a lovely day together in many ways. It's hard to explain that, after nearly a year of him being so angry, aggressive, controlling, paranoid and full of fear, to see him calm and accepting brought a very special kind of peace to us both. I admit I wished he could have had something like this peace all the way through, but I was taking anything I could after the past year of so much being taken from us. I could talk of my love for him, my gratefulness for all we'd had together, and he could absorb and accept it. To me this was a gift from him and it nurtured my feeling of calm and acceptance.

His children arrived together. I met them outside and very quietly told them he was seriously ill and I did not think he would rally. I did not want to panic them about it but I wanted

261

them to understand. I let them know he was taking a lot of medication and was fully aware of everything going on around him, but he was not able to communicate very much and was sleeping a lot.

For the first time in two days I could just sit outside and not wonder if he was still breathing. After about half an hour, however, I felt that the extra energy of having three young people in the house was unnerving me a little. I had settled into acceptance, and a peace in myself, in how I could help him remain calm and peaceful. I could feel it being a little rattled. It's very different for the primary carer, who has watched and lived this every single day, to be in the moment of where we were. But for his children who had not come here often, it was distressing. They were covering their distress well, but I think I was so sensitive at the time it felt like it was bouncing off the walls.

I was pleased when they were ready to leave, as I knew Chris needed more medication, and some soothing touch and quietness. He indicated, however, that he would like to get out of bed and come out on the verandah, if his son would help me get him up. Again I was awed by the striking difference it was for him to actually ask for help from one of his children.

So he came out onto the verandah, his children left and he requested a cigarette. I set it up for him but he could barely breathe or sit up. I understood that he knew how close to the end he was. In truth, he held the cigarette holder in his mouth and he breathed smoke in as it curled off the cigarette, but he didn't have enough in him to actually suck on it. When he finished, he wanted to speak so I got his chart and he spelled out to me, 'I am SO spaced out!' I laughed a true laugh and looked him in the eye saying, 'Yes you are, and you are going to stay that way darling.' He smiled.

Then he asked to see the dogs. He had not really been near the dogs in weeks, so again I was surprised but happy to do this for him. He actually seemed to have rallied a little bit. He was delighted with the dogs but he never moved. Cetta lay at his feet wriggling against his foot to simulate him patting her. Cero came behind him, gently put his paws up on his shoulders and kissed him on the cheek many times. He sat with them for around fifteen minutes, just soaking up their love, and I knew he was saying goodbye to them. When I brought him back in he asked to be put back into bed. I was sad that I was no longer able to lie in the bed beside him because he had to be positioned so exactly, with so many pillows propping and supporting every joint.

When I updated palliative care, I was again reassured of how well I was caring for him, told what increases could be tolerated in his medications if needed overnight, and again that I could call at any hour.

We watched more *Breaking Bad* and when the episode ended he said the last word I ever heard from his mouth. As a single word it was clear enough to understand. He simply said, 'More.' I asked if he wanted another *Breaking Bad* episode and he grinned and nodded. He needed more morphine and Clonazepam before it started, and fell asleep halfway through the episode. I lay on the recliner beside him again, but I only dozed between giving him medications and doing gentle calming things for him, swabbing his mouth and stroking his hands, limbs and face. He woke more frequently during the night, always needing some combination of his medication to settle again.

Monday I rose early but, as he was still sleeping, I sat outside with a cup of tea. I watched the day beginning and felt so calm that I realised how tense I had been for so long, as we had battled the monster. Chris woke and he was aware but far weaker, and I knew he would not leave this bed again. It's hard to explain how I knew this. I could have thought this the day before or I could have believed he would get up for a short time again in the afternoon. But I knew he was far worse than the day before. He could no longer use the charts to communicate; in fact, he could not truly communicate beyond answering yes by raising his eyebrows a little or no by frowning slightly. I could only ask very basic questions, as he couldn't follow full sentences. When I entered the room or spoke he would look directly into my eyes. However, he did not seem to be as settled after I had done his personal care.

I made my call to palliative care and she advised that I could safely increase his medications a little more. She asked me to call her again in the middle of the day rather than wait until the night. After half an hour she phoned back and said it had just occurred to her to ask when he had last passed urine. I realised that twice during the night he had wanted to go but had been unable, and he had not yet been this morning. She said his restlessness could be a full bladder and we talked of a few tips to try to help him empty it. She suggested he might be best to have a catheter inserted. Now, remember, this was Easter Monday morning!

I tried tricks of placing the urinal and lightly pressing on his lower abdomen, placing a warm pack on it, but no result. He was not able to say if he definitely felt the need to pass urine, as though he could not tell if his bladder was full or not.

I wondered if lifting him in the hoist would allow gravity and change of position to help but, for the first time, I did not feel confident in getting him hoisted on my own. He was so frail I worried that I may hoist him and he could panic. So I phoned his son and asked if he would help me. Together we were able to get the sling under him as I explained to him that I felt he needed to try to empty his bladder. Again he was aware of what we were doing, and was not objecting to what we wanted to try, but that was about all. We lifted him in the sling and I wasn't fully happy with the positioning but we seemed to have him more upright, and yet all was in vain, nothing happened. I kept him in the sling for fifteen minutes, just in case, and to give him a little position change and take pressure off his bum. I changed his bed linen as he hung gracefully, and then gently positioned him back in the bed.

The only resource I could draw on over a public holiday weekend was to see if the on-call doctor would do a house call, check him and maybe insert a catheter.

The doctor's first response was that he had not inserted a catheter for many years, and I should call an ambulance so it could be done in the ER. My feelings of peace and calm began to dissolve a little but I held my patience as I explained he would not tolerate a trip in the ambulance, let alone being in the ER. He asked why I thought this and, even as I replied, I wondered if I was sounding like a rambling lunatic. I said in a rush, 'He weighs less than fifty kilograms, he can't breathe unless upright, he can't stand, he has frozen shoulder joints and is developing a pressure sore. He is covered in all manner of fungal infections and is confined to a hospital bed with an alternating mattress, which is all he can barely tolerate. A ride in a jolting ambulance won't be possible.' He reluctantly agreed it would not be wise to attempt to move him and he would come and check him.

The doctor checked Chris over very gently and spoke to him directly, which I truly appreciated, as too many talk over a patient's head as though they don't exist, especially when in the kind of state he was in. He pronounced he only had a moderate amount in his bladder. He could wait until the next morning for the palliative care nurse to come and place a catheter then, if he still could not empty it himself. I asked him to write a short report in the communication book used by the home care staff and myself and as he did this we spoke quietly. He said he felt Chris had pneumonia again, and pointedly told me that I was doing a brilliant job looking after him. He suggested a further increase I could safely make in his medications if I felt it was needed.

I decided to phone the home care worker who had worked the most with us and let her know, as she was not due to come until Wednesday. I felt she would want to know the situation. She was grateful and, as she was working, asked if she could stop in to see him on her way home. I did not tell him she was coming.

When she arrived, indeed he had enough understanding of time and place that he was surprised to open his eyes to a quiet voice and see her standing beside him. She sat and talked quietly with him for some time and I was able to go and sit outside for a little while. It felt good to be able to sit outside knowing she was with him, as she had brought further peace and calm into the house and I knew he could feel it too.

After some time she came out and just held me in a long hug. For the first time in those four days I cried. She asked if I would like a cup of tea and sat me down outside again as Chris's daughter arrived and went in to sit with him. She brought the tea out and as I started to drink it she went silently inside and retrieved my brush. Without a word she undid my matted hair, brushed it through thoroughly and made a beautiful braid. I drank tea, cried, and felt tension draining from me by the simple kindness of being touched.

Once we were alone again I curled on the recliner beside Chris. About two hours later, after we had both rested a little, we had success with the urinal and he passed a reasonable amount. I felt such relief that at least we would not need any intervention on this. He was now only taking a little water with each dose of medication so I knew he would not build up large amounts of urine again. I updated the palliative nurse and she was very pleased that he had been seen to. She could tell that it had been comforting to be told again that I was doing everything possible for him in a competent way.

I kept lots of candles burning in the house and lovely music playing. He was no longer able to concentrate on the TV and did not seem to want it turned on. I hoped the music would enhance the effects of the medication. As I sat with him, I contemplated the many gifts he had bestowed on my soul during our first years together. I spoke softly as memories of love and beauty came to me, or sat silently touching him, allowing us to feel each other through that element of touch.

That evening his daughters returned and brought me dinner. I was so grateful as for the past few days I had only really been eating muesli or throwing something onto a slice of bread every now and then. I could not even think to prepare food while Chris lay there. A meal was indeed welcome.

They did not stay long, for which I was grateful, as I longed for the lights to be off again, just the candles burning, and quiet music so my attention could be focused purely on my man. I updated the palliative nurse, and again she was a great comfort.

I felt the calm and peace deepen as the evening wore on.

Around midnight I felt strongly that it was time to apply the homeopathic remedy that helps cope with the fear of dying. I crushed the remedy and mixed it with some water. I spent half an hour gently rubbing it into his temples and the backs of his hands. I talked of all my memories of our short time together and my love for him. He was aware and calm, but unable to make any real response except to look into my eyes. And then he smiled.

I took a deep breath and told him that he was gravely ill now, and was not going to rally this time. I told him it was time to let go. I told him I did not ever want him to die, but he had endured far more than any human being should ever have to endure. He had fought an amazing fight, but he did not have to hold on and fight any more. He looked into my eyes. He could see I had tears though I did not weep openly, just silent tears slowly trickling.

At 1 am I gave him his medication, and settled myself into the recliner and held his hand. I must have moved in and out of a partially asleep state, but I remember often opening my eyes and just looking at him.

At 2 am I realised that his breathing was less noisy, and by 2.30 it was slowing. Just before 3 am he took his last breath. He did not make any other move in those last two hours, did not make any attempt to communicate with me. He peacefully and quietly let go and slipped away. I think I held my own breath for a while, it wasn't a conscious thing; rather it was more a matter of suddenly realising that I needed to take a deep breath of my own. I was staring fixedly at him, expecting him to take one more breath, but it never came. When I did draw a breath I half-expected him to as well.

I kissed his forehead gently, then made a bowl of scented water and washed his face gently. I told him how very, very, very sorry I was that he had been taken hold of by such a vicious monster and I had not been able to do anything to stop it. I spent about half an hour with him, saying many of the same things I had said the past few days, then I went outside, trying to absorb that this really was the end. He really was gone and, finally, he really was free of the hideous agony he had suffered.

I had a mental picture of him flying away, free and high into the air with that monster held in his hands until he flew over the edge of a high cliff and flung the monster over it. It wasn't that I felt this was happening but the imagery seemed fitting. There were no tears, just such a silence. It wasn't an empty silence; it was a silence that was a place to be for the moment.

I think I went back and forwards and maybe even paced the house a little, once I returned inside, as it was a very strange couple of hours. I couldn't seem to quite keep still, but kept returning to sit with his body, saying things as they came to me. There was no fear that he would misunderstand or that what I was saying would lead the conversation awry or end in anger. There was just this place of silence that allowed me to say aloud some of the things I truly felt about the man he had been, how much I had missed him for a long time, and would now continue to miss him.

I didn't have any feeling like he was hovering around the room listening. I think it was my own way of finally saying those things out aloud, without fear. As I gazed on the ravaged body that had been left behind I was so glad he was freed from it. I wanted him so much, but the monster had prevented us, and every day he had been trapped by the monster had proven to be a living hell for both of us.

I will never believe that I truly knew what he went through. I can tell my story, what I witnessed and how I interacted with that. But every single day I knew that his own personal journey, trapped in there, was a far worse nightmare than what leaked out of him. And still I talked a bit, walked up and down and in circles, and returned to sit by his body again.

I did not want to phone any of the children and wake them in a panic and then immediately tell them he was gone. There was time enough, I felt, for them to sleep a couple more hours before they would have to start their first day without their father.

Finally I got into the shower and washed my hair. I felt a need to hurry, to check on him, even though I knew he was gone. I forced myself to make it a long luxurious cleansing. When I came out, clean and in fresh clothes for the first time in days, I had to check on him, even though I knew he would be exactly how I had left him. I put on the kettle and realised it was nearly sunrise. A most amazing colour was building on the horizon.

As a child

time is so slow

we seem always to wait

As an adult

time is short

we want more

we run to catch it

When it is gone

we lament

that we wasted it.

27. A new day dawns

A perfect day was awakening, with a sunrise over mist-shrouded lowlands greeting me when I walked out to the front yard. As I drank my tea, the sky lightened and the sun peeked over the horizon, and I took some photos. There was a serene feeling in the birth of a new day that washed over me with the growing light. It wasn't a feeling of excitement or joy, but the serenity of knowing that the earth keeps turning, causing the sun to appear in the sky again every morning, no matter my loss through the previous night. That hour of allowing myself to wake up with the new day refreshed me in a way that felt like I had actually slept for hours, rather than sitting vigil with the love of my life as he flew free.

I had calculated what time various family members would be likely to wake and leave for work. I wanted to call them early enough to prevent them walking out the door or arriving at work, but not so early as to wake them.

I decided to first post to my online support teams and let them know he had been set free and thank them for their support.

Next, I emailed the funeral director and let him know that he would now be actually collecting the body. It was good to be able to practice telling people that he was gone with text rather than a possibly shaky voice and having to hear immediate reactions.

Even though it was still very early, I knew our home care worker would be up and leaving earliest of all. I phoned and let her know. This was another good kind of test as she was close to me but it wasn't like having to tell his children. I then phoned each of his three children and they all took it quietly. I told each of them, in a voice that I hoped came across gently, that I was exhausted and needed to have this day to myself, and would talk to them the next day. They all seemed to understand and I was grateful because I knew that I still felt calm and at peace with how gentle his passing had been.

I could not imagine being put in the middle of other people's reactions and the range of energy changes that would create.

I phoned each of my own children and two of them offered to drive straight to me. Again I asked to have the day to myself. I truly appreciated their offers and had not expected them to do this. I told them I would love them to come, just not today and I would call them that night or the next morning.

Lastly I phoned the palliative care nurse. She was beautiful in assuring me yet again of how wonderful it was that I had been able to keep him here and so comfortable, and then to see him pass so peacefully.

I barely had time to sit with another cup of tea before the funeral director arrived. Here we go, someone else is going to see his body and it is about to become real.

He was very sensitive, and only looked briefly at Chris's body as we went out to the back verandah. He explained procedures and the services he could offer. We phoned the doctor's surgery together and after I spoke with our GP, the funeral director spoke to him. He organised to drop in to the doctor's surgery on the way through town with the body and do the death certificate. I was catching on that this meant I would not have to see another single person, answer no more questions, other than the forms I was already filling out, as they spoke on the phone. What a beautifully simple system. Definitely the last thing I felt up to handling today was a lot of people going over anything more. Everything was settled and signed within half an hour. I spent a few last minutes with Chris's body, and then walked out into the back yard while he put the body into the hearse and left.

It is hard to describe that day as it has become very fuzzy in my memory. The intensity of the caring, the way my mind was constantly in overdrive, the lack of sleep and decent food were all beginning to catch up with me in their own ways. My mind was in a tug-of-war. One part wanted to just shut down completely; the other insisted it had to be alert, thinking ahead and listening out. I had been in such a heightened state of 'carer mode' for so long, part of me was refusing to accept it was no longer needed. Feeling numb immediately after the death of a loved one is a normal and common reaction, and I was certainly there.

It's hard for the mind to grasp that the person you have cared for all this time is truly and finally gone, even when you have held and washed the body afterwards. Part of me still expected it was something temporary, no matter that my conscious brain knew everything that had just happened.

In many ways that day was important to me as I slowly wound down and the numbness settled in. Maybe it was numbness, but I still felt so peaceful in myself. I could still feel the peace that had enveloped us both over the last days. I did not want to lose that peace and plummet into an emotional whirlpool that others may set in motion. I knew I would only have this day before I would have to face the world again, so I allowed myself the important space to simply be.

Later that afternoon I received a text message from our wonderful home care worker asking if I needed anything from the shops, as she would be leaving town soon and coming past. On an impulse I replied that I needed milk, even though I did not, and she arrived with milk and one good stiff drink each. We sat together on the verandah and drank and talked through what had happened over the past months, and in her usual gentle way she was just there with me.

After she left I felt I was ready to see people and move forward into what the next short period would bring – removal of equipment, putting back all the furniture, cleaning up the gardens and holding a memorial service. I phoned my son and daughter, who had been ready to come straight to me, and they both agreed they could arrive the following day. Another two friends came and helped with the large furniture next morning so all the equipment could be ready for the truck, and the house put back into some kind of order. MND NSW were fantastic and everything was collected the next day so I did not have to sit looking at all the equipment.

My stepdaughter's twentieth birthday was only two days after Chris's death. We all went out for a lovely beach picnic, and I think we were a little amazed at how beautiful the day was, and how much we enjoyed each other's company and could smile and enjoy ourselves. It was important to me that we celebrated her birthday. I didn't want her birthdays overshadowed by the loss of her father, remembering that first one as a day of pain, misery and solitude.

My children came and went in shifts of a few days each during the next two weeks, and I began to organise and formulate the memorial service for the love of my life.

I couldn't bare a large public affair as we had always been so connected to our property and had been married here. I felt the most fitting way to say goodbye was a small personal gathering here, in the same kind of format we had used for our wedding.

I put all the effort I could into making each item and involving family in all aspects of the day, just like we did for our wedding. I created a personal invitation and included on the back a menu of the items Chris had been most famous for cooking. Each person selected an item from the menu, cooked it at home, spending some quiet time remembering Chris, and then brought it on the day to share for lunch.

I made a bookmark for each person who attended as a small memorial gift. I was sent such a forest of flowers, during the previous week that I used these as the decorations for the service.

I selected from a range of beautiful keepsake urns, an urn for each of our seven children, his mother and myself. When Chris's ashes arrived I was able to borrow the ashes of his first wife, the mother of his children. I carefully placed half of his and half of her ashes into each keepsake urn for his three children. I then placed some of his ashes into the rest of the keepsakes. I kept aside the remainder to bury under our engagement tree, on our wedding anniversary only four days later.

My two sons ran the service, the same way they had run our wedding breakfast speech, but with such solemnity instead of joyous celebration. I felt intensely proud of their ability to stand up this way, even with a small gathering, supporting me and honouring their stepfather. I realised they were both men, rather than the young lads I perceived them, as a mother does.

Nearly every person who attended came up for a few minutes and spoke about their connection to, and memories of Chris. There was no celebrant and no one read anything out. We all came up singly or in small groups and spoke from the heart.

His younger daughter put a great effort into collating photos and making electronic copies for a beautiful slideshow. It contained all the typical photos covering many aspects of his life up until MND began its ravaging. I added a selection of his favourite music to go with the slideshow and loaded it onto his iPad, which could then be displayed on the TV screen, playing the music through the sound system.

These things just wouldn't be complete without one scary moment in the process. I decided I should test out the slides and music display early so it would be ready to just turn on later in the morning. The slides were perfect but the music sounded decidedly like it was coming down a piece of string and through a tin can. We fiddled with settings and volumes and my younger son was handed the problem to solve. After trying several unsuccessful, though logical, solutions he checked to see if the iPad itself was running poorly. I had not used it since Chris had passed, as it was his, and my son discovered that nearly every app was open in the background. So he methodically closed them all and rebooted the iPad and perfect sound erupted from the stereo. The relief was palpable in the air and I couldn't turn it off again as the slideshow began to display.

The effect was enthralling. I found myself still standing and watching half an hour later. It made no difference that I had been over the slideshow several times when setting it up.

There was something powerful about seeing it on the big screen and hearing the music through the stereo that had me spellbound. All through the morning I found myself lingering nearby or moving very slowly past. During the hours the guests were here, there was barely a time that you would not find two to five people sitting in the lounge room transfixed by the show. I noticed most people stayed there in silence for around half an hour. It was easy to do, as there were hundreds of photos, so it seemed they were never-ending.

The meal was a particularly special success. Here were all these dishes that connected us to Chris. Most had been made with some personal variation, and there was plenty of laughter as people compared how Chris would have made each dish, or some memory of him in his café life with a funny story. His connection to food, talk and laughter had been such a focal point of his life that this final feast in memory of him felt like the best way to send him off I could imagine.

Nearly every person present commented that they had never been to a funeral or memorial service that had felt so personal, intimate and celebratory, even in such sadness. Everyone left knowing a little more of my beautiful man through the sharing of others that day.

My favourite memory that was shared about Chris was to describe him as the perfect blend of enlightenment and yobbo.

I had put my soulmate to rest, but had absolutely no idea what life could possibly look like from that day forward, and was still too numb to even realise it.

The kettle is boiling
as I pour it over the tea leaves
I whisper my fears into the steam
and am soothed
by the liquid gold that envelopes me

28. The lowdown (medical stuff)

If you have to deal with a diagnosis like MND, it helps to understand what is happening in front of your eyes. You are inundated with information, but somehow none of it makes a lot of sense.

However, at some point after diagnosis you kind of get your head around it and realise things that were happening well before you thought anything was happening.

All the strange things I described leading up, realising something was wrong, actually have a name and are known symptoms of this disease.

Two terms are often confused: 'upper', thought of as the top half of the body, and 'lower', thought of as from the waist down. This is incorrect. MND involves both upper and lower motor neurones and the death of these neurons cause different symptoms.

Some people have more upper or more lower motor neurone effects and this causes more of some symptoms, and less, or even an absence, of others.

Upper motor neurones (UMN)
These neurones (nerves) reside in the brain and spinal cord.

Symptoms characteristic of UMN damage include: increased muscle tone (spasticity), weakness, increased reflexes, up-going plantar response (known as the Babinski reflex) and sustained muscular contractions (known as clonus).

Running a blunt instrument along the underside of the foot tests the plantar response. A normal response is for the foot to curl in (down-going).

We often laughed about his strong reflex, years before MND. We didn't know it was abnormal and had a name. I noticed it when massaging his feet. I would have to take hold of his feet firmly beforehand and hold them until the Babinski response settled.

Lower motor neurones (LMN)

These reside between the spinal cord and the muscles that we move voluntarily.

Symptoms characteristic of LMN damage include: decreased muscle tone, weakness, atrophy, arreflexia (absence of reflex) and fasciculations (twitching).

Atrophy is a decrease in muscle mass and can be partial or complete. Neurological atrophy is when the muscle dies and wastes away as a result of damage to the nerve that stimulates the muscle.

We did not understand any of this when Chris began to have issues with his shoulders and we noticed muscle atrophy. We just thought it was something that went along with getting older, even though he was only fifty-two years old and very active.

Laryngospasm

Early on, even before he started slurring his speech, I had noticed him giving these odd little coughs. I could never describe them because they seemed totally involuntary and nothing to do with his chest, it was totally in the throat. Laryngospasm is an uncontrolled or involuntary muscular contraction (spasm) of the laryngeal cords. I had never even heard the term, but the name was enough to tell me that this was what had been happening.

Jaw clonus

Clonus is a series of involuntary, rhythmic, muscular contractions and relaxations. It is a sign of certain neurological conditions, particularly associated with UMN lesions, and is often accompanied by spasticity, which can be described as another form of hyperexcitability. Unlike the small, spontaneous twitches known as fasciculations (which are usually caused by LMN pathology), clonus causes large motions that are usually initiated by a reflex.

From early in his bulbar symptoms Chris noticed any breeze, even a warm one, blowing across his face would cause his jaw to shudder, like uncontrollable teeth chattering.

In the later stages this clonus increased especially if he became upset and tried to speak. He developed leg clonus as his leg atrophy advanced.

Emotional lability

Pseudobulbar affect (PBA), or emotional lability, refers to a neurologic disorder characterised by involuntary crying or uncontrollable episodes of crying and/or laughing, or other emotional displays.

This should not be confused with depression or frontotemporal degeneration (FTD). Sometimes for someone watching a loved one it can be difficult to understand what is going on and what is causing such behavioural changes.

The person may begin crying uncontrollably at something that is only moderately sad, being unable to stop for several minutes. Conversely they may laugh hysterically at something only mildly funny, and again be unable to stop for several minutes. Often they may laugh uncontrollably when angry or frustrated, or suddenly cry at something funny.

It became increasingly cruel for Chris as his bulbar symptoms progressed, as he could aspirate saliva when uncontrolled laughter began. We had some very scary episodes. This caused us to become very cautious about just relaxing and having fun.

A study designed specifically to survey the prevalence of this symptom found that 49 per cent of patients with MND also had PBA.

While not as profoundly disabling as the physical symptoms, this emotional lability can have a significant impact as sudden, frequent, extreme and uncontrollable emotional outbursts may lead to social withdrawal.

Chris remarked in the early stages of the disease that it felt like his brain had become disconnected from his body. He could hear and see things, and form an opinion and response in his brain, but his body would react in a way he did not intend it to, and he would have to fight to get it under control.

Fasciculations

Everybody twitches somewhere, at some point, for some reason. Some people twitch in many places, and as a symptom on its own, without it being an indication of any neurological disease. Fasciculations caused by MND are always associated with other symptoms that progress. They are focused on an area of the body or, more specifically, a muscle or group of muscles.

Fasciculations originate at the very tips of the nerves, called axons, as they come close to being in contact with the muscle. The tips of the axons are thought to be overly sensitive to the electrical firing that triggers a muscle to contract. When a nerve fires, an electrical impulse starts in the nerve, moves out towards the muscle, triggers the release of a chemical that 'swims' across the gap between the nerve axon and the muscle, and binds to a receptor on the muscle, causing it to fire. This complicated process takes a small fraction of a second.

When the muscle is still working and strong, the fasciculations tend to be simple and quite stable, and can be caused or increased by actively using the muscle. Once the muscle is weak and atrophy is present, the fasciculations become complex and unstable, and are not usually affected by muscle activity. Once the muscle has died, there is no nerve impulse left and fasciculations cease altogether.

The fasciculations do not cause the muscles to waste; they are simply an indication that the nerves are overreacting to the impulses being sent through them as a result of damage.

Bulbar symptoms

The medulla oblongata is the lower half of the brainstem, which is continuous with the spinal cord. It is often referred to simply as the medulla. Cone-shaped, it was once known as the 'bulb', hence the reference to bulbar symptoms. The medulla controls the involuntary functions of breathing, heart rate and blood pressure.

Bulbar symptoms relate to the nerves and tracts connected to the medulla, as well as the muscles affected by those nerves, such as the tongue, pharynx and larynx.

When MND is bulbar onset, the first symptoms the person will experience connected with difficulty in speaking or swallowing. Speech may become slurred or sometimes start sounding nasal in character. There will be difficulty in swallowing and loss of tongue mobility. Most people experience difficulty with liquids first, particularly water, progressing to difficulty swallowing anything.

Most people with MND will progress to develop bulbar symptoms. In a way, onset is just a way of classifying where the disease starts, rather than describing that only a part of the body will be involved.

However, bulbar onset, on average, is generally more aggressive and therefore more rapidly progressing. There is a documented higher incidence of FTD in bulbar onset people.

Spasticity

The nervous system is incredibly complex and takes years to learn about after regular medical training. Every neurologist worth their salt admits that we know very little about the brain and nervous system at all. I will try to explain spasticity in layman's terms using illustrative examples.

Our most obvious movements could be thought of as basically two muscles at a joint, for the sake of simplicity. Taking two muscles most people know, such as the biceps and triceps, we know they are both in the arm but are used for opposite functions. To bend the arm, the biceps is pulled tight so it gets shorter, while the triceps gets longer and stretches, allowing the joint to move. To extend the limb, the opposite happens – the triceps shortens and the biceps lengthens. In reality there are more muscles at play but, if you hold your arm out and bend your elbow, so that your hand comes towards your face, you can feel the biceps contracting and the triceps stretching. Now straighten your arm out again and you feel the opposite happening.

When spasticity is involved, as the brain sends the command to the biceps to contract, there is background noise like static. The muscle hears static over the real message, and so hears 'Contract – no, get longer – no, contract.' However, the static is also getting in the way of what the triceps is hearing and so it is hearing much the same. Both muscles try to contract and the result is some crazy, jerky movements.

This is why spasticity causes a lot of stiffness and deep muscle aching.

Medications can help reduce and control spasticity. They usually work by reducing the amount of static, which was confusing the muscles. As a result, people often complain they are weaker when on these medications, because the static was masking a lot of their true weakness with all the extra contractions. Now, without the static in the background, the muscles are more relaxed and so the weakness is more apparent.

Frontotemporal degeneration
Frontotemporal degeneration (FTD – is also known as frontotemporal dementia) has become more widely recognised and understood in recent years.

Researchers are recognising an important connection between FTD and MND. FTD is a syndrome of progressive changes in behaviour and language due to loss of function of neurones in the frontal and temporal lobes of the brain. Many researchers now say that up to 50 per cent of people with MND will display some degree of FTD. This means some degree of change in behaviour and the ability to make complex decisions.

FTD has an insidious onset, typically in those aged in their fifties and sixties. There is relative preservation of memory, but impairment of behaviour, language and/or personality.

Patients characteristically lack insight into their problems. The immense importance of this statement is that, as far as the patient is concerned, they are not showing any change of behaviour, and their perception is completely valid so there is no problem. When a carer or health professional tries to talk to them about their behaviour, they are met with a brick wall and complete indifference.

Most commonly the initial symptoms may include changes in behaviour, difficulty with expression of language and impaired comprehension.

In what is known as 'executive dysfunction', problems arise with planning, organising, abstracting and prioritising, along with impaired verbal fluency. Most researchers agree that bulbar onset more often results in MND-FTD compared with those with MND alone.

Survival in patients with MND-FTD is generally shorter compared with those with MND alone, especially when the executive functions are highly impaired.

A caregiver questionnaire avoids the limitations posed by the patient's physical disabilities. In addition, caregivers can better identify behavioural changes than patients with FTD because they are frequently oblivious to those changes. To ask a patient a question like 'Do you find x more difficult now than you used to?' is fairly meaningless as a diagnostic tool. The patient will either answer no or answer yes but state it is because of a physical limitation of the disease. Caregivers can answer a variety of questions about change in behaviour, mood and attitude that can quantify the level of behavioural change.

Interestingly, in the past, before FTD was widely recognised, the following list was commonly reported in MND patients:

- withdrawn due to depression
- stubborn
- seeking control in some area of life
- anger outbursts due to frustration
- denial
- language problems due to dysarthria.

The symptoms on this list were considered to be understandable and normal, rather than symptoms of further involvement of the brain in the disease process and degeneration.

For carers, the disinterest by medical practitioners and dismissal of FTD symptoms has been a major issue. They were left unsupported and not understanding why they were being subjected to so many behaviours that had never been a part of the person they knew before the disease.

For myself, even though I came to understand FTD and what was happening to Chris, it was extremely difficult not to take the lack of empathy, the paranoia, anger and lack of insight into the whole situation to heart and feel like a total failure as his wife and carer. How anyone caring for a person with MND-FTD, without understanding this aspect of the disease, comes out of the situation without severe scarring is beyond me.

I didn't have Chris formally diagnosed because of his intact memory and severe paranoia. As we were never going to be able to treat it when he was so rapidly progressing with the MND, it felt cruel to put him through testing and tell him that he also definitely had FTD

When executive functions are affected, the person begins to think more slowly than they used to. So health professionals find themselves constantly saying to the person at each visit, 'We are worried about you falling', 'We are worried about you choking', and the patient has a lot of difficulty understanding the impact of this. When the family is brought in on this they say, 'My loved one just doesn't seem to be the same person any more and he doesn't seem to understand. He does not want to listen to me and does not want to do anything that is being suggested as the best for his health and quality of life.'

For me as a carer, the very worst part was that I could not talk to friends, most health professionals or family about the FTD, as my view was immediately discounted as me just not understanding what an awful thing Chris was going through. Time and again the items on that list were thrown at me until I stopped talking about this side of the horror at all.

However, with my online peer support there were three other people dealing with the same types of behavioural issues. As we shared stories and feelings together we felt as though any one of us could write any of our posts. The relief of having these people who understood every part of the horror of watching the person waste away, just as their body was wasting away, was profound. Others caring for their loved ones without the addition of FTD marvelled that we continued with a loving attitude as situations unfolded.

Writing this book has been an enormous struggle, as I was tempted to leave out any parts that disclosed his behavioural symptoms because I felt I was speaking ill of the dead. I worried that his children would find the book and believe I was making up a lot of awful things about their father. I worried it would sound like I actually had been an awful wife and carer, who never understood and maybe never truly loved my husband.

It took a lot for me to get past these fears. The story needs to be told so that others can understand what is happening and survive the role of carer.

Chris was the most amazing man. I loved him completely, and all the emotional horror we lived through was because this disease was degenerating the frontotemporal area of his brain.

Memory is not always affected by FTD. I never had the blessing of him forgetting any of the terrible situations that developed, or forgetting his attitude towards any of them. For this reason, many of these symptoms increased as he built on them and convinced himself I did not care about him as a person, and that my problems in trying to cope were insignificant.

I will always think of Chris as the man he was before MND-FTD, but I can never forget what the disease did to him, and took away from us, as it ran its course. I can only hope that as research understands FTD better, perhaps until a cure is found, the medical profession is better able to diagnose FTD early, and provide true support to the carer as they battle the monster.

29. My own support

I went for my first counselling session two months after diagnosis. I was nervous, as I was not convinced that a counsellor would really do much good.

First, I wasn't sure how open I would be talking about everything I was feeling, without just sitting and crying about my situation. Second, although possibly even more important, I wondered if this person would have the skills to actually help.

As I entered the room it struck me that the counsellor would have no idea why I was seeing him. It dawned on me how difficult his job must be – meeting a new client without knowing what kind of person this would be, what they wanted and what kind of issues they were facing.

When I told him I was here because my husband had received a diagnosis of a terminal illness with no hope of a cure, I could see a flicker of shock. Of course it's hard to say what it was, but I did get the feeling he had not been expecting this. The first session was basically an hour of explaining what MND is, and what that would mean for both Chris and me. In some ways it felt like a waste of time. I didn't want to explain all these facts to yet another person.

I was able to express my feeling that we were no longer equal partners, that I was scared of what was to come, and angry about the disease taking our life together away, like I had been ripped off. I felt the need to have someone outside any emotional connection to help give me perspective. I remember I said to him that I wanted someone who could tell me if I was just weird. We both laughed when I said this and then, after a moment, it seemed to have been perfectly appropriate.

I came away with two important things from that first session. At one point, what I was saying and the language I used caused him to ask if I was feeling trapped. That made me pause, as I wasn't sure exactly what I had said. I looked him in the eye and said it wasn't that I felt trapped. I knew there were always choices. He gently offered that we could explore choices at our next session. The second important thing came at the end of the session. He said, 'Okay, now you have filled me in on the situation, I know that I can't make things better for you. I can't help you solve this, but I do know how to walk beside a person on their journey.'

For a couple of hours after that session, as things slowly sifted down, I found myself thinking about the 'feeling trapped' part of the conversation. It occurred to me that he had touched something very deep and powerful. I could say in truth I did not feel trapped. I had not been able to control the fact that Chris had been stricken by this nightmare terminal illness, but I did have choices. And I knew, very clearly in all of my being, that my choice was to stick by my husband, through the worse and through illness, as we had promised in our marriage vows.

There are people who do not choose to do this and either run, leaving the person to deal with this on their own, or put them into a nursing home. Their reasons may be many and varied; they may even be completely understandable. But I was going to stick by my husband and face this nightmare with him, not because I felt I had to or because I couldn't do anything else. I was choosing to do this because I wanted to live my love for him completely. From that moment on, no matter how hard things got, every single day I made that choice afresh. I could have chosen on any day after that to change my mind and choose something else. I consciously chose to stay every single day. I believe that love is not a feeling; it's an act of your will.

I cannot overemphasise how that simple understanding sustained me through everything that came afterwards. Feeling trapped, feeling that you have to do this, robs the love and the giving from your soul. Knowing that I chose to be there allowed me to tap into a well of love, and be thankful for everything we had together before the disease hit, and be thankful I could care for this man who had given his life over to me.

The fact that this counsellor had the sensitivity not to minimise anything that I was facing and offer to just be there with me also told me clearly that amazingly, first go, I had been given the kind of counsellor I needed. As our counselling relationship developed, and Chris continued to rapidly degenerate, I did have one person who was just there for me, a time each month when I could stop and look at myself, when otherwise nearly all my thoughts were on Chris.

One of the approaches we explored in early sessions is called Voice Dialogue therapy. I worked to identify a name for the different voices that spoke within my head. I found I could really identify with this approach, as I know I have conversations with myself all the time. It sometimes feels like I am split into different people, because of the opposing views I can put forward and argue with.

He observed that my carer voice was the loudest but there were other parts of me that needed to have a say in my life. We worked to identify them and let them talk too. We focused on the paradox of love for Chris versus a willingness to do anything for him, without totally giving up my 'self'.

It's not easy when that carer voice is so loud and strong, and for me it's so familiar – I raised four children, had a herd of goats, a pack of dogs, a flock of chickens and a small property to run. There are so many great rewards to caring, but with this disease it is the reverse of the caring I'd done. Raising children was a situation where I helped them develop and they went on to mature and gain their own independent lives. With this caring I was giving slowly escalating levels of care, and independence was dropping. The rewards were not the same at all. In fact, with each passing month he became more childlike in his attitude and behaviour, so we went backwards in many ways.

I was impacted by the difficulties in talking with Chris. He was defensive so often, but at other times would be exhorting me to open up and share myself fully instead of filtering my thoughts before I spoke. I could not find a way to explain to him that his defensive reactions and hurtful statements were restricting my ability to open up. I felt that my feelings were ignored, and if I spoke about them he felt I was speaking about myself, as a criticism of him. If I spoke of my fears he reacted by saying he would soon be dead, so it didn't matter.

It was a relief to be able to say these things plainly to someone who listened without becoming defensive, and then could talk it through with insight. I did not want someone to say Chris was being awful; I wanted someone to hear my side, acknowledge what I felt, talk with me about how I could cope.

Within months, I admitted that I couldn't take care of everything for everybody and I needed to start accepting help. Even more importantly, I needed to start listening to some of the other voices inside me, as the carer voice was yelling over the top of others. The effect of this was that I was putting Chris's needs totally above my own.

We often admire someone who seems to have a huge capacity for giving to others, and the altruism we see is applauded and commended. The simple fact is that one person cannot neglect themselves for another's needs as a long-term situation. There was no blame associated with any of this; rather it was some insight into my own responses.

If I did not look after myself, I risked something breaking along the line and stopping me by force. The car accident had cemented the reality of this and I knew I needed to learn from it right now, as it had been such a close call. The next time I was unlikely to be let off the hook.

I could talk openly about the oppression I felt with the increasing isolation as Chris withdrew from the world, and friends and family in that world withdrew from us.

I was still battling guilt and could discuss my guilt with someone who was incredulous that I was even coping at all, let alone that I was feeling I wasn't doing enough or well enough. It became a hallmark of my situation, that I could discuss the decline in his condition with my counsellor, and it was clear I was doing all I possibly could. Yet the moment I was back with Chris, I was faced with apathy towards my role and needs, and paranoid accusations, which immediately fuelled my guilt to heights again.

Chris wanted me to give the care he needed and yet ignore that his body was wasting and failing at the same time, and somehow pretend that we were a normal married couple.

We explored strategies I could use to discuss my obvious need for help looking after him. Sometimes I would even rehearse ways to approach the subject. It seemed so much easier in this setting to explain my needs and the solutions that were available, because there was no emotional reaction to deal with. The worst was the look in Chris's eye that would drive a spear through my heart. How could I put my needs on an equal level when my situation was temporary and his was terminal?

During the session before his first serious fall, discussion centred on the decline in Chris's behaviour, and my counsellor used the word 'abusive'. It was such a relief that someone identified the serious nature of what I was experiencing. So many people justified his behaviour and spoke as though I was heartless. This would leave my head reeling, with waves of despair and guilt flooding over me. At night I wondered if they were right. Was I truly heartless, neglecting his emotional needs and therefore deserving of his cruel responses?

A skilled counsellor pays attention to the language used and identifies so much behind a sentence, cutting to the core of what is being said. I could talk and he would cut through and pluck out the core issues, so we could address them. Therefore, for him to call out the behaviour as abusive allowed me to accept that this was the case, no matter what others may think or suggest.

He told me that, regardless of whether Chris died tomorrow or lived for years, he still had the opportunity to keep growing as a person, and was accountable for his actions and attitudes.

We discussed boundaries I could set for my own sanity and to return some respect to the relationship, and how I may be able to put those boundaries into place.

One boundary I put in place was to respond to spiteful and sullen behaviour by removing myself from his presence to have breaks during the day. Until this time any break was spent sitting with Chris with a cup of tea or coffee. I had identified that he could use this time to inflict cruelty by pointedly refusing to make eye contact or engage in any kind of conversation. He would give me the silent treatment and I would sit beside him in despair.

This small step was immediately beneficial because I could truly take a break by myself once again. When I removed myself from the effect of it, I realised his silent treatment had been an effective punishment. When a period of silent treatment ended, I would resume taking most of my breaks with him. I hoped he comprehended that I was not retaliating. I was simply not going to be punished this way.

I had worked alone at home for many years, and had devised many ways to take a break from my work, alone, that would provide a feeling of refreshment. I had stopped giving myself these breaks because Chris expressed such a need for me to be with him.

I learned about 'when … then …' statements and told Chris that 'when' he used silence and withdrawal 'then' I would remove myself from the situation rather than suffer through it.

By the time Chris returned from palliative care for the pain control regime and resumed his unreasonable behaviour, I was beyond exhaustion and talked about the wearisome journey that I felt unable to complete. I was bewildered by his ability to swing seemingly from one personality to another in response to people who were present or absent. I felt I had to be constantly vigilant about my facial expressions, tone of voice and words if I were to avoid his outbursts. Yet I knew there was no escaping the outbursts, as he would accuse me of things he imagined once in a tirade. All I wanted was to care for my man with love and tenderness, but the stumbling blocks of his accusations left me bruised and bleeding.

We discussed my conviction that I was dealing with FTD, rather than a man having trouble dealing with his diagnosis or depression. I certainly believe he was also depressed, but FTD prevented the depression being confronted and dealt with.

I began the counselling session after the second serious fall with my head in my hands, repeatedly saying I just knew this would happen and could do nothing to prevent it. I did not know how I could return home and face this any more. I was angry that he would continually ignore all pleas for safety from everyone involved in his care, and yet I felt I had failed to bring him to this understanding. I was terrified that he would continue to fall, and suffer a terrible, painful death while I waited for an ambulance. I could not understand how he could take such a stand on his physical situation. I had given him all my support, even when I did not agree with his choices, and stood by his decisions.

Once the festive season was over I wondered how much longer he would go on. I felt a growing sense of the end approaching. He was barely mobile and my fear of him falling had lessened but was not removed. Walking with a walker and assistant was no guarantee he was now safe. All health professionals had advised me that, if he were to fall, I must step back and let him go over. Injuring myself in attempting to catch him would only put us in a serious situation that could see him in a care facility.

My concerns shifted to bafflement that he was walking at all and how he could bear the day-to-day existence he had locked himself into. His day consisted of spending all his energy on the most basic tasks of moving between furniture and toilet.

He could not communicate anything beyond his immediate needs and the television was his only real companion. I had little sense of my own self now. Each day was consumed with providing personal care, organising rosters of care services, making appointments, getting him to them, anticipating and planning for the next stage, and keeping staff trained in the latest adjustments as he deteriorated.

The counselling sessions changed from counselling to simply reporting on all the declines we had experienced since the last session. I was dismayed when my counsellor told me he was taking a couple of months' leave. I knew in my heart when he gave me the dates that Chris would be gone before he returned. I was offered another counsellor, and I tried to open myself to the possibility that a new person at this point could be a positive thing.

The session with the other counsellor was, for me, a disaster. As it happened, it was only weeks before Chris passed and I found myself explaining MND to a new person. I left the session wishing I had simply gone and done something nice for myself with that hour, as I felt drained.

The sessions I had on my counsellors' return took on a whole new perspective as, finally, I was able to return to focusing on myself as my process of grief progressed.

I continued to see my counsellor regularly for nearly a year after Chris died. I spent much of my time with him identifying the threads I was trying to unravel and weave into my new reality. The sessions often involved a lot of laughter, as we both marvelled at what had happened and how life continued to unfold as I tried to keep up with it.

30. Living with or dying from

I was often asked how I coped with this.

I could never find the words to explain how I coped. To be honest, how I answered depended on the day I was asked! Coping is not a straight line or a simple answer, and there are no rights or wrongs. I used different coping mechanisms at different times, depending on just what I was coping with and what my energy reserves were like at the time.

Love is the key to surviving every crisis. I believe this to the depth of my being. I would still be alive no matter what coping strategies I had used during my time as a carer, but I can only wonder what kind of state I would be in now if I had not been determined to live my love every single day.

A common reaction to this diagnosis is to wonder why. I learned quickly to put this aside as a pointless question. It was, and that was enough to cope with and accept, the 'why' seemed like something that would only take away the energy I needed to devote to coping. After the first month or so I began to formulate some kind of answer to why, without immersing myself in worrying about it.

I would hate to imagine him going through this alone, with his children – who lost their mother so young – trying to look after him. I held to a strong belief that I met him so I could learn deeply and truly about love and show that to him so he could find comfort and dignity in his journey through the ravaging of this awful disease.

There were many days and times when I felt I could not cope, could not do this day-in and day-out. I had to consciously bring myself to a halt and meditate inwardly on the fact that only by how I lived now could this be truth. I would realise that I always had the choice to react to any given moment in a very different way, and could change this to anything else. I could also choose to hold this in front of me and use it to concrete the way I would respond, and that this would bring that statement to the light of being truth.

People all around the world, every single day, are being struck by all manner of disease and disaster. Why would I think we should be exempt from this when so many other good and beautiful people are not? That question is one that will mess your mind up and take away energy needed for the day-to-day business of loving and living.

An untreatable, terminal illness does not create a situation of hope. There was absolutely no hope for us that Chris would somehow recover, or that a cure would be found in time, or that he would even just level out and live with the illness.

I had to accept that a cure was not something I could afford to hope for, but surely there were other things I could hope for. This is what brought me to the conclusion that I could hope to come through this tragedy as a better person, with something to offer as a result of what I experienced, and that I could hope to learn to love without receiving in return.

I have witnessed many people going through the same illness, and the wide range of reactions of the affected person, their carer and their families. The mixture of coping strategies always fascinated me; sometimes it also dismayed me.

In truth, I had many hopes, and some of them were dashed along the way, but many were outside my control. For example, I hoped he would progress slowly and we would find a way to enjoy much of life and each other for at least a couple of years, if not more, as we learned to live with the disease. I could not control that his progression was rapid and we were barely able to keep up with the daily losses.

My most important hopes, however, were around how I could care for him, and how I could survive the situation. I had to learn to let go of the things I could not control, and the things that were not going to be as I hoped, and learn to accept. Oh, how hard it is to accept that which every fibre of your being does not want! Acceptance does not mean you are happy about a particular thing; to me it is about how you will spend your energy. When a person is not in a state of acceptance, they spend energy in anger, frustration, futile attempts to change, fighting against the current. When a person is in a state of acceptance, they spend their energy loving, upholding dignity and moving with the current. Even if you don't like where it is taking you, fighting against a strong and swift current is the best way to exhaust yourself very quickly.

From the earliest realisations that something was seriously wrong, even with so much denial at work, through until his death, I battled a range of emotions. It was a battle as great as the one of providing the highest level of care possible.

Despair was an ogre always crouching in the shadows waiting to grab and capture me. I was constantly aware of it lurking and had to be vigilant against it. Certainly the use of antidepressants was critical to elude its grasp. I had to look after my own mental health actively.

The paths holding the most shadows for this ogre to lurk in were Chris's emotional withdrawal and paranoia about my intentions. This man, who had been so lovingly expansive in his empathy towards others, changed so dramatically and so suddenly, it took time to realise it was a personality change that would persist.

In the early months I worked on strategies I hoped would help him to deal with his emotional turmoil so we could become a unified team, leaning on each other. As he became increasingly childlike and all efforts of mine backfired, I eventually moved to an acceptance of the ruination of our relationship as husband and wife.

No matter how deeply I was being impacted, Chris and his needs were always the centre of my attention. No one else truly saw the desperation I experienced, attempting to arise each day with a bright smile and find the energy to look after someone who was going to be yet more disabled in some way that day. People would listen sympathetically if I explained some bodily function he had lost or some new care he needed. They didn't understand it in a real 'this is your life' way, but they could sympathise if I cared to talk about that. They would kind of glaze over, however, if I mentioned my own despair and fear. Too often it would be met with comments about how much worse it must be for Chris.

The stark contrast when talking with my online peer group could not have been greater. In this space we were all equal, and we were all just as important as the people we cared for. We had full rights to our own feelings without it detracting from the plight of the one we cared for. There was constant encouragement for each of us to clearly and fully state how we felt and what we were going through inside ourselves. This was met by a relieved empathy from others, unable to explain this to anyone else. Some days it was sheer madness in these support groups as long-pent-up feelings of despair were aired, understood and shared. The relief as I both received and gave true empathy was exactly what I needed. The very act of admitting your feelings, and having them accepted as valid, was all that was needed to cope with having the feelings.

The group was made up of many people feeling those same things and battling the very same goblins in the shadows. Some of the worst things suddenly became perfectly normal. As I got to know these friends, some of the things that had caused great despair in the beginning became subjects of hilarious black humour. We could laugh at and joke about terrible things as ways to cope. The relief that came from these interactions was so intense I could find myself laughing internally at awful situations, reminded of stories others had told. Sometimes I almost couldn't wait to tell a story from my day, because I knew these peers would 'get it'.

We also shared practical solutions to providing a high level of care and coping with our own needs.

The ogre of despair holds its greatest power by keeping you isolated down dark corridors. Coming out into the light of a street full of other travellers was truly liberating.

As Chris accused me of wanting him to die, wanting to be free to live my own life, it seemed he was slowly convincing me that I did actually want these things. The more often he lashed out verbally or completely withdrew from me, the more I had treasonous thoughts of how much I wanted this behaviour to stop, knowing it would only stop once he was dead. It seemed that the nastier he became, the more he trampled on my own self and spirit, and the more he was making his own words come true.

I was terrified to talk about this with anyone in my circle of friends or family because I was scared they would agree with his deranged rantings and tell me I was indeed selfish or making him unhappy.

One thing that proved his paranoia true, for him, was any desire I expressed to have any time to myself or to pursue anything pleasant for my own enjoyment. I knew other carers whose partners actively encouraged them to maintain friendships and things they enjoyed. They realised they provided better care if they had these critical breaks and fulfilments. Chris isolated us both and wanted my sole focus to be on him. He did not consider any personal loss for me was valid to mourn. He was the centre of our world, and my concerns were discounted because he would soon die, so it was no real sacrifice for me to dedicate myself solely to him.

He did not realise I had willingly dedicated myself to his care. However, if he became my sole world, I would quickly burn out. It was the way a child demands constantly from their mother, with no concept of their mother being a separate human being with her own needs.

As his condition deteriorated and his withdrawal increased, I found so many ways to feel guilt. I felt guilt just for having my own health, when he was facing death. I felt guilt if I found something terribly funny and laughed out loud, as he could not laugh without fear of aspirating. I felt guilt for enjoying a meal, as he could not eat. Indeed, I found cooking itself a source of guilt, as he had loved to cook. My meals became increasingly simple as his ability to eat declined, because I felt too guilty to make some favourite meal.

301

On respite days I would go to a café for lunch and order steak and eat a marvellous meal. I had to work hard not to feel guilty. I knew I needed these high-quality meals, but my guilt would remind me that he would never again eat a meal like this.

With each thing the disease robbed him of, I seemed to develop some corresponding guilt about my ability to still have that.

Chris was fond of saying to other people that he was living with MND, not dying from MND. He was often hailed as some kind of hero for his amazing attitude to the disease and held in the highest regard. I experienced incredible battles with guilt and despair over this very statement. There was such a difference between the person people saw on their infrequent visits, or read on Facebook, and the person I experienced daily, and I was the only person who knew the reality. I was expected to fully back him up on his claims of how well he was doing, how positive his attitude was and how he was fighting.

I was the one who spent hours preparing him for a visit, painstakingly presenting him as best as was possible, while he complained bitterly that he didn't want to see anyone. I was the one who witnessed his persona change as soon as people arrived, and watched him carefully sitting in one place, doing as little as possible, so he could try to fool them that he was not as disabled or frail as he was in truth. I was the one who saw him collapse in exhaustion when they left and immediately withdraw once we were again alone. I was the one who witnessed him complain incessantly about every aspect of the visit, even though at the time he had appeared to both enjoy the visit and display his wonderful attitude. I was the one who witnessed him constantly refuse the amount of care he needed if he was actually going to fight this disease at all.

I could have better accepted these things if he were not deliberately portraying a different image to everyone else.

I longed to freeze time so I had this smiling, positive man to myself for just a little while, but he was gone like a puff of smoke with visitors' car doors closing.

No matter what I did, I was only 'keeping him comfortable' until the inevitable end. I couldn't 'fix' this situation, he could not be cured and, even more than that, I couldn't even slow his progression. On top of this, if I had full control of what was done and how, I would have done things differently. So I constantly felt guilty to be standing by while he made bad decisions that would only result in him progressing faster, living with less quality of life and maybe even dying earlier.

Oh, the guilt this one piled on me. The further we went into the journey, the further Chris progressed, the heavier the weight of this particular guilt became.

I also knew that a few facts of life had to be understood, logically and reasonably. A person with MND lives with a lot of fear. They are facing that they have a terminal disease that is going to progressively do very frightening things to their body. Not only is it going to kill them, but they fear it could be a very frightening death. I think the fear of choking to death is top of the list for most. For Chris, the fear of falling asleep and not waking up rated high as well. I felt it would be the best way to go. However, every time he was trying to fall asleep he was gripped by this fear.

These fears obviously affect the way a person with MND approaches the disease but, in general, there are three main ways people deal with this (or any) terminal illness.

The first is to give in. Sadly some people become majorly depressed and do give up very quickly, thinking 'What is the point of anything?' This is not about how you might feel one day or when some particular thing happens, but the broad outlook taken. When people give in they usually become severely withdrawn and morose, refusing food and assistance. They may refuse their medications or want larger quantities of pain relief or sleeping medication to escape their distress.

People who give in often die quickly because they lose the will to live and assist the disease in doing its work.

A second response is that they want to fight. The person feels guilt at being ill, or their loved one being ill, and feel they must fight the illness. This is going to take a *lot* of energy. What does it mean to 'fight' an illness that is incurable, terminal? If there were some hope, even a small hope, we may feel that a fight to win is worthy. If there isn't hope of winning, if the beast is going to devour no matter what, is fighting the right way to approach it?

The third approach is to accept. The first and second responses are opposites and are therefore extremes. So if we are not going to just give in and we are not going to fight, what else is there? Acceptance is the middle ground, and a more peaceful path for the soul. It should never be confused with giving in. Chris only believed in two stances – giving in or fighting. I could never discuss acceptance with him as he interpreted it immediately as giving in and giving up.

Here are a few examples from our own situation of how it can pan out in practical terms.

In experiencing loss of muscles in the hands and arms, if you give in, you sit down and say, 'I can't do anything with my hands.' Now you rob yourself of any pleasure in achieving or doing something for yourself, and your depression will feed on this.

If you fight, you insist you can do more than you really can. With MND this is dangerous, because overusing muscles that are wasting can easily damage them and speed up progression of the wastage and total death of the nerves. So this type of fighting can actually produce the opposite effect you are looking for and cause you to lose functionality even faster.

If you accept, you will be conscious of your limitations and find ways to modify things so you can continue to do as much as possible, without risking hurting those muscles. You will accept help with some things, so you can use your energy for other things. You will look to aids and technology to replace what you could do with your body.

In experiencing loss of speech, if you give in, you may withdraw and refuse to try to communicate anything beyond immediate needs. If you fight, you may try to use verbal speech all the time, finding yourself in constant frustration when people can't understand you. If you accept, you will look at other ways of communicating and learn to use as many methods as are available, and be thankful for technology.

In regard to safety, you need to conserve energy and avoid falls. I can never say this enough. Injuries through falls often happen because someone believes they are fighting the disease and not giving in. But each injury hastens the progression of the disease. Acceptance allows the person to look at safety as a bigger concern than embarrassment at using equipment or being in a wheelchair. Truly, it is less embarrassing to be seen in a wheelchair than face down on a hard pavement.

Chris may not have lived any longer but, if he had taken in enough calories, conserved energy and avoided falls, he may have had a better quality of life. I know that the underlying FTD was the reason he didn't do things wisely, and I know that it allowed MND to attack his body ferociously.

It is horrible watching your body failing, and being unable to do things you want. But learning to accept the limitations and make the most of what you do have every day, so that you have the energy to enjoy little things, is what I've seen many other people with MND do.

I have marvelled at how much enjoyment in life some with this disease have maintained. I celebrate with a happy dance when I hear any of these friends test out a PWC and choose one with every possible feature, and exclaim they now have incredible mobility with safety, and their lives are opened up to new possibilities again.

I cry with joy when I hear carers, or their loved ones, talk openly about the disease and how it limits them, and then describe all the ways they have learned to adapt and find new pleasures together.

Chris was dealt a particularly cruel hand with the combination of rapid progression and FTD. It robbed us of all joy in each other, from so early into the disease, that I was utterly alone as I cared for him in his withdrawal from me.

I still have to work hard to turn my memories of him back to the amazing man he was before MND. I refuse to think of the disease as 'him'.

Every month since he was taken physically from this world, I regain more precious memories of my soulmate. Writing this book has helped me put to rest many of the traumas I suffered, as a bit of me died along with every progression and loss, in his muscles and his personality.

I have come through this experience with a new perspective on life and love. As I adjust to being a widow I am learning to look forward to what will unfold, rather than being fearful of the future.

And so I have finally written my story. I have brought together the words that explain my journey. I have faithfully written the years and have explained my world, both to myself and to all who read it. I put this to the world and trust that I have captured the meaning of my days with MND.

Will I return to these words one day to find that the past still holds the same meaning, or will my perspective have changed? Is history really dead and fixed?

Or do we find new meaning to our future as we discover that the past is no further away than each precious memory that unfolds anew?

The things that happened in our past cannot be changed, but our perception of them and the learning we can derive from them are timeless and endless.

Overcoming a loss by 1000 deaths

Being with the one you love
as they journey through death
is the last
and most intimate thing
one soul can have with another

The loss is great
but I am strengthened
rather than defeated
because I know the meaning of love

31. Postscript

We never *get over* losing someone we love deeply. True, as time passes I find the loss is a little easier to deal with. My despair is not as deep. Eighteen months after losing Chris, I laugh and find great pleasure in my life. I was wounded however, and will carry the scar to the end of my own days.

For several months I teetered between feeling numb, relieved his suffering was over, and haunted by the accusations thrown at me during his illness.

I continue to live alone on the dream property we purchased together. A few months after Chris was taken from me I went for a walk. It had been 8 months since the tractor had left the shed. It had been at least a year since any real slashing had been done. I had concerns over my ability to look after the property alone, and I wondered what it would look like after the neglect.

Not even in my wildest dreams could I have imagined what I discovered.

Amongst the long grasses (which I have now learned are beautiful native grasses important for our bird life) I discovered thousands of young koala food trees that had self-sown. I was in awe as I gazed on the results of the amazing healing power of nature.

Left alone, the land was healing itself of the wounds forced upon it by the intervention of man.

This discovery began a metamorphosis within me.

I am learning to work with nature, rather than trying to impose my will on the land. I am learning to value an approach that works with cycles and seasons.

I have obtained approval for an environmental facility on the property and am actively assisting the regeneration of the native habitat. I have been successful in securing grant funding for this purpose. Endangered koalas are here on the property every day. Discovering mothers with joeys brings an overwhelming thankfulness to my heart.

My hope is to build enough business around the environmental facility to fund spending most of my time working with the land. I have met many wonderful new friends doing volunteer work for koala care and rescue.

I am also involved as a volunteer supporting local carers and sufferers of MND.

I have remained in the online support networks that sustained me as a carer. I receive comfort from offering support to others suffering with the disease or caring for those suffering.

I give trees to these people in a virtual sense. I label the trees and send photos when a koala is in their tree. It is a place for them to escape to when their days are particularly hard.

A new shape is being defined for my life without Chris. I feel peace in trusting that this new shape is beautiful. Cycles and seasons – life is about change and adapting. Life is about the beautiful things that can grow out of any amount of decay.

Life is a gift, while death is a certainty. It's living that is uncertain, as it is ours to embrace or waste. I miss Chris, but I can only change and influence the future. So I set my eyes forward and throw my arms open wide as I embrace life and whatever my time on this earth offers.

It is only by turning my inner eye
to face my fears
that allows me to know my own ability
to overcome

This too, yes even this sorrow
shall pass into the shadows of the past
to be wrapped in the stillness
of silence and surrender

It is a grave error to look back in anger
Worse to look forward in fear

Would I miss my whole life
consumed from both sides?

Be aware
Be still
The future is in the palm of my hand

32. Another story

It began as "little things" hardly worth attention... a stutter step that turned into a fall... difficulty getting into a friend's SUV... a leg that collapsed getting out of the car... hands that too quickly would tire when typing. Taken individually, they seemed insignificant. But in November of 2012, when suddenly unable to get up from a seated position without help, the dots began to connect. Something unexplainable was happening. It was time for Darcey (my wife) to visit her doctor.

And so began the game of tag as each doctor passed Darcey off to the next. There were blood and urine tests, MRIs, EKGs... and still no answers. Moving to the neurologist there were EMGs, nerve conduction studies, more MRIs and the lumbar puncture. The uncertainty while awaiting a diagnosis is one of the most terrifying of times and experiences... and we'd secretly begun to question whether it might be something terminal like "ALS". November had now become April when a diagnosis was finally handed down. The neurologist was ready to begin treatment for a recoverable autoimmune disorder called "CIDP". And so life was put on hold as she began treatment.

The months continued to come... and pass. Hands, arms and legs all continued to decline in function. Walking became difficult and driving was no longer a safe venture. The use of a "walker" migrated to the electric scooter... until the threat of falling mandated use of a power wheelchair. With each new challenge and loss of function, we found new ways to accomplish previously normal tasks.

With life still on hold, 2014 arrived. And with it came the realization that we might be dealing with something altogether different than CIDP. We were accepted for evaluation at Johns Hopkins and a whole new slew of tests were conducted. In March of 2014, Darcey's diagnosis was officially changed to ALS. Even though such a possibility had been lurking in the background, the actual diagnosis was still a shock.

Shock gave way to disappointment that we'd put life on hold for a year, expecting that Darcey would soon get better... and that we were now having to make the difficult transition to "time's running out". To keep from falling into the trap that despair can encourage, we sought to come to terms with this new reality and find our own way to cope; individually and as a couple. And so we likened it all as being akin to riding on a train. Let me see if I can explain...

We imagined that we were now travelling on a train. We didn't ask to be on this train but we're here anyway. We know where the train is headed... yet for as much as we'd like to get off, there is *no* getting off. It is a ride we'll share to its end. With so much out of our control, we desperately needed something we COULD control. We might not be able to get off, but we did have control over how we elected to make this ride.

We accepted that Darcey wasn't going to get better. And because we now knew exactly what we were dealing with, we sought to become better educated. Knowing what to expect allowed us to get the equipment that we now knew we'd need... and to do so BEFORE we actually needed it. And most importantly, with time counting down, *we took life off of hold*. We began to do all the things that we could still do while we could still do them. And when those things could no longer be done, we found new things to do. And we treated each new problem as a puzzle to be solved... believing that there was a solution only waiting for us to find it. Some solutions we found on our own and others from online ALS specific forums; learning from those who had gone before us.

Today, as I write this, we're celebrating our 31st Wedding Anniversary. We are about 3 years into this ALS ride and still make every day the very best it can be. I don't believe that we have ever loved each other more. Because of ALS, we've been encouraged to communicate better (at *everything*)... to be more respectful, thankful and appreciative of each other... and to work more closely (together as a team) with everything that has needed to be considered and done. We've been privileged to have finally learned what really *is* important... and what is not. We were great before. But we're *awesome* now!

I hope they soon find a cure for ALS. Good people should not have to go through all that this disease brings with it. But if you do find yourself on this ride, Darcey and I hope that you will find your own way to squeeze every bit of love, life and laughter out of the time that still lies ahead... and that you can make your ride as good as ours has been and still continues to be!

With love and hope for great tomorrows...

Jim & Darcey Bird

As a gold sponsor during the indiegogo campaign to publish this book, Jim gained a place to tell his own story as a carer.

Jim has become an awesome friend as our journeys unfolded. Personally I love the contrast stories like this have to my own story. They highlight so clearly the difference when FTD is combined with this disease. They have also been blessed with far more time to learn to live with, and love through, a terminal illness.

I love how Jim and Darcey have become that kind of inspiration.

When Chris was first diagnosed I had a vision of our story being one that would inspire others to live well through a terminal illness. Eleven short months and the addition of FTD changed that story in ways I could never have imagined. Yet I have emerged with a story of hope in overcoming the loss of the 1000 deaths this disease brings.